Public Policy Challenges Facing Higher Education in the American West

HIGHER EDUCATION & SOCIETY

Series Editors:

Roger L. Geiger, Distinguished Professor of Education, Pennsylvania State University

Katherine Reynolds Chaddock, Professor of Higher Education Administration, University of South Carolina

This series explores the diverse intellectual dimensions, social themes, cultural contexts, and pressing political issues related to higher education. From the history of higher education to heated contemporary debates, topics in this field range from issues in equity, matriculation, class representation, and current educational federal acts, to concerns with gender and pedagogy, new media and technology, and the challenges of globalization. In this way, the series aims to highlight theories, historical developments, and contemporary endeavors that prompt critical thought and reflective action in how higher education is conceptualized and practiced in and beyond the United States.

Liberal Education for a Land of Colleges: Yale's "Reports" of 1828
By David B. Potts

Deans of Men and the Shaping of Modern College Culture
By Robert Schwartz

Establishing Academic Freedom: Politics, Principles, and the Development of Core Values
By Timothy Cain

Higher Education in the American West: Regional History and State Contexts
Edited by Lester F. Goodchild, Richard W. Jonsen, Patty Limerick, and David A. Longanecker

Public Policy Challenges Facing Higher Education in the American West
Edited by Lester F. Goodchild, Richard W. Jonsen, Patty Limerick, and David A. Longanecker

PUBLIC POLICY CHALLENGES FACING HIGHER EDUCATION IN THE AMERICAN WEST

Edited by
Lester F. Goodchild
Richard W. Jonsen
Patty Limerick, and
David A. Longanecker

PUBLIC POLICY CHALLENGES FACING HIGHER EDUCATION IN THE AMERICAN WEST
Copyright © Lester F. Goodchild, Richard W. Jonsen, Patty Limerick, and David A. Longanecker, 2014.

All rights reserved.

First published in 2014 by
PALGRAVE MACMILLAN®
in the United States—a division of St. Martin's Press LLC,
175 Fifth Avenue, New York, NY 10010.

Where this book is distributed in the UK, Europe and the rest of the world, this is by Palgrave Macmillan, a division of Macmillan Publishers Limited, registered in England, company number 785998, of Houndmills, Basingstoke, Hampshire RG21 6XS.

Palgrave Macmillan is the global academic imprint of the above companies and has companies and representatives throughout the world.

Palgrave® and Macmillan® are registered trademarks in the United States, the United Kingdom, Europe and other countries.

ISBN: 978–1–137–38197–2

Library of Congress Cataloging-in-Publication Data

    Public policy challenges facing higher education in the American West / [15 authors] ; Edited by Lester F. Goodchild, Richard W. Jonsen, Patty Limerick, David A. Longanecker.
      p. cm.—(Higher education & society)
    Includes bibliographical references and index.
      ISBN 978–1–137–38197–2 (hardcover : alk. paper)
      1. Higher education and state—West (U.S.) 2. Education, Higher—Economic aspects—West (U.S.) 3. Education, Higher—West (U.S.)—Finance. 4. Federal aid to education—West (U.S.) I. Goodchild, Lester F., editor of compilation. II. Jonsen, Richard W., editor of compilation. III. Limerick, Patty, editor of compilation. IV. Longanecker, David, 1946– , editor of compilation.

LC173.P825 2014
379.78—dc23
                                                          2013047585

A catalogue record of the book is available from the British Library.

Design by Newgen Knowledge Works (P) Ltd., Chennai, India.

First edition: March 2014

Contents

List of Figures and Tables vii

Editors' Preface xi

Dedications xvii

Introduction xix
Lester F. Goodchild, Richard W. Jonsen, Patty Limerick, and David A. Longanecker

Part I Public Policy Demographic Background

1 A Demographic Profile of Higher Education in the American West 3
   Cheryl D. Blanco

Part II Seven Regional Public Policy Challenges

2 Assessing College Access and Success in the West 31
   Mikyung Ryu

3 The Federal Government, Research Funding, and Western Higher Education Policy 59
   David A. Longanecker

4 State Policy Leadership in the Public Interest: Is Anyone at Home? 71
   Aims C. McGuinness Jr.

5 Higher Education Finance Policy in the Western States 91
   Dennis P. Jones

6 Public Financing of Higher Education in the Western States: Changing Patterns in State Appropriations and Tuition Revenues 107
   Charles S. Lenth, Kathleen J. Zaback, Andrew M. Carlson, and Allison C. Bell

7 Technology and Distance Education: Challenges Facing the American West 143
   Sally M. Johnstone and J. Ritchie Boyd

8 The Growth of Community Colleges in the West:
   Conditions and Public Policy Challenges   159
   Cheryl D. Lovell

Part III A Concluding Commentary

Afterword Where Do We Go from Here: The Policy Nexus
           between the West and the Federal Government   187
           David A. Longanecker

Notes on Contributors   191

Index   199

Figures and Tables

Figures

1.1	Total population by region, 1900–2010	5
1.2	Distribution of population by age groups, US 1900–2030	5
1.3	Projected numerical and percentage distribution of population by age groups, WICHE region, 2000–2030	6
1.4	American Indian/Alaska native population by US region, 1900–2000	11
1.5	Asian/Pacific Islander population by US region, 1900–2000	12
1.6	Black population by US region, 1900–2000	13
1.7	White population by US region, 1900–2000	14
1.8	US public and private schools with secondary grades (9–12), 1929–2008	18
1.9	US public and private institutions in the West, 2009–2010	22
1.10	Total fall enrollment in degree-granting institutions, US, 1970–2010	23
1.11	College enrollment rates of high school completers, US, by race/ethnicity, 1960–2009	23
1.12	Degrees earned by level, 1869–2010	24
1.13	Total fall enrollment in degree-granting institutions, West, 1970–2008	25
1.14	Total degrees awarded by level, US and West, 2008–2009	25
2.1	Changing racial/ethnic make-up of young population (aged 18–24) between 2000 and 2020	36
2.2	Racial/ethnic gaps in education for selected states	38
2.3	State overall category scores in *Measuring Up 2006*	41–42
2.4	High school graduation rate in four years, 2002	44
2.5	Immediate college-going rate of recent high school graduates, 2002	45
2.6	Total expenditures for state need-based aid as a percent of total Pell Grants awarded in the state, 2005	46
4.1	Changes in underlying assumptions about the state role in higher education	74
5.1	Percent of total undergraduate headcount in the public sector, Fall 2010	92
5.2	Percent of high school graduates going directly to college, Fall 2008	93

Figures and Tables

5.3	Family share of funding for public higher education, FY 2010	94
5.4	The decision space for state funding of higher education	98
5.5	Competition for state resources based on projections of service loads	100
5.6	Total state grant expenditures as a percentage of appropriation of tax funds for higher education operating expenses by state, 2009–2010	102
5.7	Public 4-year in-state average undergraduate tuition and required fees, 2009–2010	103
5.8	Public 2-year in-state average undergraduate tuition and required fees, 2009–2010	104
5.9	Finance policy—the options	105
6.1	Percent change FTE enrollment growth and population, 1980–2010	113
6.2	Public FTE enrollment, educational appropriations, and total educational revenue per FTE, United States—fiscal 1980–2010	115
6.3	Public FTE enrollment, educational appropriations, and total educational revenue per FTE, all WICHE States—fiscal 1982–2007	116
6.4	Public FTE enrollment, educational appropriations, and total educational revenue per FTE, Alaska—fiscal 1982–2007	119
6.5	Public FTE enrollment, educational appropriations, and total educational revenue per FTE, Arizona—fiscal 1982–2007	120
6.6	Public FTE enrollment, educational appropriations, and total educational revenue per FTE, California—fiscal 1982–2007	122
6.7	Public FTE enrollment, educational appropriations, and total educational revenue per FTE, Colorado—fiscal 1982–2007	123
6.8	Public FTE enrollment, educational appropriations, and total educational revenue per FTE, Hawaii—fiscal 1982–2007	124
6.9	Public FTE enrollment, educational appropriations, and total educational revenue per FTE, Idaho—fiscal 1982–2007	126
6.10	Public FTE enrollment, educational appropriations, and total educational revenue per FTE, Montana—fiscal 1982–2007	127
6.11	Public FTE enrollment, educational appropriations, and total educational revenue per FTE, Nevada—fiscal 1982–2007	129
6.12	Public FTE enrollment, educational appropriations, and total educational revenue per FTE, New Mexico—fiscal 1982–2007	130
6.13	Public FTE enrollment, educational appropriations, and total educational revenue per FTE, North Dakota—fiscal 1982–2007	131
6.14	Public FTE enrollment, educational appropriations, and total educational revenue per FTE, Oregon—fiscal 1982–2007	133

6.15	Public FTE enrollment, educational appropriations, and total educational revenue per FTE, South Dakota—fiscal 1982–2007	134
6.16	Public FTE enrollment, educational appropriations, and total educational revenue per FTE, Utah—fiscal 1982–2007	136
6.17	Public FTE enrollment, educational appropriations, and total educational revenue per FTE, Washington—fiscal 1982–2007	137
6.18	Public FTE enrollment, educational appropriations, and total educational revenue per FTE, Wyoming—fiscal 1982–2007	138
8.1	Share of state budget allocated to all of higher education and share of higher education budget allocated to community colleges—graphical representation	168

TABLES

2.1	*Measuring Up* report cards evaluate states on the following measures	33
2.2	WICHE state grades in *Measuring Up 2000–2008* by category	34
2.3	Highest education level attained among adults (aged 25–65), by race, 2000	37
4.1	Examples of state higher education reforms, 1996–2013	77
6.1	Attainment and participation rates 2010 western states, western region, and nation	113
7.1	Summary of principles of good practice for electronically offered academic degree and certificate programs	149
7.2	Selection of issues in *The Distance Learner's Guide*	155
8.1	Number and type of two-year institutions, by decade	161
8.2	Percent of state enrollments in community colleges for the WICHE states	165
8.3	Share of state budget allocated to all of higher education and share of higher education budget allocated to community colleges	166
8.4	Examples of public policy issues involving community colleges in the WICHE region, 2003–2011	171

Editors' Preface

American public higher education is at a crossroads; its future is uncertain. The twenty-first century financial demands on states for improved services to their citizens have outstripped the public determination and will to support postsecondary education during the recent Great Recession. Many states have reduced their support for their public universities and colleges in the face of the current difficult times. A new consensus needs to be built around one of the most powerful resources the states have to overcome their current economic woes—their universities and colleges. The higher education development engine has succeeded in the past to boost the economic productivity of the states. If the current public leadership had an understanding of higher education's past successes and a vision for appropriate policy strategies to move forward using these great educational plants, a more productive way forward might emerge.

Two comprehensive books on higher education in the western states seek to provide this understanding and vision. One volume, *Higher Education in the American West: Regional History and State Contexts,* offers the first regional overview of the history of postsecondary education in the United States. In that book, we crafted a new portrait of the development of western higher education to see how in previous eras these institutions provided part of the means to overcome tough times. This companion volume, *Public Policy Challenges Facing Higher Education in the American West*, explores major public policy directions needed to utilize this higher education enterprise to educate and train the West's citizens for future careers to move the state economies forward. National policy experts made assessments of postsecondary access, finance, federal funding, state governance, institutional tuition, technology and distance education policy, as well as community college issues for 15 western states and their systems of higher education. In this way, postsecondary history in the first volume provides a context and a vision that informs public policy directions in the second companion volume.

This two-volume project thus offers an overview and assessment of public and independent higher education in the West, from the very earliest American efforts to bring scholarship along the overland migration trails and sea routes to the Pacific and beyond in order to create a future that built the region's higher education sector. Subsequent major immigrations to the West over the past 50 years have made it the most diverse region of the country. Now its 71.5 million citizens support over 1,200 universities and colleges to educate its people, to train its professionals, and to advance knowledge through its researchers and scholars. The West's historic importance in supplying natural resources for the country, and its more recent history of dynamic technological innovation and resources for the country and the world, makes what happens in the West, and how its colleges and universities develop, important signals for the future of the nation's economy, society, and culture.

These books are intended for a variety of audiences who are interested in higher education, particularly in the western states. State and higher education policymakers will be especially interested in this companion book, which focuses on the difficult issues facing higher education policymakers in the West and indeed the nation. They will find that the first part provides a valuable context for understanding these policy commentaries and seeing how different eras used higher education to foster state development. State political leaders will find this comprehensive treatment of postsecondary education a useful study for crafting new public policy directions. Faculty and graduate students in the field of higher education will find this regional history and policy overview a useful addition to their study of public policy and the development of American higher education. Those engaged and interested in higher education in other parts of the country will find this portrait helpful in seeing their own regional postsecondary needs and directions.

One major initial question introduced this project: How should one define what states constitute the American West? The scope of this two-book project was influenced initially by the coming of the fiftieth anniversary celebration of the 15-member state compact, the Western Interstate Commission for Higher Education (WICHE), which occurred in 2003. The 15 states comprising WICHE's membership are: Alaska, Arizona, California, Colorado, Hawaii, Idaho, Montana, Nevada, New Mexico, North Dakota, Oregon, South Dakota, Utah, Washington, and Wyoming. This WICHE West and its states' higher education stories, traditions, histories, and policies became the main focus of the project's undertaking. With a view toward this anniversary, the late Michael Malone, president of Montana State University, proposed in 1998 to engage a collaboration of scholars, policy researchers, and administrators associated with or interested in WICHE and its state higher education systems to explore an appropriate project, and discussed the idea with then Executive Director Richard Jonsen. They then consulted with Patty Limerick, director of the Center of the American West and Professor of history at the University of Colorado at Boulder, whose center joined the collaboration. David A. Longanecker, who succeeded Jonsen at WICHE in 1999, warmly endorsed the project. At Jonsen's invitation, Professor Lester F. Goodchild, then director of the Higher Education Program at the University of Denver, assumed the leadership of the project. His coedited book, *Higher Education and Public Policy* (1997), suggested a way of doing policy history and analysis as its key framework. With the untimely death of Malone, Goodchild, Jonsen, Limerick, and Longanecker became the gang of four editors who oversaw this two-book project to its conclusion.

Discussions with members of the Western Historical Society also aided in identifying themes, possible authors, and the western scope for the project. Early chapter drafts of the book were vetted at a WICHE symposium in 2002 and then presented at an authors' conference the following year to mark the anniversary. Along the way, generous support had been received from The William and Flora Hewlett Foundation, followed later by support from the Wyss Family Foundation of Portland, Oregon.

Over the next ten years, Goodchild and Jonsen worked closely with authors, enhanced by the able efforts of our content editor, Jason Hanson, at the Center for the American West, our copy editor, Paul Albright, formerly with WICHE, and graphic designer Candy Allen of WICHE. Their combined work with the volumes' nationally recognized policy leaders, researchers, historians, and administrators led to these two companion volumes. Eventually, 22 authors wrote 18 chapters and produced this first regional history and public policy study of higher education in the western United States, which blended the historical character, current status, and public policy problems and perspectives into a narrative picture that is unique, both in the West and among the other regions of the country. Many thanks are owed to the authors and editors who have made these volumes possible.

In fall 2010, critical support for publishing this extensive project came from Professors Roger L. Geiger of Pennsylvania State University and Katherine E. Chaddock of the University of South Carolina who believed the work was highly appropriate for their Palgrave/Macmillan series "Higher Education and Society." At the November 2010 History of Education Society meeting in Boston, Goodchild, on behalf of the other editors, met with them to discuss the project and with their endorsement proposed the project there to Burke Gerstenschlager, Palgrave/Macmillan's higher education editor. He liked it and wanted WICHE's story and contribution to higher education in the West to be more well known. He welcomed a full prospectus. His enthusiasm for the project over the next two years and then Sarah Nathan's, his successor as associate editor, continued support enabled it to be realized. The four-book editors extend their grateful thanks to them and their appreciation to the Palgrave/Macmillan's Editorial Board for making this two-volume project a reality. With the project's completion in 2013, the editors see the work now as part of the sixtieth anniversary celebration of the founding of the Western Interstate Commission for Higher Education.

A Critical Commentary

In his appraisal of America in a "post-American world," Fareed Zakaria (2008, p. 186) called higher education "America's best industry." Perhaps. However, the political consensus to support this growth and development industry has always been a struggle. Nevertheless, higher education in the American West represents a new wave of responsive postsecondary education. Zakaria focused on the global predominance of the major research universities, and this is surely true of the West. Five of the top ten US universities with the most research and development revenues—all world-class institutions, as noted in Arthur Cohen's Chapter 2 in the *Higher Education in the American West: Regional History and State Contexts*—are located in the West. Of course, there are pinnacles of excellence in the West among the public and private institutions at each level and of each type. Community colleges are undoubtedly portals of opportunity to millions of western students, where the 15 WICHE states have some 259 of them, or 25 percent nationally. Among the fewer primarily baccalaureate public institutions and the many public master's and limited doctoral-level institutions, there are likewise many exemplary institutions. Twenty-three of the 37 Tribal Colleges and Universities (TCUs), or 62 percent nationally—the West's truly unique institutions—serve the distinctive needs of Native American students on their tribal lands, both with respect to deepening their cultural knowledge and preparing them for further education. The 119 Hispanic-Serving Institutions (HSIs) in the West represent approximately one-half of the US institutions that enroll more than 25 percent Hispanics in their student populations. Lastly, alternative higher education has a significant home in the West with nonprofit online higher education being represented by the Western Governors University, Regis University, and National University and with for-profit higher education being led by the University of Phoenix and Jones International University in Denver. In total, according to Cheryl Blanco's demographic chapter 1 in this *Public Policy Challenges Facing Higher Education in the American West* book, the West is home to over 1,200 colleges and universities, whether they are public, independent, proprietary, or for-profit.

It may be best to depict the West as a region of regions, and look at common qualitative comparisons in this higher education landscape. However, even within those subregions (such as, the Pacific West with its states of Oregon, Washington, Alaska, and Hawaii), there exist huge differences among and within the states regarding the development and strength of higher education. History, culture, demography, wealth, and surely, the role of visionary and strong leaders, all affect those institutional and subregional profiles, as can be seen in the chapters reviewing Southwest States, the Middle Border States, or Pacific West higher education in the companion volume of this project.

What is at stake for these various kinds of institutions and their constituents in each part of the West? Looking at the future, Roger Geiger claimed that "despite recurrent financial pressures and demographic pressures looming in the next century, the immeasurable contribution of colleges and universities to American life should sustain them through the inevitable challenges lying ahead" (Altbach, Berdahl, and Gumport, 2005, pp. 65–66). However at the close of the twentieth century, Clark Kerr was less sanguine about future prospects or their predictability. In the final edition of his definitive work, *The Uses of the University* (Kerr, 2001), referring to accurate predictions in the first 1963 edition, Kerr wrote: "I wish that today I might again be so prescient about the shape of things to come, but I cannot... I think having a clear view of the future is now much more difficult, perhaps impossible. We live in an age of too many discontinuities, too many variables, too many uncertainties, as almost any university president today can certify" (p. 201). And, in the economic conditions that exist at the time of this writing in mid-2013, those uncertainties seem daunting indeed.

True, there are commonalities and common strengths among our western institutions. The land-grant institutions are high quality, close to their constituents, and oriented to public service. The famed "Wisconsin Idea"—that of a progressive, collaborative relationship between that land-grant university and its state and community—during the first half of the twentieth century surely inspired the later development of those institutions in the West. There are world-class research institutions in the public and private domains, and among smaller private institutions, enormous diversity, especially in value-oriented and church-sponsored institutions. The West took leadership early on in the community college "movement" with some of the first and some of the best. Our western institutions serve an increasingly diverse population—the most diverse in the country. Some have done so admirably, some fall far short of reflecting their communities or states. In fact, the tribal colleges and universities represent a unique example of institutions serving a specific clientele, and most of these institutions are in the western WICHE states. Initially, the classical New England–inspired liberal arts model existed in only relatively limited numbers in the West, because many of that genre sprang out of untilled colonial soil some 350 or more years before the West's development. While some early institutions may have "looked like" the small liberal arts colleges of New England, there was too much of a gap in time and geography for that model to be widely replicated here. Public higher education became dominant in the West. For this reason, the future of higher education in the West remains largely in the hands of state government and public higher education decision makers.

Summing Up

There are major differences between the West and other regions of the United States in terms of higher education institutions, faculty, students, and curriculum, although there are elements within institutional types that are more "uniform" with other parts of the country. Western higher education is a complex enterprise: over 1,200 institutions overlay the enormous and magnificent landscape and the political history of the states. Those institutions, collectively and individually, have a distinctive history that includes thousands of leaders, faculty, and students. It took a myriad of individual decisions in public and private higher education to create and comprise this world.

The enterprise is magnificent, but many of its promises remain unfulfilled. Access is far from universal, and far from equitably distributed across socioeconomic groups. Access to higher education is also greatly hampered by weak links between higher education and K-12 education. Financial resources may or may not be sufficient, but they clearly are distributed unevenly across institutional types and vary enormously among states. Institutions carrying the greatest burdens of access seem to be those least well financed, especially the community and tribal colleges. Though much attention has been paid to striking the "right" balance between research and undergraduate education, we are not there yet. Similarly, efforts to revise and renew curricula are often victims of entrenched interests, or at a deeper level, the absence of a contemporary consensus among the state and campus leaders of higher education.

So, what we may have originally intended as a "celebration" of western higher education and WICHE's contributions has become a more ambiguous and ambitious exercise. It may be that the uniqueness of western higher education with its spirit of innovation, as discussed by Patty Limerick in the companion volume, is as much about its challenges as its triumphs. The challenges of a vast area to serve (one-half the landmass of the United States, larger than all but six of the world's nations); the diversity of a population that includes more than one-half of the US Asian Americans, more than one-half the Native Americans, and more than one-half the non-Cuban and non-Puerto-Rican Hispanics; and, most critically, a political landscape that includes several of the country's most restrictive state tax–limitation laws.

To confront these challenges, much work needs to be done at a time when it looks like the country's resources will be seriously constrained in the short or even medium-range future. We encourage our readers to review both the history of western higher education book (Goodchild, Jonsen, Limerick, and Longanecker, 2014) and its public policy issues in this companion volume, *Public Policy Challenges Facing Higher Education in the American West*. Here our authors address policy concerns related to postsecondary access, federal research funding, state higher education governance, fiscal challenges facing states and public higher education systems, rising costs of tuition, distance education and technology, as well as challenges facing community and tribal colleges. In spite of these concerns, the West has always been a land of hope, promise, and innovation. There is no reason why it should be different for higher education tomorrow.

References

Altbach, P. G., R. O. Berdahl, and P. Gumport. *American Higher Education in the Twenty-First Century: Social, Political, and Economic Challenge*, 2nd ed. Baltimore, MD: Johns Hopkins University Press, 2005.

Goodchild, L. F., R. W. Jonsen, P. Limerick, and D. A. Longanecker (eds.). *Higher Education in the American West: Regional History and State Contexts*. Higher Education and Society series. New York, NY: Palgrave Macmillan, 2014.

Goodchild, L. F., C. D. Lovell, E. R. Hines, and J. I. Gill (eds.). *Public Policy and Higher Education*. Association for the Study of Higher Education Reader Series. Needham Heights, MA: Simon and Schuster Custom Publishing, 1997.

Kerr, C. *The Uses of the University*, 5th ed. Cambridge: Harvard University Press, 2001.

Zakaria, F. *The Post-American World*. New York: Norton, 2008.

DEDICATIONS

With great affection, this book is dedicated to the memory of Michael P. Malone, president of Montana State University from 1991 to 1999, whose idea this book was, to Phillip Sirotkin, executive director of WICHE from 1976 to 1989, whose leadership improved western higher education during his important tenure in office, to Thomas T. Farley, Colorado legislator and board member, who was a generous supporter of both public (the Colorado State University System) and private (Santa Clara University) higher education, and to Loren Wyss, whose leadership as commissioner and chair took WICHE to the next stage.

The words and works of leaders like these echo throughout the companion volumes of this new western regional history and policy study of American higher education:

> *With the economic downturn of the 1980s, westerners came more and more to realize that education was the key to their social, cultural and economic future—just as, in truth, it always had been.*
>
> Michael P. Malone and Richard W. Etulain, *The American West: A Twentieth Century History* (1989, p. 214)

> *Sirotkin proved himself the right person for the WICHE directorship at the right time. His convictions about the needs and potential for regional interstate collaboration and his energy and courage in dealing with governors and legislators inspired responses from commissioners and other WICHE friends and transformed threat to opportunity.*
>
> Frank C. Abbott, *A History of the Western Interstate Commission for Higher Education: The First Forty Years* (2004, p. 247)

> *Thomas T. Farley...dedicated himself to public service and to helping the underdog...(and) in the death of Thomas T. Farley the people of Pueblo and the State of Colorado have lost an outstanding citizen and dedicated public servant.*
>
> House Memorial 11–1001, State of Colorado, August 23, 2010

> *When scholars of the future compile a list of Oregon's most wise, passionate and effective citizen leaders, the name of Loren Wyss will surely be prominent on the list...Loren will be missed for his good-natured wit, generous and caring spirit and his unyielding integrity.*
>
> Bill Allen, from tributes on Loren Wyss, Obituary Notice in the *Portland Oregonian*; Loren Wyss became involved in WICHE programs in 1977, and served as a WICHE Commissioner from 1984 to 1990, as chair of the Commission in 1988–1989.

DEDICATIONS

IN GRATEFUL APPRECIATION

Our grateful thanks to The William and Flora Hewlett Foundation for its generous support of the project that produced this book, and to Sally Tracy for her personal support and patience in approving an interminable journey to its conclusion. We would note the role played by the foundation, and also by the Hewlett family in their support of western higher education. That generosity, as well as William Hewlett's pioneering role in Silicon Valley, has greatly strengthened the economy of the West as well as its colleges and universities. The Wyss Foundation of Portland Oregon also made a generous contribution in the memory of Ann M. Jonsen, late wife of one of the editors, to support the publication of these volumes.

We wish also to acknowledge the valuable assistance of the University of Denver's staff of its Sponsored Programs Office and Mordridge College of Education in assisting with the management of the Hewlett Foundation grant.

We would be remiss not to acknowledge the support of WICHE and the assistance and participation of David Longanecker, its president, in helping to bring this two companion volume project to completion.

Introduction

Lester F. Goodchild, Richard W. Jonsen, Patty Limerick, and David A. Longanecker

In *Public Policy Challenges Facing Higher Education in the American West*, the authors take a wide-angled public policy snapshot of western higher education today. Using some historical comparative demographic data, they reflect on pressing policy issues. The complexity of public and independent higher education confounds any attempt to paint a comprehensive picture, especially across such an enormous region. The challenges facing most states in terms of rapidly changing demographics, added to the recent and current problematic history of finances in most states, and the burdens of rapidly increasing tuition are spine-chilling. This book thus looks at public policy issues today and options for the future, describing the hard choices that will need to be made to strengthen higher education in the West in response to issues of access, quality, efficiency, and affordability. Here the authors address most pointedly the various education scenarios that might unfold in the new millennium.

Most of the book's chapters focus on critical public policy issues facing the western states, their systems of higher education, and the political climates and cultures. In chapter 1, Cheryl Blanco provides a broad demographic portrait of higher education in the 15 WICHE West states over time and profiles the enterprise through the use of data about institutions, enrollments, tuition, and student aid. Distinctive contributions of TCUs and HSIs are also highlighted in this chapter. In chapter 2, Mikyung Ryu paints a picture of western higher education's lagging performances on some measures, especially the declining affordability of western institutions over the past decade and dropping college-going rates of high school graduates, with mixed results in the category of college completion. In chapter 3, WICHE President David Longanecker explores the federal role in funding research during the contemporary era with a focus on how such agencies as the National Science Foundation, the National Institutes of Health, Department of Defense, the Department of Energy, and others have provided critical research funding for faculty at research universities to advance scientific and medical discoveries. Many of these developments have unique western aspects. In chapter 4, Aims McGuinness examines the structures of higher education governance in western states and the nation, which have been particularly affected by the change in political climate during the Great Recession, and finds them inadequate for the tough decisions needed ahead. In chapter 5, Dennis Jones realistically describes the policy trajectory of western states in funding higher education and lays out the stark policy options to provide a positive future direction. State economic downturns during the Great Recession since 2008 have made higher education's funding more problematic. In chapter 6 Charles Lenth, Kathleen Zaback, Andrew Carlson, and Allison Bell fill out the statistical fiscal picture by looking at the past 25 years and the evolution of the relationship of state-to-student financing of public higher education, with the former shrinking as a proportion of total revenues and the latter growing to place strains on families and sources of financial aid. In chapter 7 Sally Johnstone and Ritchie Boyd document the explosive growth in technology-based higher education, but they make no prediction about the likelihood of these technologies solving some of the basic problems of access, affordability, and completion. In chapter 8, Cheryl Lovell looks specifically at policy issues related to the community and tribal colleges, and at the distinctive role those institutions have played in the West, providing a great deal of the initial access, particularly to public higher education, and making up an important aspect of the character of higher education in many of these states.

Finally, David Longanecker's Afterword ponders what we have learned from this exercise. He offers some alternative scenarios and the policy actions that will propel them as western higher education enters perhaps its most challenging era. That challenge can fairly be described as a perfect storm of economic recession, growing and changing demographics, and an unprepared state higher education enterprise. Longanecker writes that in an "all else being equal" need not be the only vision or reality of the West's future. Diversity is an advantage in relating to a global economy. The West's strength in securing federal funding promises continued leadership in innovation, which so characterizes the West. Community colleges also provide a powerful tool for both access and workforce training for a rapidly evolving economy. The centrality of public policy creates potential for marshaling both planning power and political will. Longanecker contends that we must improve in almost every facet of the higher education enterprise—if we are to succeed in this regard. Perhaps the current profound recession can supply the motivation and the political will to rethink the organization, funding, and operation of this vital higher education enterprise, and make the next decades a time of renewal, energy, and new success for the West's colleges and universities.

This first major public policy study of a region in American higher education offers a comprehensive commentary on that region's challenges and opportunities. The successes of efforts over the past 130 or so years is amply demonstrated by the robustness and excellence of the research sector (a remarkable 5 of the top 25 research universities worldwide, as ranked by the *Times of London*, are in this region), as well as the diversity of the enterprise, with its robust community college systems, urban-service universities, independent colleges and universities, tribal colleges and universities, Hispanic-serving institutions, and the growing for-profit sector and burgeoning virtual university movement. These institutions continue to be vigorous and innovative, even in a time of great financial difficulties. Visionary educational and political leadership will be required to forge an even stronger future.

Part I

PUBLIC POLICY DEMOGRAPHIC BACKGROUND

1

A Demographic Profile of Higher Education in the American West

*Cheryl D. Blanco**

This chapter provides a limited set of data to outline a statistical profile of higher education for the western states. There was no attempt to gather all possible information that might inform the development of higher education in the West. Rather, data were selected to help the reader put other chapters of this book and the complementary policy papers in a context of numbers related to higher education as it serves the increasingly large and diverse population of the West.

The most comprehensive source for population data is the US Bureau of the Census, and much of the information in this section is taken from its reports and internet web pages. The Bureau of the Census presents data regionally in four sections. The region identified as the West by the bureau does not include North Dakota and South Dakota. As these states are members of the Western Interstate Commission for Higher Education (WICHE), information for these states has been incorporated in the regional data as part of the West whenever possible. The chapter begins with general population and demographic information on the United States and the western region, followed by data on educational institutions, enrollments, and degrees.

General Demographic Trends

Population: United States

The first national population census occurred in 1790, more than a century after the establishment of the nation's first institution of higher education at Harvard, chartered in 1636. The first census reported the population of the United States as 3.9 million.[1] By the beginning of the twentieth century, the population had reached 76.2 million (Hobbs and Stoops, 2002, p. 17; Thelin, 2011, p. xxii).

Census data reveal tremendous growth in the US population in the 100 years that followed, as the population more than quadrupled from

76 million to 308.7 million people in 2010. This growth, however, was irregular, with two periods experiencing lulls and spurts: the Great Depression decade of the 1930s with the lowest numerical increase and the post–World War II baby boom with record population growth in the 1950s and the baby-boom echo following in the 1990s (Hobbs and Stoops, 2002, p. 17).

As the general population increased dramatically between 1900 and 2010, the nation also began experiencing several demographic shifts. According to a Census Bureau analysis, "As the United States entered the 20th century, most of the population lived in the Northeast or the Midwest, in non-metropolitan areas, was male, under 23 years old, White, and rented a home; nearly half lived in a household with five or more other people. One hundred years later, as the United States entered the 21st century, most of the population lived in the South or the West, in metropolitan areas, was female, at least 35 years old, White (but much less so), owned a home, and lived alone or in a household with one or two other people" (Hobbs and Stoops, 2002, p. 12).

The developments of interest for this book include the move from rural to metropolitan areas, the shift to the West, and the increasing racial/ethnic diversity of the American people. The implications of these trends and additional information are covered in more detail in later sections. Briefly, however, the census documents how the population became more metropolitan over the decades. From a predominantly rural nation in the 1790s, the city had come to dominate the country by the 1990s. "Metropolitanization" particularly characterized the demographic change of the United States in the twentieth century. Before World War II, the majority of Americans lived outside metropolitan territory. By the end of the century, four of every five people in the United States resided in a metropolitan area. The US population has shifted toward the South and West, and these regions dominated the last century's population growth. Together, the West and the South increased by 471 percent during the twentieth century, compared with the combined increase of 149 percent for the Northeast and Midwest.

Population: The West

In every decade of the twentieth century and the first decade of the twenty-first century, the West's population increased more rapidly than that of any other region. The West's population was more than 18 times larger in 2010 than in 1900, increasing from 4 million to 73.4 million in that period (see figure 1.1; Hobbs and Stoops, 2002, p. 23; US Bureau of the Census, Population Distribution and Change, 2000–2010).

At the state level, several individual western states outpaced states in other regions and accounted for nine of the ten fastest-growing states between 1900 and 2000. In the first decade of the twenty-first century, four of the top five growth states have been in the West, with Arizona and Nevada consistently in this group.

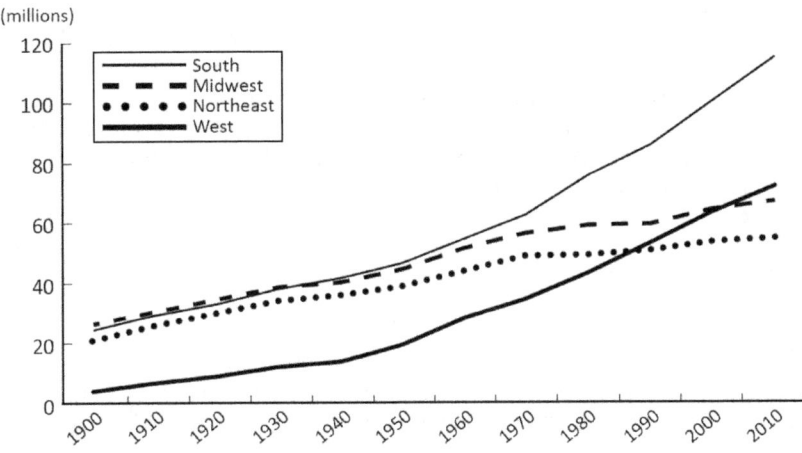

Figure 1.1 Total population by region, 1900–2010.
Source: US Bureau of the Census, *Population Distribution and Change: 2000 to 2010*, Table 1, p. 2.

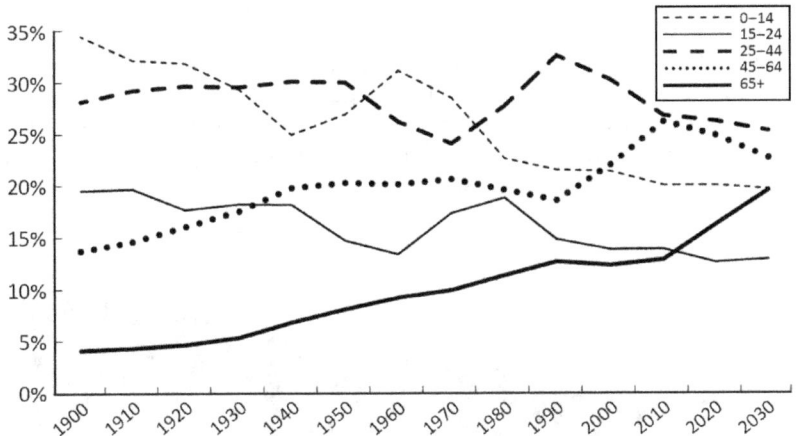

Figure 1.2 Distribution of population by age groups, US 1900–2030.
Source: Hobbs and Stoops, *Demographic Trends in the 20th Century*, Table 5, 2002.

Age: United States

Age data provide essential information in understanding the potential size and distribution of the pool of individuals entering college as traditionally aged students or as adult learners. Data since the beginning of the twentieth century document the changing age patterns in the national population (see figure 1.2).

The shift in the precollege-age portion of the population is most notable: in 1900, approximately one-third of the population was under age 14; by

2010, that proportion had dropped to about one-fifth. The members of the population aged 45–64 and those 65 and over have each increased their share of the population.

As the twenty-first century progresses, the share of the nation's youngest population, those from 0 to 24 years of age, will decline modestly. The largest decline in share will occur among those aged 45–64, as that group will move from 26 percent of the total population to 23 percent. The only increase in percentage share will be in the nation's oldest population group; by 2030, nearly one-in-five people in the United States will be at least 65 years of age.

Age: The West

The western states also experienced significant population shifts across major age groups during the twentieth century. The age group under 15 years numbered 1.2 million in 1900, but had grown to more than 16 million by 2010. The population in the West between the ages of 16 and 64 was 2.7 million in 1900 and 48.5 million in 2010. Proportionally, the share of the population in the West under age 15 declined between 1900 and 2010 from close to 35 percent to 22 percent. That loss transferred into growth in both of the other age groups.

Projections for the western states suggest that some of the trends in age groups will continue well into this century. Numerically, all age groups will be larger in 2030 than they were in 2000 (see figure 1.3). While all age groups will grow in number, the percentage increase varies considerably. The oldest group, those aged 65 and over, is projected to see growth of 145 percent. The group projected to increase at the lowest rate is 25–44-year-olds at 23 percent.

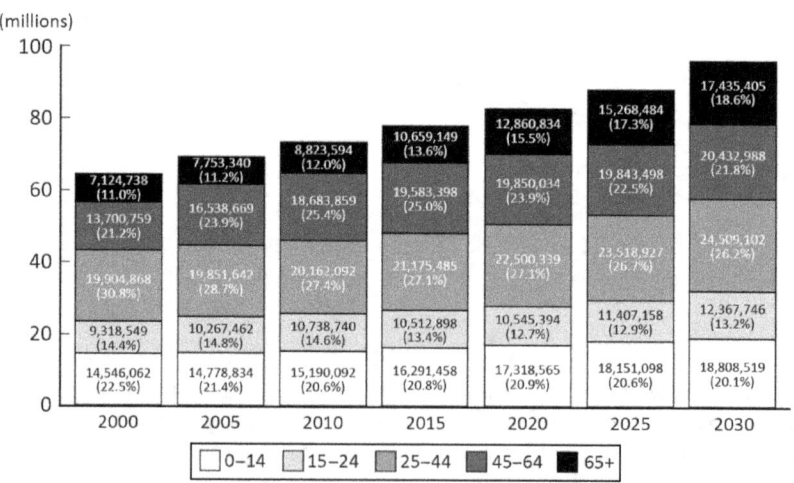

Figure 1.3 Projected numerical and percentage distribution of population by age groups, WICHE region, 2000–2030.

Source: US Census Bureau, *Interim State Population Projections*, 2005. File 3.

Proportionally, the West is expected to follow age trends similar to those at the national level (see figure 1.3). The youngest population group—those aged 0–14—will be a share of the population similar to the oldest group at about 20 percent, but this older group will have increased as a percentage of the total population. The largest decline will occur among those aged 25–44, as they will account for 26 percent of the population in 2030, a drop of nearly 5 percentage points from 2000.

Race/Ethnicity: United States

The phenomenal change in the racial/ethnic fabric of the United States started slowly in the early twentieth century and gained considerable momentum by mid-century. In 1900, approximately one out of ten Americans was of a race other than White; early in the twenty-first century, the ratio is approximately one out of four. Hispanic populations have experienced dramatic increases nationally and regionally. In many states, the Asian and Pacific Islander population more than tripled. The Census Bureau notes that "the vast majority of growth in the total population came from increases in those who reported their race(s) as something other than White alone and those who reported their ethnicity as Hispanic or Latino" (US Bureau of the Census, *Overview of Race and Hispanic Origin, 2010*, p. 3).

Until 1970, the US population was predominantly classified as either White or Black; those portions of the population that were of other races numbered fewer than three million, or approximately 1.4 percent of the population. By 2000, there were 35 million people in the United States who were of races other than White or Black (Hobbs and Stoops, 2002, p. 72). When considered collectively, minorities as a group (including all races other than White or people of Hispanic origin) grew by 88 percent between 1980 and 2000. By 2010, minorities accounted for one-third of the US population. Hawaii had become a majority minority state by 1980, when more than 50 percent of the population was minority. Among the western states, California and New Mexico had joined Hawaii by 2000.

The complexity of reporting and analyzing racial/ethnic data took a new turn with the 2000 census when, for the first time, respondents were given new options to report their racial/ethnic background. One of the more challenging options allowed respondents to self-identify as "Two or more races." In Census 2010, 2.9 percent of respondents listed "Two or more races," which may be any combination of the individual races, including combinations with White. The percentage of the population identifying as two or more races varies among the regions. For purposes of this chapter, data after 2000 are not comparable to earlier data due to these changes in reporting.

Race/Ethnicity: The West

Some of the regional concentrations of populations by race/ethnicity that characterized the beginning of the twentieth century changed over time, as

Blacks relocated from the South to other parts of the country and Asian/Pacific Islanders moved out of the West in larger numbers, particularly to the East and Midwest. The American Indian and Alaska Native populations continued to remain predominantly in the West. Reflecting these movements, the South had the highest percentage of races other than White in every census from 1900 to 1980. The West has had the highest percentage of races other than White since 1980. In 2010, nearly 46 percent of the population in the West was minority (people who reported their ethnicity and race as something other than non-Hispanic White alone in the decennial census). The marked increase in the West's minority population since 1980 increased the gap with other regions on the share of the population that is minority. The groups comprising the minority populations among the regions also vary, with Blacks accounting for the largest share in all regions outside the West. During the twentieth century, Blacks became an increasing presence in the West, as did Asian/Pacific Islanders.

Hispanics in Western Higher Education

Now the largest ethnic minority, Hispanics (the census term) are also the fastest-growing. This is particularly true in the southwest states, including the western states of Arizona, California, and New Mexico. In those three states (and Texas as well), WICHE projects that by 2021–2022 Hispanics will constitute almost one-half of high school graduates. They already do so in New Mexico (WICHE, 2012).

This profound demographic shift, seen against the persistently lagging high school and college completion rates of Hispanic students, as well as their lower socioeconomic status, poses a profound challenge to higher education throughout the country, and especially so in the WICHE states. Santiago and Brown (2004) point out that in 2000, only 22 percent of Hispanics were enrolled in colleges and universities, compared with 40 percent of White, non-Hispanics and 56 percent of Asians.

Nationally, fewer than one-half of Hispanic high school graduates go on to enroll in undergraduate degree programs (WICHE, 2008; *The Chronicle of Higher Education*, 2008). In California, the Hispanic student population is huge, both numerically and proportionally. In 2009–2910, when 41 percent of the state's public high school graduates were Hispanic, very few of California's four-year institutions approached even one-half of that figure. The notable exception: more than one-half of the California State University campuses exceeded that percent and several enrolled more than 45 percent Hispanics (WICHE, 2012; *US News and World Report*, 2013).

Although Hispanic students exist in every state and institution, they are concentrated both institutionally and geographically, with most enrolled in community colleges in the western states. The Hispanic Association of Colleges and Universities (HACU) estimates that its 350 college and university members enroll more than half of Hispanic college students (HACU, 2013). Through HACU's efforts, the federal government began recognizing institutions with more than 25 percent Hispanic enrollment as Hispanic-Serving Institutions (HSIs) in 1992. More than one-half of these institutions are in California and Texas.

As a result of HACU's continuing advocacy, several federal programs open to HSIs began supporting those institutions after 1995. In 2008, $93 million was appropriated for HSIs under Title V of the Higher Education Act (HACU, 2009). However, the larger issue is the amount of financial aid available and actually awarded to Latino students, whether in HSIs, or HACU institutions, or not. The picture is not encouraging. In a report for the Pew Hispanic Center, Santiago and Brown (2004) found that, "Latinos receive the lowest average amount of financial aid awarded—by type and source of aid—of any ethnic group...Latinos also received the smallest grants of any ethnic group, larger loans than Black or American Indian/Alaska Native students, and lower work-study awards than White or Asian/Pacific Islander students" (p. 8). Even after factoring in the concentration of Latino students in lower-tuition community colleges (more than one-half), this finding is disheartening.

Unlike Tribal Colleges and Universities (TCUs), which are also federally recognized, HSIs are defined by proportion of Hispanic students, and HACU members are self-selected. Thus, there is no profile that fits all such institutions with respect to mission, curriculum, composition of enrollment, or location. However, a majority of HSIs are community colleges, whose districts exist in heavily Hispanic communities. And the 25 percent criterion means that many institutions serving large numbers of Latino students (e.g., UCLA with more than 4,600 Hispanics, representing 17 percent of its undergraduate enrollment) are not HSIs.

Unlike the TCUs which represent an imaginative and entrepreneurial solution to the problem of equitable access to college opportunity for an important and historically underrepresented minority group, the HSIs and HACU institutions also represent more traditional institutions that are responding in more conventional ways to the same issue on behalf of a minority group that is large and rapidly growing. However, among leading institutions educating Hispanic students, there are such practices as developing strong linkages with feeder schools, community colleges, and community-based organizations (Santiago, Andrade, and Brown, 2004).

Already the majority of students in New Mexico, Hispanics will continue to increase their share of the college-age population in the coming decade. In some other states they will become majorities or near-majorities. This means that to the issue of equal opportunity is added a critical issue of workforce representation and economic development. In those heavily Latino states, these students represent the future workforce at all levels. At their current level of educational progress, Latinos will not make the contribution to a highly educated workforce and vibrant economy that is critically needed to restore and to keep that economy humming. That contribution cannot be made without strengthened support, both for the students and the institutions that enroll them.

References

Chronicle of Higher Education. "2008–2009 Almanac Edition," August 20, 2008.

Hispanic Association of Colleges and Universities (HACU). Retrieved from www.hacu.net, in December 2013.

Prescott, B. T., and P. Bransberger. *Knocking at the College Door, 2008, 2012.* Boulder, CO: Western Interstate Commission for Higher Education, 2008, 2012.

Santiago, D., and S. Brown. "Federal Policy and Latinos in Higher Education." Washington, DC: Excelencia in Education, 2004. Retrieved from www.edexcelencia.org.

Santiago, D., S. J. Andrade, and S. E. Brown. "Latino Student Success at Hispanic Serving Institutions: Findings from a Demonstration Project." Washington, DC: Excelencia in Education, 2004. Retrieved from www.edexcelencia.org.

US News & World Report. *America's Best Colleges.* Washington, DC: US News & World Report, 2013.

—*Richard W. Jonsen*

American Indians/Alaska Natives

Unlike other minority groups, American Indians and Alaska Natives have tended to remain primarily in the West. The proportional representation of this group in the national population was the slowest to increase early in the century, when the group represented from 0.23 percent to 0.31 percent of the population and their numbers ranged from 237,000 to 343,000. The population grew more rapidly in the last one-half of the twentieth century and reached nearly 1 percent of the population and over 2.2 million people. The Bureau of the Census suggests that changes in reporting may account for the large statistical change (Hobbs and Stoops, 2002, p. 86; US Bureau of the Census, *Overview of Race and Hispanic Origin*, 2010).[2]

The American Indian/Alaska Native population in the West numbered close to 124,000 in 1900, about 2.5 percent of the total population then.

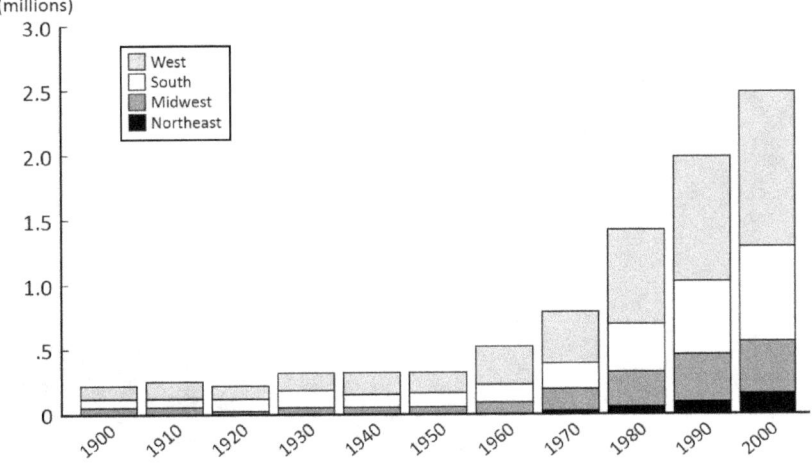

Figure 1.4 American Indian/Alaska native population by US region, 1900–2000.
Source: Hobbs and Stoops, *Demographic Trends in the 20th Century*, Tables 8 and 9, 2002.

Gradual increases brought the number to nearly 1.3 million in 2000 or 2 percent of the population in the West (see figure 1.4). By 2010, the American Indian/Alaska Native population had grown to more than 1,445,000 million and accounted for 2 percent of the population.

In 1900, the western states with the highest percentages of American Indian and Alaska Native people were: Arizona, Nevada, New Mexico, Montana, Idaho, North Dakota, Washington, and Wyoming. By 2010, Alaska was in this group, while Nevada had dropped out of the top tier of states.

Asians/Pacific Islanders

Data have been available for Asians and Pacific Islanders throughout the last century. Population trends indicate that this group has experienced dramatic growth, from 114,000 in 1900 to nearly 10.6 million in 2000 (see figure 1.5). As noted earlier, immigration has been a significant factor in this increase, and the entry of Hawaii to statehood during the 1950s also contributed to the increase.

The Asian and Pacific Islander population also had a strong regional concentration. From 1900 to 1940, about four out of five Asians and Pacific Islanders lived in the West, but the numbers dropped noticeably between 1940 and 1950, primarily due to the forced relocation programs enacted during World War II (Hobbs and Stoops, 2002, p. 80). By the beginning of the twenty-first century there were 5.3 million Asians and Pacific Islanders in the West, nearly 9 percent of the population. In 2010, the Asian population alone in the West was nearly 6.7 million or 9 percent of the population.

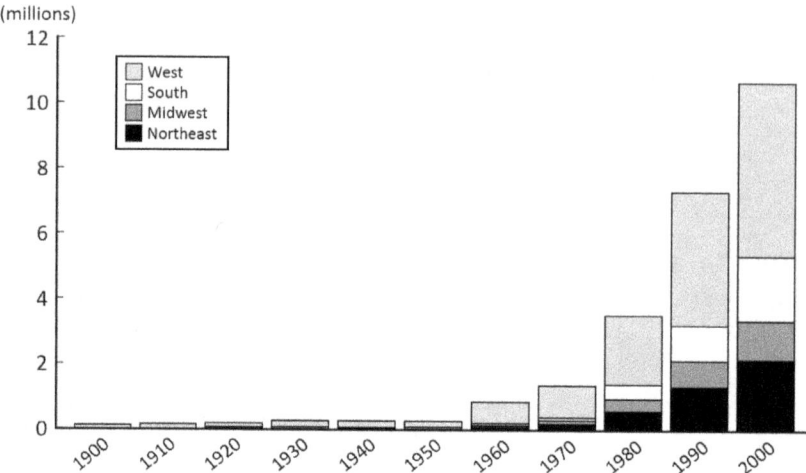

Figure 1.5 Asian/Pacific Islander population by US region, 1900–2000.
Source: Hobbs and Stoops, *Demographic Trends in the 20th Century*, Tables 8 and 9, 2002.

The Native Hawaiian or Other Pacific Islander population numbered nearly 408,000, or less than 1 percent of the population.

Blacks

Data on Blacks were collected at the national level much earlier than other race or ethnic information. To maintain consistency with the presentation of information on other groups, however, the trend analysis of the Black population here covers the period from 1900 to 2000. During that century, the size of the Black population grew steadily from 8.8 million in 1900 to almost 34.7 million in 2000 (see figure 1.6). Although the numbers escalated after 1960, the proportion of the total population that was Black increased only 1 percent over the twentieth century—from 11.6 percent to 12.6 percent—due to increased numbers of other minority groups. In 2010, the Black or African-American population alone or in combination in the United States numbered 42 million and represented 13.6 percent of the population.

The West has historically had fewer Blacks than other regions, and they have made up a smaller proportion of the population. In 1900, the West counted only 31,000 Blacks, accounting for less than 1 percent of the population. Following the national pattern, their numbers increased steadily until 1960 when the number of Blacks in the West jumped from close to 171,400 to 571,800—a 234 percent increase in one decade. Growth continued throughout the later part of the century, and Blacks numbered close to 3.1 million in 2000, representing nearly 5 percent of the population in the West. In 2010, the West counted 4.1 million Blacks alone or in combination—or 10 percent of the region's population.

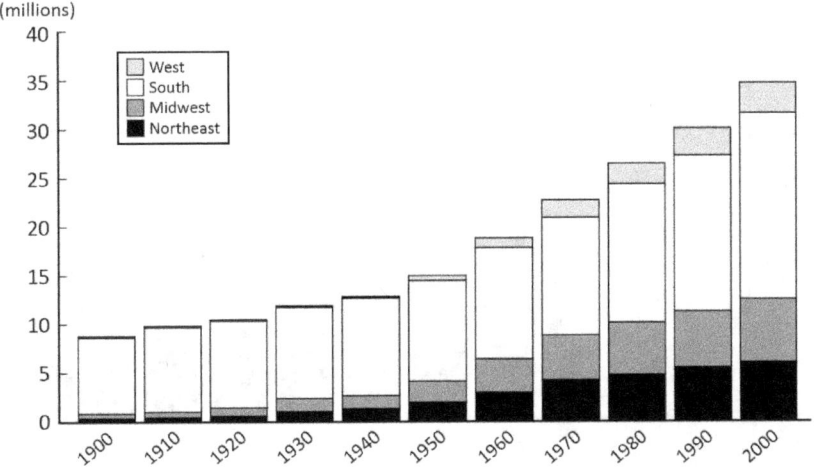

Figure 1.6 Black population by US region, 1900–2000.
Source: Hobbs and Stoops, *Demographic Trends in the 20th Century*, Tables 8 and 9, 2002.

Whites

Although the numbers of Whites in the general population dominated all other racial groups' numbers for years, that trend diminished during the twentieth century with unprecedented growth in most other races. Growth in numbers and share of the total population peaked in 1930, when the White share was just under 90 percent. Gradual decline in the share of the population marked the remainder of the century. Even though the number of Whites grew annually, the growth rate weakened so that by 2010 Whites alone or in combination made up 75 percent of the United States population.

The story of the White population in the West has been similar to that of the nation, but occurring somewhat later (see figure 1.7). In 1900, Whites in the West represented nearly 95 percent of the region's population. By 1940, this group reached its peak at 96 percent of the population in the West. By mid-century, increasing numbers of people from other races were migrating to the West, and the share that Whites represented in the population began to decline at a steady and growing pace. In 2010, the 50.6 million Whites (alone or in combination) in the West were 78 percent of the population.

The significant changes in the West's population are nowhere better illustrated than in the demographic makeup of the region's high school graduates. Between 1991–1992 and 2004–2005, the number of high school graduates in the western states increased by 217,000, or nearly 42 percent. Like other regions, this growth rate will taper off for a few years before picking up again in 2015. Hispanics will account for the majority of the growth in the elementary and secondary school population, resulting in potentially

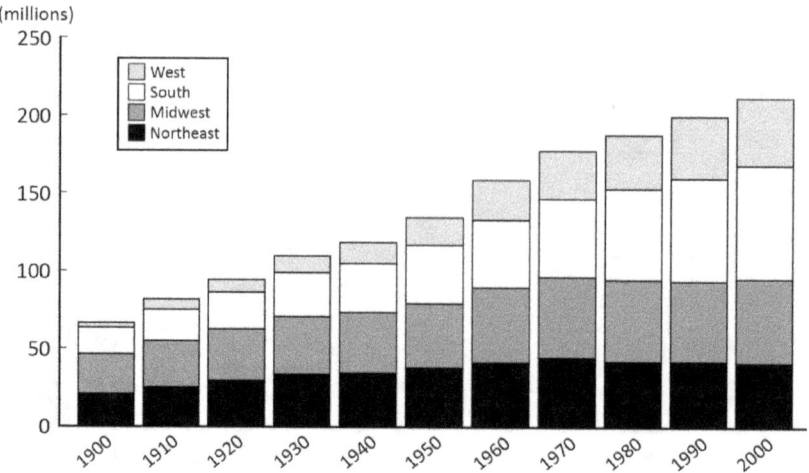

Figure 1.7 White population by US region, 1900–2000.
Source: Hobbs and Stoops, *Demographic Trends in the 20th Century*, Tables 8 and 9, 2002.

large increases in the number of high school graduates who are of Hispanic origin. In a very different trajectory, the number of high school graduates who are White non-Hispanic has already begun to decline, a trend that is projected to continue (WICHE, 2012). While the economic recession that began in 2007–2008 may have shifted these patterns among Western states, it is clear that the region remains subject to the powerful forces of growth and accelerating diversification.

Hispanics

The population of Hispanic origin is defined as another group for federal statistical purposes and may be of any race (US Bureau of the Census, *Overview of Race and Hispanic Origin: 2010*).[3] The Bureau of the Census reports information from 1980, 1990, 2000, and 2010 which disaggregates the data; in the 2010 census, federal agencies were required to use a minimum of two ethnicities: "Hispanic or Latino" and "Not Hispanic or Latino." Nationally, Hispanics alone grew in number from 14.6 million to 50.5 million or by 246 percent between 1980 and 2010. During that period, people of Hispanic origin more than doubled their representation in the total population from 6 percent to 16.3 percent; by 2010, one in six individuals was of Hispanic origin. The Bureau of the Census notes that, "High levels of immigration contributed to this rapid growth, coupled with relatively high fertility levels" (Hobbs and Stoops, 2002, p. 74).

The growing dispersion of Hispanics beyond western states was becoming evident by the end of the twentieth century. The West has reported the largest proportion of Hispanics in the nation since 1980. At that time, nearly

43 percent of all Hispanics in the United States (6.3 million) lived in the West, with another 31 percent (4.5 million) in the South. The West's proportion increased to 45 percent in 1990, but declined in 2010 to 41 percent, which equaled 20.6 million people. Conversely, the South saw an increase to 36 percent, or 18.2 million, in 2010 (Hobbs and Stoops, 2002, Tables 8 and 9, p. 74; US Bureau of the Census, *The Hispanic Population: 2010*, Table 2, p. 6).

Several western states have experienced considerable growth in the numbers of people reporting Hispanic origin. In California, for example, 19 percent of the population was of Hispanic origin in 1980, but that proportion had increased to 38 percent three decades later, equaling Texas in that over one-third of the population was Hispanic by 2010. Only New Mexico has a higher proportion of Hispanics, which grew from nearly 37 percent in 1980 to 46 percent in 2010. Arizona is another western state that has reported significant growth; there, the Hispanic portion of the population increased from 16 percent to 30 percent in the last three decades (Hobbs and Stoops, 2002, Table 10, p. 74; US Bureau of the Census, *The Hispanic Population: 2010*, Table 2, p. 6).

The Census Bureau reports that the Hispanic population is projected to more than double between 2000 and 2050. While international migration has had an important effect on the growth in the Hispanic population, it is not the only factor. A higher fertility rate relative to other racial and ethnic groups and a much lower median age relative to the total population also are significant reasons for the projected dramatic growth (US Bureau of the Census, "United States Population Projections: 2000 to 2050," pp. 3–4).

Age by Race/Ethnicity: United States

Some of the general aging trends seen in the national population are also present in the various racial/ethnic groups. All portions of the population, regardless of race or ethnicity, are aging, although Whites and Asians and Pacific Islanders have higher proportions of their populations in the older age groups, while Blacks, Hispanics, and American Indians and Alaska Natives are somewhat younger (Hobbs and Stoops, 2002, p. 71). In 2000, the "two or more races" population, only available in Census 2000, had the highest percentage (36 percent) of its population under age 15 (Hobbs and Stoops, 2002, p. 70).

During the twentieth century, race groups in the United States had varying rates of fertility, the principal factor determining the proportion of young people in a population. Even so, nearly every race group experienced a general decline in their young populations (Hobbs and Stoops, 2002, p. 106). The proportion of the youngest age group, ages 0–14, in the population has generally declined since about 1960 for all races. The 0–14-year-old group comprised a large share of the population in 1960, but in the four remaining decades of the last century, the proportion of the population in this age group dropped steadily. The 15–24-year-old group comprised a smaller share of the population and has fluctuated throughout the decades. Again, compared with other races in 2000, American Indians/Alaska Natives had the largest share in this age group and Whites had the smallest share. Those aged 25–44 represented a large proportion of the population among all races, with American Indians/Alaska Natives and Blacks experiencing growth in the representation of this group in their populations. In contrast, Asians have seen a steady decline since 1900. The age group 45–64 has contained a smaller percentage of the population than most other age groups since the twentieth century began. In 1900, Asians saw the largest proportion in this age group compared to Blacks with the smallest share.

The oldest age group shows some of the greatest variations among the four races and across the decades. Among American Indians/Alaska Natives, only about 5 or 6 percent of the population every decade has fallen in this age category. Whites have experienced the greatest change in the share of its population in this age group: while 4 percent of Whites were 65 or over in 1900, that share had grown to 14 percent by 2000.

As noted earlier, data on all Hispanics have been collected since 1980. Nonetheless, in the short span of two decades, noticeable changes are apparent in the size of the age groups in the population. The youngest age group made up 32 percent of the Hispanic population in 1980 and 30 percent in 2000. The proportion of the population 15–24 years old also declined by 3 percent in that period. On the other hand, the 25–44-year-old group saw a 5 percent increase in the two decades, while the oldest age groups saw little change in their share of the population.

Mobility

Population mobility is a very real issue for higher education and a key component of demographic trends. As state higher education entities develop or update master plans and enrollment projections, they are concerned not only with population changes within the state but also trends for in-migration patterns. Population and student mobility concerns also impact a wide range of related issues; the implications for public policy are many and varied—touching issues of tuition setting, financial aid, appropriations, housing, faculty, facilities management, residency requirements, transfer, student outcomes, efficiency, and linkages with K-12.

According to the Bureau of the Census, approximately 37.5 million Americans moved between 2009 and 2010. Approximately 16 percent of all movers in 2010 reported that they moved for work-related reasons, and the percentage of movers listing this reason generally increased as the educational level of the respondent increased. For example, work-related reasons prompted 12 percent of movers with less than a high school education to relocate, compared to 24 percent of those with a bachelor's degree (US Bureau of Census, 2010).

The West has become a destination for persons who are relocating. Between 2009 and 2010, 631,000 people moved into the West. However, 478,000 people left the West for other regions—most of them headed south.

Migration trends are linked to higher education enrollments, particularly of first-time freshmen. Six western states—Idaho, Montana, North Dakota, South Dakota, Utah, and Wyoming—have high percentages (more than 25 percent) of freshman college students who come from other states. In addition, 20 to 25 percent of students attending institutions in Oregon come from other states or countries. High percentages of students from WICHE states also elect to attend institutions in other states. Hawaii, Idaho, North Dakota, and Washington send between 20 and 30 percent of their residents to other states for college (WICHE, "Regional Factbook for Higher Education in the West", www.wiche.edu).

National research shows that large shares of undergraduate students attend more than one college or university. Recent data from the National Student Clearinghouse Research Center indicate that nearly one million mobile students—those attending more than one postsecondary institution concurrently or consecutively—attended a combination of two- and four-year institutions between August, 2010, and August, 2011. Additionally, many mobile students cross state lines to attend postsecondary institutions: on average, 15.1 percent of all US postsecondary students who received undergraduate degrees in 2010–2011 had previously attended college in at least one other state or territory (National Student Clearinghouse Research Center, 2011).

The demographics presented above trace the rapid shift in the profile of the nation and, most particularly, the western states. By 2010, the West had become a majority minority region in terms of the racial/ethnic background of its high school graduates (WICHE, 2008). The impact on higher education is well underway, as individual states and institutions reassess their capacity and their ability to adequately serve students who may be very unlike the traditional college freshman of the past. As the following section also shows, the profile of the nation's collection of higher education institutions also has changed remarkably in the past century.

Education

Secondary Schools: United States

The nature of the nation's changing population is reflected in growth trends in the number of public and private schools with secondary grades over nearly eight decades between 1929 and 2008 (see figure 1.8). Private schools experienced moderate growth through the end of the 1950s, but their numbers grew much faster in the twenty-first century.

Enrollments in grades 9 through 12 reflected the trends in the number of schools between 1869 and 1999. The US Department of Education reported 80,000 students in public schools for grades 9 through 12 in 1869; that number had reached 6.6 million by the beginning of World War II and dropped to 5.7 million as the nation entered the 1950s. By the end of that decade, however, enrollments had jumped to nearly 8.3 million students and to 13.6 million by the end of the 1970s. The decline in the number of

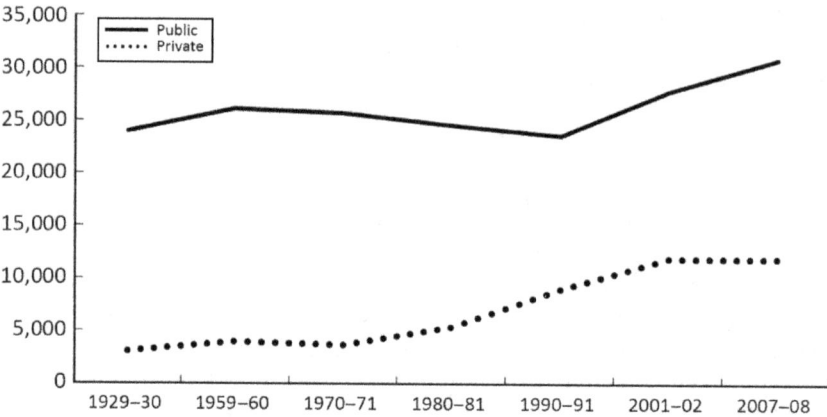

Figure 1.8 US public and private schools with secondary grades (9–12), 1929–2008.
Source: US Dept. of Education, *Digest of Education Statistics 2010*, Table 90.

schools for grades 9 through 12 that marked the 1980s and 1990s was also seen in enrollments, as the number of students in those grades dropped to 11.3 million. Enrollments rose again and approached 15 million in 2008 (US Department of Education, "Enrollment in Educational Institutions," Table 3, 2009 and 2010 as well as Table 2).

As noted earlier, the number of children between the ages of 0 and 14 is projected to increase from 60.25 million in 2000 to 68 million in 2030. This growth has the potential to place increased demands on higher education institutions, especially if the states are successful in graduating more children from low-income groups and families of color and guiding them to higher education.

Institutions of Higher Education: United States

Since 1869, the total number of institutions of higher education in the United States increased from 563 to 4,495 in 2010. While growth was relatively constant throughout the period, with the exception of the last decade of the nineteenth century and the first decade of the twentieth century, the greatest increase occurred as baby boomers began to graduate from high school in large numbers in the 1960s and campuses expanded to meet the demand. Between 1960 and 2000, approximately 500 new institutions opened each decade, resulting in twice as many colleges and universities in 2000 than the nation had in 1960.

Tribal Colleges and Universities

Among the richest areas of diversity in the tapestry of western higher education are the tribal colleges and universities (TCUs). While the establishment of an American Indian university was proposed as far back as 1911 (Stein, 2003, p. 30),* the actual founding of the tribal colleges and universities is of recent origin. Diné College, founded in 1968 as Navajo Community College, in Tsaile, Arizona, is the oldest of the TCUs.

The motivation for the tribal college movement came largely from the recognition that the standard postsecondary educational programs available to American Indian students were not serving them well, and, at the most basic level, did not provide access to these students on geographically isolated tribal lands. Another important factor was that the strengthening and advancing of American Indian tribes and culture, most importantly language, had inadequate institutional vehicles on or off the reservations and tribal lands. The larger context for the TCU movement is the push for self-governance on the part of the Indian tribes—tribal sovereignty and self-determination, which have constituted a growing aspect of American Indian culture and society since the rejection of the Federal Termination Policy of the 1950s.

At present, there are 37 US members of the American Indian Higher Education Consortium (AIHEC), which was founded in 1972 to support and represent the TCUs. Of those 37 TCUs, most are regionally accredited, and 29 are recognized as federal land-grant institutions, a status secured for them by the AIHEC in 1994. The TCUs are imbedded in the tribes they serve, but they are governed for the most part through independent boards of trustees, which provide a buffer between the institutions and tribal politics.

AIHEC members report a total of about 19,000 students (Fall, 2010). Although this represents less than 10 percent of the total enrollment of American Indian students nationwide—which in Fall, 2010 was 196,400, or about 1 percent of all US college and university students (USDOE, 2013), the AIHEC institutions fill a vital niche for the students and communities they serve. Two-thirds of their students are women, and AIHEC characterizes the typical students as "a single mother in her early 30s" (AIHEC). Furthermore, about 20 percent of students at AIHEC institutions are non-Indian, signifying the broad-based contribution to access represented by these often geographically isolated TCUs.

The objectives of the TCUs commonly include the following six, which reflect their overall institutional missions:

- Providing vocational, career, and academic opportunities, including transfer programs to four-year institutions;
- Preparing tribal leadership;
- Preserving, promoting, and developing American Indian culture, especially Native languages;
- Serving community needs through continuing education and other programs;

- Providing opportunities for research; and
- Preparing professionals, especially teachers and nurses, to serve Native American students.

Many of the TCUs have developed effective and creative relationships with four-year institutions in their home states and elsewhere. These relationships are extremely important for the 40 percent of students who express their intent to transfer. This articulation between the four-year public institutions and the TCUs seems to be especially effective in Montana, North Dakota, and Minnesota (Stein, 2009), having benefited TCU students transferring into four-year programs and providing some upper-level and graduate courses delivered to the TCU. Several TCUs now have their own baccalaureate programs, and even graduate study, particularly in teacher education. Some, such as Salish Kootenai College in Montana, have harnessed information technologies to provide distance learning and other opportunities (O'Donnell and others in Benham and Stein, 2003).

Funding is a continuing struggle for most TCUs, a difficulty reflected in the very low structure of faculty salaries in most of these institutions (Tippeconnic, 2003). Funds for the institutions come from tribes, foundations, states, and several federal programs. A notable instance of foundation support has been a $30 million grant from the W. K. Kellogg Foundation to support the multiyear Native American Higher Education Initiative (Benham and Stein, 2003). State funds are generally proportionate to non-Indian student enrollment. The establishment of AIHEC in 1972, and later the American Indian College Fund (AICF) in 1988, provided a voice for national advocacy and an instrument for providing student aid to the TCUs. Today, the most important source of funding is federal at about $4,500 per student (though higher in a few institutions).

The TCUs provide a true model of the organic conception, growth, and development of colleges out of local soil, meant to serve particular needs of their tribes. Many difficulties remain: the ongoing struggle for funding; the need to articulate more effectively with four-year institutions; and the need to overcome some of the problems created by isolation. However, the remarkable progress made by the TCUs in the relatively short time span of little more than a generation attests to the persistence and imagination of dedicated leaders. Their success thus far promises even greater strides in the future.

Note

*It should be noted that several colonial colleges were established with some intent of providing higher education opportunity for American Indian students, but these efforts bore little fruit in the seventeenth century.

References

American Indian Higher Education Council (AIHEC). Retrieved from www.aihec.org., n.d., in December 2013.

Benham, M. K. P., and W. J. Stein, (eds.). *The Renaissance of American Indian Higher Education: Capturing the Dream.* Mahwah, NJ: Laurance Erlbaum, 2003. (See in particular the essays by Michael O'Donnell, Michelle Mitchell, Al Anderson, Lori Lambert, David Burland, Wayne J. Stein, and Kim Barber in this book.)

Stein, W. J. "Developmental Action for Implementing an Indigenous College: Philosophical Foundations and Pragmatic Steps." In M. K. P. Benham and W. J. Stein (eds.), *The Renaissance of American Indian Higher Education: Capturing the Dream.* Mahwah, NJ: Lawrence Erlbaum, 2003, p. 30.

Stein, W. J. Personal communication (telephone conversation). March 2, 2009.

Tippeconnic, III, J., and S. McKinney. "Native Faculty: Scholarship and Development." In M. K. P. Benham and W. J. Stein (eds.), *The Renaissance of American Indian Higher Education: Capturing the Dream.* Mahwah, NJ: Lawrence Erlbaum, 2003.

US Department of Education (USDOE). National Center for Education Statistics. Digest of Educational Statistics, 2010. Retrieved from http://nces.ed.gov., in December 2013.

—*Richard W. Jonsen*

This dramatic change in the landscape of higher education was characterized by different growth patterns in public and private institutions and between two-year and four-year institutions. Since 1949, the number of Title IV degree-granting four-year institutions, both public and private, more than doubled, from 1,327 to 2,774 in 2010.

Private institutions historically have outnumbered public institutions over the past 50 years. In 1949, there were 641 public institutions and 1,210 privates (not-for-profit and for-profit); in 2010, those numbers were 1,672 and 2,823, respectively. Although privates have outnumbered publics, the growth rate among publics since 1949 has exceeded that of privates, with a 161 percent increase in the number of publics versus a 133 percent increase in the number of privates.

Also since 1949, the number of two-year institutions more than tripled, growing from 524 to 1,721, after peaking at 1,833 institutions in 2001. Although the public and private sectors each had nearly the same number of institutions in 1949, the public sector now accounts for the majority of two-year colleges. From 297 colleges in 1949, the public sector increased its numbers by 237 percent to 1,000 institutions by 2010. Conversely, growth among the private two-year colleges was 218 percent between 1949 and 2010, from 227 institutions to 721.

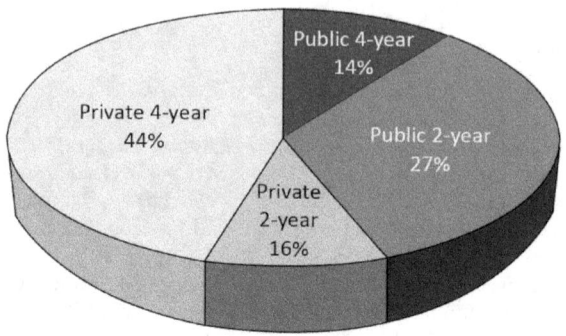

Figure 1.9 US public and private institutions in the West, 2009–2010.
Source: US Dept. of Education, *Digest of Education Statistics 2010*, Table 276.

Institutions of Higher Education: West

Of the 4,495 degree-granting public and private (not-for-profit and for-profit) institutions in the United States in 2010, more than one-in-five were in the western states. A slightly higher proportion—23 percent—of all public institutions was in the West. Of the 197 public baccalaureate institutions in the nation, 40, or 20 percent, were in the West. The West has a higher percentage—23 percent—of all doctoral intensive (very high research) institutions and a smaller percentage—16 percent—of master's institutions. Nearly 26 percent of public two-year colleges are located in western states. Among private four-year institutions, the West has one-in-five, or 20 percent. Only 18 percent of the doctoral extensive (research high) and 24 percent of the doctoral intensive (research very high) institutions are located among the 1,229 colleges and universities in the West (Goodchild, Jonsen, Limerick, and Longanecker, 2014).

As figure 1.9 illustrates, western postsecondary education is characterized by more private institutions than public, with private two- and four-year colleges and universities accounting for 60 percent of all institutions. Proportionally, four-year institutions, both public and private, represent more than one-half of all colleges and universities in the West.

Enrollment and Degree Completions in Higher Education: United States

Driven in part by significant population growth after and accompanying demographic shifts, enrollments in colleges and universities also document the national and regional changes in higher education. As figure 1.10 shows, enrollment nationally grew by 37 percent in the decade 2000–2010.

While total enrollment is one indicator of demographic trends, it also is useful to look at college enrollment rates of recent high school completers. The proportion of high school completers enrolling in college in any state increased from 45 percent in 1960 to 70 percent in 2009 (see figure 1.11). Since 1975, Whites and Blacks have each increased their percentage of high

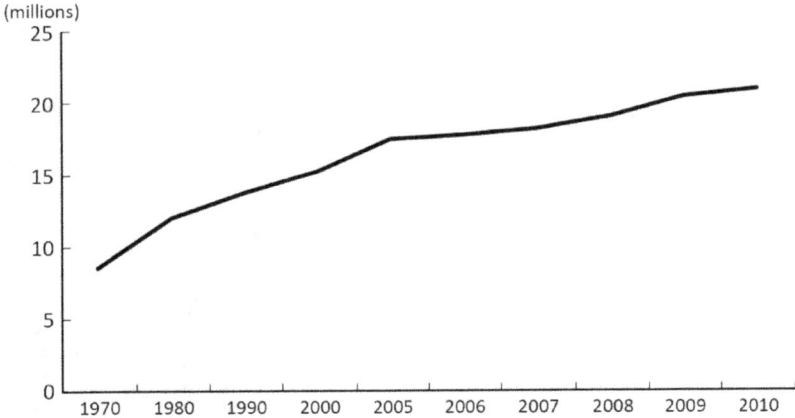

Figure 1.10 Total fall enrollment in degree-granting institutions, US, 1970–2010.
Source: US Dept. of Education, *Digest of Education Statistics 2011*, Table 216.

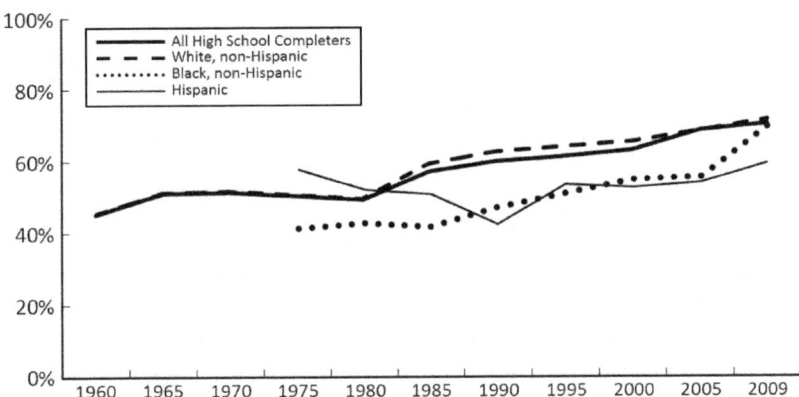

Figure 1.11 College enrollment rates of high school completers, US, by race/ethnicity, 1960–2009.
Source: US Dept. of Education, *Digest of Education Statistics 2010*, Table 209.

school completers going on to college considerably—from 51 percent to 71 percent among Whites and from 42 percent to nearly 70 percent among Blacks. Hispanics, however, have experienced very different trends. In 1975, 58 percent of Hispanic high school completers went on to college; that proportion declined steadily until 1990 when it was nearly 43 percent. In the following decades, the percentage increased and by 2009, it had reached 59 percent, surpassing the 1975 level.

As figure 1.12 illustrates, growth in the number of degrees earned also increased dramatically after the 1960s. Although growth was evident across all types of degrees, the emergence of the nation's community colleges is

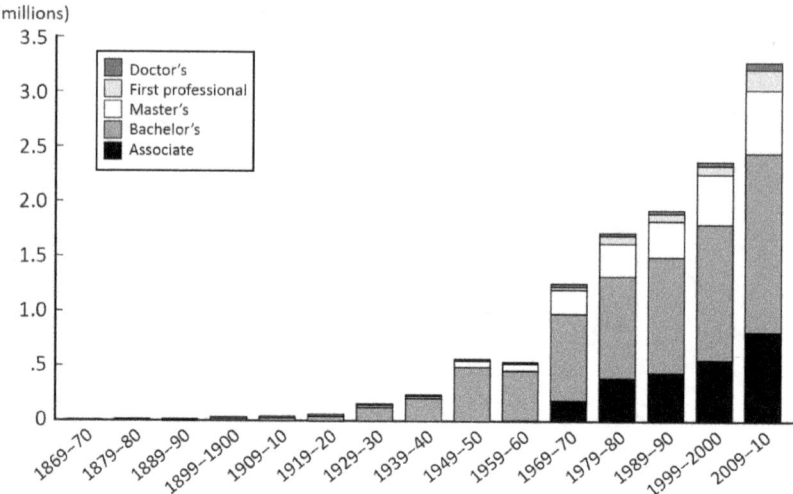

Figure 1.12 Degrees earned by level, 1869–2010.
Source: US Dept. of Education, *Digest of Education Statistics 2007*, Table 258; and *2010*, Table 279.

clearly evident after the 1970s. The number of associate's degrees earned grew by 287 percent between 1970 and 2010 compared to a growth of 109 percent for bachelor's and 130 percent for doctoral degrees in that period.

Enrollment and Degree Completions in Higher Education: West

The enrollment trajectory for western states (see figure 1.13) resembles of the United States. Between 1995 and 2008, however, total fall enrollment in the region increased by 61 percent compared to 34 percent growth in the United States. Over the 38 years illustrated, fall enrollments in the West consistently accounted for close to one-fourth of total fall enrollments in the United States. While approximately 20 percent of all public and private colleges and universities are in the West, the region enrolls a slightly higher proportion of students.

In 2008–2009, the West accounted for more than one-fourth of all associate's degrees awarded that year by public and 32 percent awarded by private institutions. More than one-in-five of all bachelor's, master's, and doctoral degrees came out of the region's public institutions. Among the first professional degrees conferred, 17 percent were awarded by western states (see figure 1.14).

The West has played an increasingly important role in providing higher education opportunity in the United States, while enrolling and graduating significant proportions of students to support the nation's economy. The combination of demographic and institutional data described in this chapter documents the importance of the region's colleges and universities

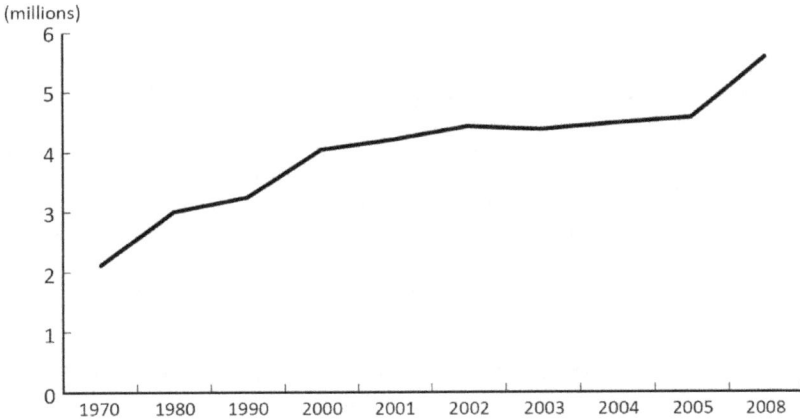

Figure 1.13 Total fall enrollment in degree-granting institutions, West, 1970–2008.
Source: US Dept. of Education, *Digest of Education Statistics 2003*, Table 190; and *2007*, Table 218; and *2010*, Table 215.

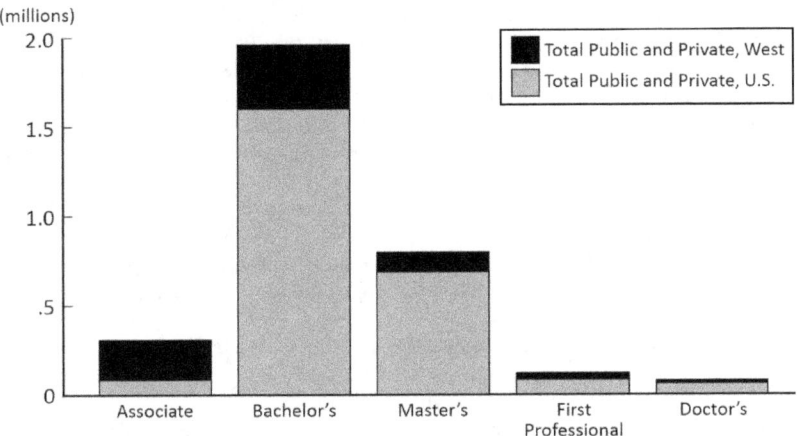

Figure 1.14 Total degrees awarded by level, US and West, 2008–2009.
Source: US Dept. of Education, *Digest of Education Statistics 2010*, Table 332.

in supporting the individual benefits that citizens gain from college and in supporting the public benefits that those higher education institutions and their students bring to the nation.

Notes

*The author thanks Brian Prescott and Michelle Médal at the Western Interstate Commission for Higher Education (WICHE) for their assistance with data collection and graphics in this chapter.

1. The Bureau of the Census reports that most trends cover the contiguous 48 states and the District of Columbia for the period 1900–1950 and include data for Alaska and Hawaii beginning with 1960, the first census after they became states. State trends based on total population size include the 50 states and the District of Columbia for the entire century.
2. "The high percentage change of the American Indian and Alaska Native population in part may be attributed to a higher tendency among respondents to report as this race in the 2000 census than in 1980, as well as changes in methodology and improvements in coverage of this population" (Hobbs and Stoops, 2002, p. 77).
3. Before 1970, determinations of Hispanic origin were only made indirectly, such as through questions on Spanish surname. The 1970 census included, for the first time, a 5 percent sample of all households who were asked a question on Hispanic origin. Beginning with the 1980 census, information on Hispanic origin was collected from every respondent.

References

Goodchild, L. F., R. W. Jonsen, P. Limerick, and D. A. Longanecker, eds. *Higher Education in the American West: Regional History and State Contexts*. Higher Education and Society series. New York, NY: Palgrave Macmillan, 2014.

Hobbs, F., and N. Stoops. *Demographic Trends in the 20th Century* (US Bureau of the Census, Census 2000 Special Reports, Series CENSR-4), Washington, DC: US Government Printing Office, 2002.

National Student Clearinghouse Research Center. *Snapshot Report: Mobility*. Retrieved from www.studentclearinghouse.info/snapshot/docs/SnapshotReport2-Mobility.pdf.

———. *Snapshot Report: Interstate Mobility*. Retrieved from www.studentclearinghouse.info/snapshot/docs/SnapshotReport5-InterstateMobility.pdf.

Schachter, J. *Geographical Mobility* (US Bureau of the Census, 2000 Population Characteristics, Series P20–538). Washington, DC: US Government Printing Office, May, 2001a.

———. *Why People Move: Exploring the March 2000 Current Population Survey* (US Bureau of the Census 2000 Special Studies, Series P23–204). Washington, DC: US Government Printing Office, May, 2001b.

Thelin, J. R. *A History of American Higher Education*, 2nd ed. Baltimore, MD: Johns Hopkins University Press, 2011.

US Bureau of the Census, 2010 Current Population Survey. "Table 1. General Mobility, by Race and Hispanic Origin, Region, Sex, Age, Relationship to Householder, Educational Attainment, Marital Status, Nativity, Tenure, and Poverty Status: 2009 to 2010." *Annual Social and Economic Supplement*. Retrieved from www.census.gov/hhes/migration/data/cps/cps2010.html#.

US Bureau of the Census. *Interim State Population Projections, 2005*. Retrieved from www.census.gov/population/projections/data/state/projectionsagesex.html.

———. *Overview of Race and Hispanic Origin, 2010*. Retrieved from www.census.gov/prod/cen2010/briefs/c2010br-02.pdf.

———. *Population Distribution and Change, 2000 to 2010*. Retrieved from www.census.gov/prod/cen2010/briefs/c2010br-01.pdf.

———. *The Hispanic Population: 2010*. Retrieved from www.census.gov/prod/cen2010/briefs/c2010br-04.pdf.

———. "United States Population Projections: 2000 to 2050," done by Jennifer M. Ortman and Christine E. Guarneri. Retrieved from www.census.gov/population/projections/files/analytical-document09.pdf.

US Department of Education. *Digest of Education Statistics: 2011*. Washington, DC: National Center for Education Statistics, 2012.

———. "Enrollment in Educational Institutions, by Level and Control of Institution: Selected Years, Fall 1980 Through Fall 2011," see Table 3, 2009 and 2010. Retrieved from nces.ed.gov/programs/digest/d11/tables/dt11_003.asp.

———. "Enrollment in Educational Institutions, by Level and Control of Institution: Selected Years, Fall 1980 Through Fall 2011," see Table 2. Retrieved from nces.ed.gov/programs/digest/d11/tables/dt11_002.asp.

Western Interstate Commission for Higher Education (WICHE). *Knocking at the College Door: Projections of High School Graduates*. Boulder, CO: WICHE, 2012.

———. *Policy Indicators for Higher Education: WICHE States*, Table 15. Retrieved from www.wiche.edu/policy/Factbook.

———. *Regional Factbook for Higher Education in the West*, in "Student Preparation, Enrollment, and Completion," see Table 15: "Migration of First-time, First-Year College Students in the United States." Retrieved from www.wiche.edu/factbook.

Part II
SEVEN REGIONAL PUBLIC POLICY CHALLENGES

2

ASSESSING COLLEGE ACCESS AND SUCCESS IN THE WEST

Mikyung Ryu

ISSUES OF COLLEGE ACCESS AND SUCCESS—WHY THEY ARE RELEVANT NOW

The United States' record in advancing educational opportunity beyond high school has been unimpressive for decades. The supply of college-educated workforce has been stagnant since 1980 and American's average years of schooling by age 30 has remained at 13, just above the high school diploma level (Goldin and Katz, 2008). The United States, once-world-leader, is now being surpassed by many member nations of the Organisation for Economic Cooperation and Development (OECD) in postsecondary enrollment as well as degree attainment rates. Business and policy leaders are increasingly concerned about the lack of much progress in higher education, and President Obama's call for the United States to once again lead the world in postsecondary attainment has spurred rethinking of college access and success.

The world we live in is becoming increasingly competitive and the knowledge and skills of a nation's citizens are at the core of this competition. To educate more citizens for college-level knowledge and skills, the United States is starting from a difficult position and its way forward is difficult due to existing disparities within the population, combined with projected demographic changes. The future young population is increasingly composed of the historically underserved segments of the population in the educational systems. The racial/ethnic gaps in education remain large and have not narrowed appreciatively over time. Data show that without closing the pervasive racial/ethnic gaps the United States cannot raise the postsecondary attainment levels sufficiently enough to meet the growing international competition.

The western region largely accounts for the future growth in the nation's young population. As a consequence, it is impossible for the country to build a strong workforce without major improvements in educational attainment of the population in the western states. Improving college access and success in this region has implications that go far beyond the region.

This chapter aims to assess opportunity for higher education that western states provide to their residents and to identify the areas where policy attention is particularly needed. It is not intended to evaluate the effectiveness of current state policies or recommend specific policy options for the future. Rather, it strictly focuses on assessing the western states' performance in higher education based on a variety of publicly available data, with the goals of providing a roadmap for state policy development. For the purpose of the chapter, the western region (or the West) is broadly defined by the 15 member states of the Western Interstate Commission for Higher Education (WICHE). And our assessments are primarily based on the information from *Measuring Up 2006: The State Report Cards for Higher Education* (National Center for Public Policy and Higher Education, 2006). When we evaluate whether states have made improvements over time, the underlying data are also derived from the 2006 state report cards.

One methodological note is worth mentioning about the 2008 edition of *Measuring Up*. Though more updated data are available through the 2008 edition, the analysis for this chapter is derived from data in the 2006 edition because the consistency in data and methodology is important in assessing changes in state performance over time. After examining the updated results in all performance measures, the author concluded that the entire nation and the western region in particular saw no notable changes in performance outcomes between the 2006 and the 2008 editions, with a couple of exceptions. First is Affordability, the area where not only the western region but also all other regions experienced further deterioration as a result of the combination of dwindling state subsidies, negative income growth, and rising college prices. (Consequently, three states in the West were saved from getting an F in Affordability in 2006, but two of them have fallen since, joining the rest of the country.)

Second, between *Measuring Up 2006* and *2008,* most of state grades dropped further in the College Participation category. Since such widespread declines in state performance are unlikely to be seen over the course of just two years (except for college affordability), these declines appear to have occurred due to some of the data and methodology improvements made for the 2008 report cards. This means that as newer and better data became available and the validity of assessments improved, the state of states in broadening college access turned out worse than we had believed. The state grades for 2008 are provided as a reference but not used for analysis.

It would be helpful to understand what is being measured in the *Measuring Up* report cards. States are assessed in six areas that are important for gauging the extent to which higher education meets the needs of states and the nation as a whole. The six areas consist of academic preparation at the K-12 level, college participation, degree completion, affordability, benefits, and student learning. In all areas except student learning (where insufficient information made it impossible to assess state performance), states are evaluated and benchmarked to the best states on multiple measures and assigned a grade to reflect their relative standing among the 50 states in each performance area (see table 2.1).

It is usually the final grades that grab immediate attention (see table 2.2 for state grades). However, the report cards offer much more information beyond the grades that is useful if a comprehensive diagnosis is desired rather than quick comparisons among states. This analysis will look at the state's performance results underlying the grades, in order to identify specific areas where the WICHE states, individually or as a whole, have made strides or are still struggling to improve. It will also assess how WICHE compares with OECD countries.

Table 2.1 *Measuring Up* report cards evaluate states on the following measures

Preparation
- ▶ High school completion
- ▶ K-12 course taking
  - Math course taking
  - Science course taking
  - Algebra in 8th grade
  - Math course taking in 12th grade
- ▶ K-12 student achievement
  - Proficiency in math, reading, science, writing
  - Math proficiency among low-income
  - College entrance exams
  - Advanced placement exams
- ▶ Teacher quality

Participation
- ▶ Young adults
  - Chance for college by age 19
  - 18–24-year olds enrolling in college
- ▶ Working-age adults
  - 25–49-year olds enrolling part time

Affordability
- ▶ Family ability to pay
  - At community colleges
  - At public 4-year colleges
  - At private 4-year colleges
- ▶ Strategies for affordability
  - Need-based financial aid
  - Low-priced colleges
- ▶ Reliance on Loans

Completion
- ▶ Persistence
  - At 2-year colleges
  - At 4-year colleges
- ▶ Completion
  - Bachelor's degree completion in 6 years
  - All degree completion

Benefits
- ▶ Educational Achievement
- ▶ Economic Benefits
  - Increased income from bachelor's degree
  - Increased income from some college education
- ▶ Civic Benefits
  - Population voting
  - Charitable contributions
  - Volunteering
- ▶ Adult skill levels
  - Quantitative literacy
  - Prose literacy
  - Document literacy

Learning
- ▶ Literacy levels of the state's residents
- ▶ Graduates ready for advanced practice
  - licensures
  - Competitive admissions
  - Teacher preparation
- ▶ Performance of college graduates
  - Problem-solving (4-year institutions)
  - Writing (4-year institutions)
  - Reading (2-year institutions)
  - Quantitative skills (2-year institutions)
  - Locating information (2-year institutions)
  - Writing (2-year institutions)

Source: National Center for Public Policy and Higher Education, *Measuring Up 2006*.

Table 2.2 WICHE state grades in *Measuring Up 2000–2008* by category

	Preparation				Participation				Affordability			
	2000	2002	2004	2006	2008	2000	2002	2004	2006	2008	2000	2002	2004	2006	2008
Alaska	A−	B+	B−	B−	C+	D+	D+	C	C+	F	C	D	F	F	F
Arizona	D+	D	D	D	D	C	B−	B+	B+	A	C−	D−	F	F	F
California	C−	C−	C	C	C+	B+	B+	A	A	C	A	A	B	C−	C−
Colorado	B	B	A−	B+	A−	B−	B	B	A−	C+	B−	C−	D−	F	F
Hawaii	C−	C−	C	C−	C−	B−	B−	B−	C	D	C−	D	D	D	F
Idaho	D+	C−	C	C	C	D	C−	C−	D+	D	B−	D+	D−	D	F
Montana	B	A−	B+	B+	B−	D+	D+	C	C−	D	D−	F	F	F	F
Nevada	D+	D	D	C−	C	D+	C+	C	C	D+	B	D+	F	F	F
New Mexico	D−	D−	F	F	D−	B−	A	A−	A	F	B	C−	F	F	F
North Dakota	B	B	B	B−	B−	B	B	A−	A	B−	C	D	F	F	F
Oregon	C−	C	C	C−	C+	D	D+	B−	C+	B+	D−	F	F	F	F
South Dakota	C	C	B	B	B	C	B−	B+	A	D	D+	F	F	F	F
Utah	A	A	A	A	B	C	C	C+	B	B	A	B	C	C−	F
Washington	C+	B−	B−	B	C+	C−	C	C	C−	B−	A	C−	F	C−	F
Wyoming	C−	C−	C+	C	C	C−	B−	B	B+	D	B−	D	F	D−	F
US	C+	C+	B−	C+	C+	C+	C+	B	B	C−	C−	D	F	F	F

Table 2.2 Continued

	Completion					Benefits				
	2000	2002	2004	2006	2008	2000	2002	2004	2006	2008
Alaska	F	F	F	F	F	B	C+	B	B-	C+
Arizona	C-	C+	C+	B	B	B-	B-	B	B+	B-
California	C	C+	C	B	B-	B+	A-	A	A	B+
Colorado	C	C+	B-	B	B-	A	A	A	A-	B+
Hawaii	C	C	C	B-	C	C+	B-	B	A-	B-
Idaho	C	B-	C+	C+	C	C	C	C	C-	C-
Montana	C	C	C	B-	C-	B	C	C	C+	C+
Nevada	F	F	F	F	F	C-	C-	C-	C-	D
New Mexico	D-	D	D	D	D+	C	C	C+	C	C+
North Dakota	B	B	B	B	A	C+	C+	C	C+	D
Oregon	C	C	C	B-	C+	C+	B	B	A	B+
South Dakota	B-	B-	B	B+	B	C-	D+	C-	C+	D+
Utah	D+	C+	B	B	B+	B-	B	B	B	B
Washington	B-	A-	A-	A	A-	B+	B	A-	A-	B
Wyoming	B	B	B+	A	A	C	D	D	C-	D-
US	B-	B-	B-	B	B-	B-	C+	B	B+	B-

Note: Due to the new indicators, modified indicator weights, and the change in data sources, the 2008 grades may not be comparable to those from previous years particularly in the Participation Category, in which most states' grades went down further.

Source: National Center for Public Policy and Higher Education, *Measuring Up*, all five editions.

Importance of the Western States in Meeting the Nation's Educational Needs

According to the US. Census Bureau population projections, the United States will grow more diverse, particularly among the younger segments of the population. Over the next decades, America will add more than two million people in the traditional college-age population aged 18–24, which will reach almost 30 million people by 2020. Demographic characteristics of these young people are an important consideration for meeting the future educational needs of the nation:

- By 2020, the western region will represent about 30 percent of 18- to 24-year-old young people in the country (NCHEMS, 2005).
- The United States will experience major shifts in racial/ethnic makeup of the young population over the next decades; these shifts will be pronounced in the western region (see figure 2.1). Nationally, the proportion of population that is white will decrease to 55 percent. However, in the West, the growth of nonwhite young population will reverse the current racial composition, making the West the first region where nonwhite minorities will reach 56 percent of the population (NCHEMS, 2005). It should be noted also that these nonwhite populations are not monolithic and composed of individuals with highly diverse backgrounds and differing levels of educational achievement. Considering Hispanics and African Americans who have historically attained postsecondary education at lower rates constitute the vast majority in the nonwhite group, the projected demographic shifts present a huge challenge to the region.

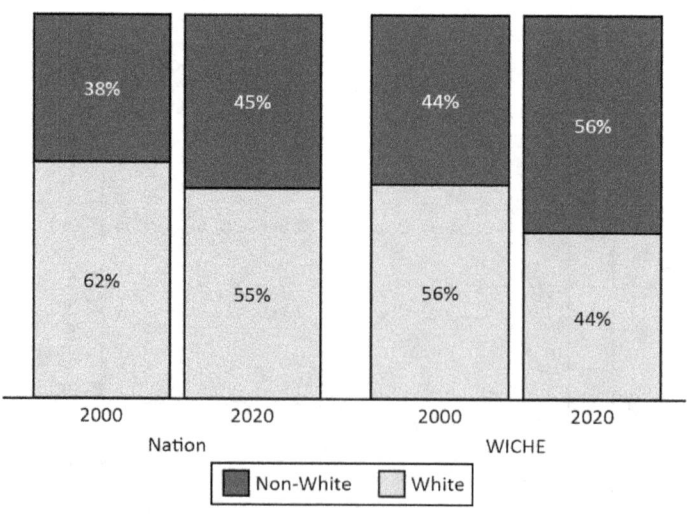

Figure 2.1 Changing racial/ethnic make-up of young population (aged 18–24) between 2000 and 2020.
Source: NCHEMS, 2005.

Table 2.3 Highest education level attained among adults (aged 25–65), by race, 2000

	Percent of adults without high school credentials					Percent of adults with associate's degree or higher				
	White %	Black %	Hispanic %	American Indian %	Asian %	White %	Black %	Hispanic %	American Indian %	Asian %
Alaska	6	10	19	23	24	38	27	28	10	28
Arizona	8	15	45	32	15	39	29	13	14	53
California	8	16	52	21	15	46	27	12	23	54
Colorado	6	13	39	19	14	48	31	16	22	53
Hawaii	4	7	15	15	13	48	33	22	26	39
Idaho	9	18	56	19	15	33	42	10	19	44
Montana	8	4	19	25	17	34	48	23	19	41
Nevada	10	19	53	20	16	30	19	9	18	37
New Mexico	7	14	31	26	13	44	30	17	17	55
North Dakota	7	5	25	21	32	38	39	31	21	40
Oregon	9	16	50	18	17	36	25	13	22	49
South Dakota	8	13	41	28	37	35	25	19	16	30
Utah	7	9	42	29	18	38	30	14	18	42
Washington	7	12	46	20	16	41	30	16	22	47
Wyoming	8	8	31	20	12	33	30	15	14	48
US	10	22	45	23	16	38	22	15	20	54

Source: NCHEMS, 2005.

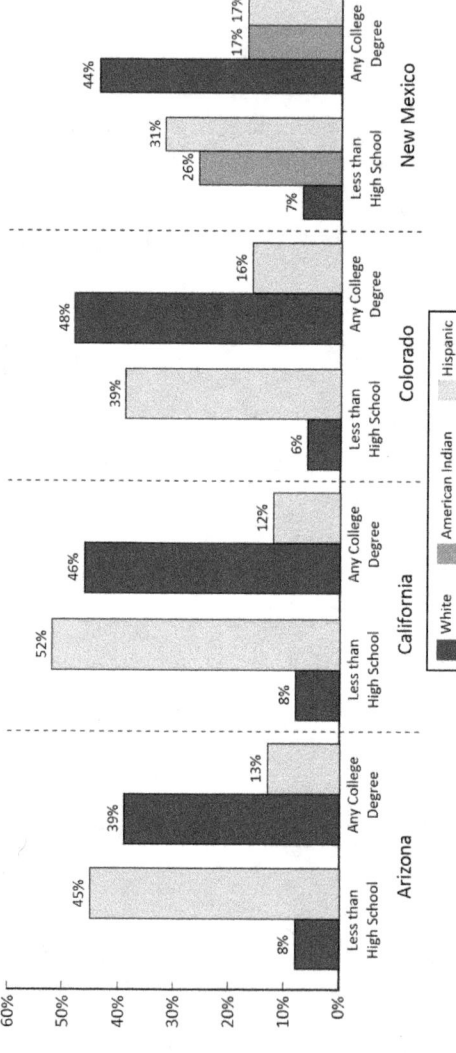

Figure 2.2 Racial/ethnic gaps in education for selected states.
Source: NCHEMS, 2005.

- Because recent high school graduates represent a large pool of entering college students, it is important to understand the nation's future high school graduate populations and the potential impacts of the western region. The United States is projected to produce a total of 3.5 million high school graduates in 2025, up 5 percent from 2009. Over this period the West and the South will produce more high school graduates, whereas the Northeast and the Midwest will experience declines (WICHE, 2012a). As with the young population, the West contributes significantly to the gross number of high school graduates to be produced: that is, one out of every four high school graduates (24%) would come from the West (WICHE, 2012a).
- The WICHE states will have an impact on changing the racial/ethnic lines among new high school graduates. Nationally, among all new public high school graduates, the share of graduates who are white is projected to shrink from 62 percent to 50 percent, 2009–2025. By comparison, the West would experience a reverse in racial/ethnic patterns, with the nonwhite minorities becoming the majority. The nonwhite share will increase from 49 percent to 59 percent, 2009–2025 (WICHE, 2012a).

The current racial/ethnic gaps in educational attainment are large in the West, as shown in table 2.3. These gaps are particularly revealing when both ends of the spectrum—the best-educated and the least-educated—are compared within each race (see figure 2.2). It is estimated that if no improvement is made to the current racial gaps in educational attainment and the minority population grows at a rate that is projected, the average educational level of the working-age population would drop in all western states (NCHEMS, 2005). As mentioned previously, the western states significantly account for the future growth in the nation's young population, particularly in the high school graduate population. Therefore, eradicating racial/ethnic disparities and improving college access and success in these states has implications that go well beyond the region.

How the Western States Stack Up in Higher Education

This section provides an overall assessment of opportunity for higher education in the WICHE states relative to other states. The overall assessments are focused on four main categories of the *Measuring Up* report that are designed to measure accessibility and completion, that is, academic preparation at the precollegiate levels, participation in higher education, completion of degrees and certificates, and affordability of college education. (The student learning category is excluded in the analysis due to insufficient data, as well as the benefits category, which is largely comprised of indirect measures of access and success.) Detailed reports on individual states are provided in Appendix below.

As the WICHE states work together to chart the way forward for improving postsecondary access and attainment in their states, the state report cards offer a useful tool by which to understand where policy attention is particularly needed. To this end, the section discusses the areas where the WICHE states are particularly similar or diverging, the areas where all WICHE states would need help, and the areas where the WICHE states appear to fall short in comparison with the OECD nations.

Overall Assessments

A closer look at each state's performance in higher education reveals more details about variation among the WICHE states. As figure 2.3 displays, the state's overall composite scores in the four categories vary across states, suggesting that the WICHE states may be more dissimilar than alike. The variability among states is particularly notable in the areas of academic preparation and college participation, in which the member states are not clustered in any particular fashion. It illuminates great variability across states in the preparation and participation categories.

In the affordability and completion categories, however, the western states tend to converge and form a cluster or clusters in the overall category scores. In affordability, the WICHE states appear polarized between the top and bottom end of the scale, which is in stark contrast with the patterns observed in the preparation or participation category. Because almost every state in the country has deteriorated in recent years in terms of making college education more affordable, this deterioration is reflected in the top state's score being 71 out of 100 (where the score of 100 refers to the top state performance in the early 1990s). Apparently, these declines were national in scope, and the West was no exception to that. What is notable is that the polarization that characterizes the college affordability in the West still persists, as indicated by the fact that while four out of the five most affordable states in the country are still in the West, five other western states are in the bottom third of overall affordability score cards.

Completion is the category that crystallizes the common challenge facing the West. In retaining and graduating students successfully in a timely manner, all 15 WICHE member states, except for Washington and Wyoming, are in the bottom half of the performance scores and 12 states fall below the national average. In short, the overall assessments illuminate a disturbing reality in the West—while there is variability within the region in the areas of academic preparation, college participation, and affordability (although to a lesser extent), poor completion rates are the most consistent problem running through the entire region.

Progress Over Time—Areas of Concern

While the overall assessments give a snapshot picture of the region based on the composite category scores, the state report cards also address the

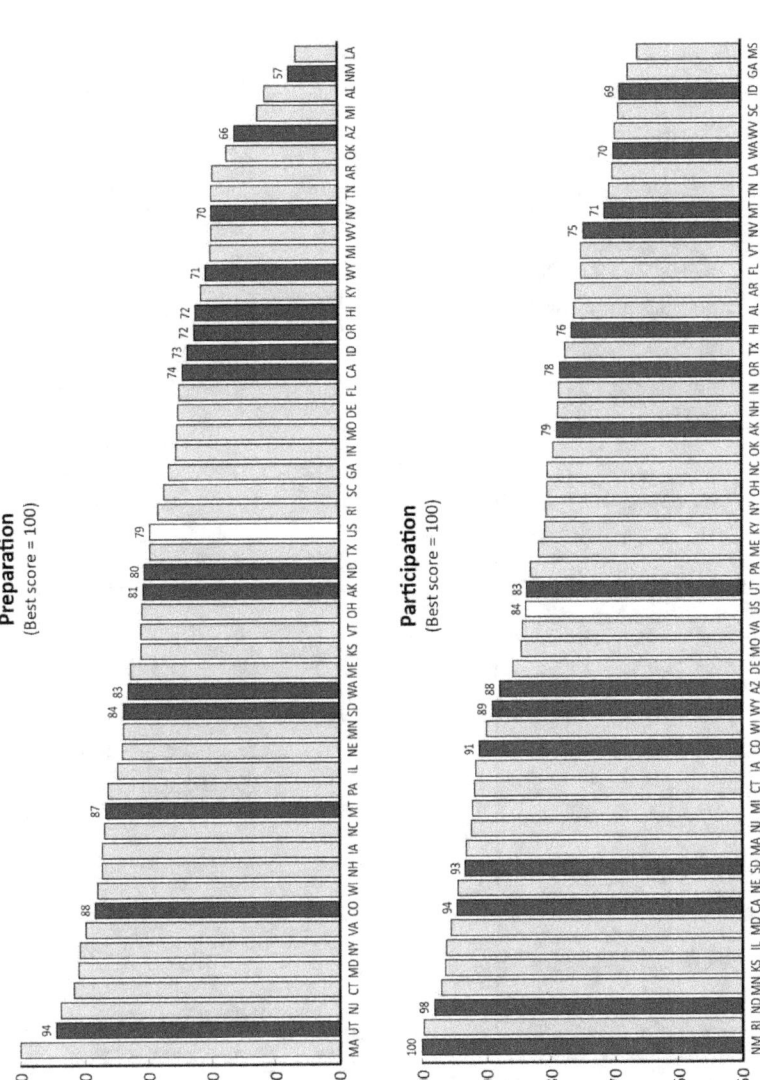

Figure 2.3 State overall category scores in *Measuring Up 2006*.

Source: National Center for Public Policy and Higher Education, *Measuring Up 2006*.

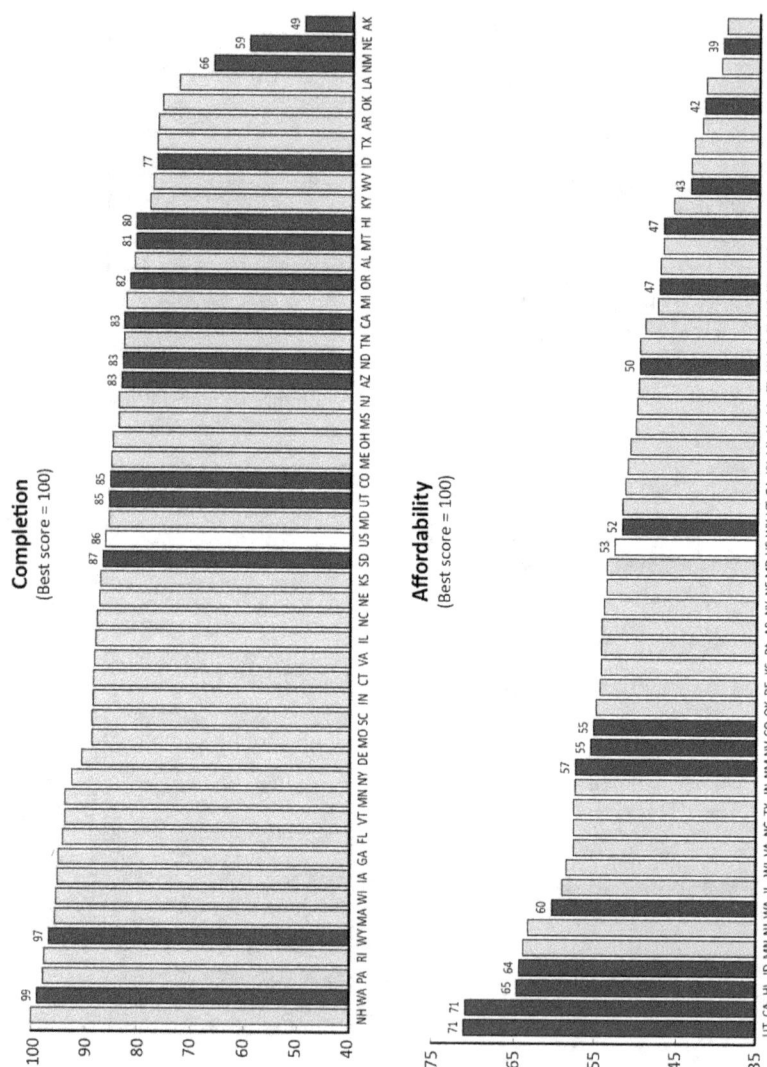

Figure 2.3 Continued

question of whether the state is on the right track in improving its performance on key indicators. To gauge progress over time, the state is being compared with itself, not with other states, but the true picture emerges when the state performance is evaluated in both absolute and relative terms. For example, among the WICHE states that did improve the performance over time on the given measure (i.e., they made progress in absolute terms), many are still struggling to close the gaps with top-performing states in the nation that are continuing to move ahead of the curve (meaning, they made no progress in relative terms).

Evaluating western higher education both ways, its meager current status and sluggish progress over time stand out in the following arenas. First, the WICHE region generally does a poor job in getting students out of high school and enrolling them in college at a timely pace. The high school graduation rate in four years across the region is no better or worse than the already low national average rate (67%). More importantly, none of the WICHE states has improved on this measure over the past ten years. As a consequence, except for a handful of states, WICHE members rank in the middle to the bottom of the 50 states on this measure (see figure 2.4). High school to college transition is even more problematic when compared with other regions. Only 52 percent of high school students (the WICHE average) go on to college immediately after high school, which is below the national average rate, and only four WICHE states are above the national rate (see figure 2.5). Over the past decade, eight of the 15 member states have improved on this measure but this is the case in point—despite the gains made by every other state in the region, the vast majority is still in the middle to the bottom of the 50 states on college continuation rate. Second, there has been little change in the college enrollment rate among the traditional college-age youth (aged 18–24)—the age group that has the best chance of attaining a college degree. Progress is also absent in the working-age adults population (aged 25–49). On the whole, most of the western states (13 out of 15) have not improved in college participation since the early 1990s.

Finally, in spite of continuing tuition and fee increases, the state financial aid for the needy has been extremely low in the region, perhaps, with the exceptions of California and Washington. The vast majority of WICHE states—including South Dakota, which offers no aid at all—have not advanced their student aid policies in order to improve college access for low-income students. As shown in figure 2.6, 11 of 15 WICHE states spent no more than 20 cents for every federal dollar awarded to low-income students in their state.

Although there are other barriers in addition to the rising costs, it is plausible to relate the cost issues to the decade-long lack of gain in college participation. Historically, the "low tuition, low aid" approach has dominated the West, but this model is no longer relevant. Steep tuition increases, coupled with the states' low investment in financial aid, have weakened college affordability in the WICHE region.

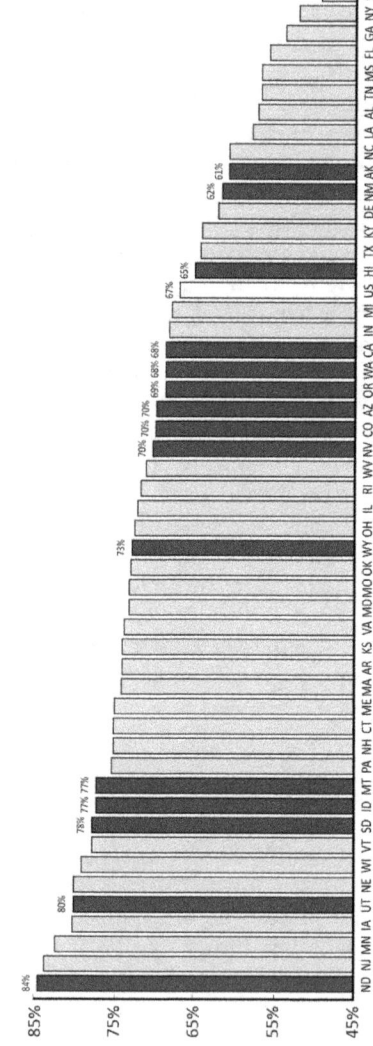

Figure 2.4 High school graduation rate in four years, 2002.

Source: National Center for Public Policy and Higher Education, *Measuring Up 2006*.

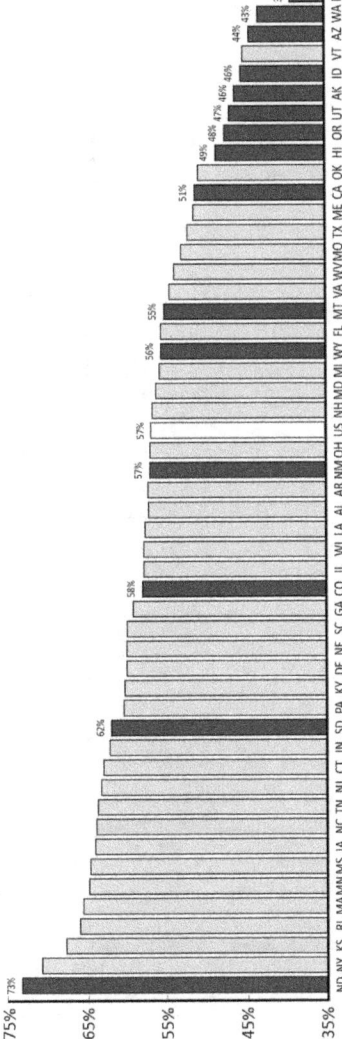

Figure 2.5 Immediate college-going rate of recent high school graduates, 2002.
Source: National Center for Public Policy and Higher Education, *Measuring Up 2006*.

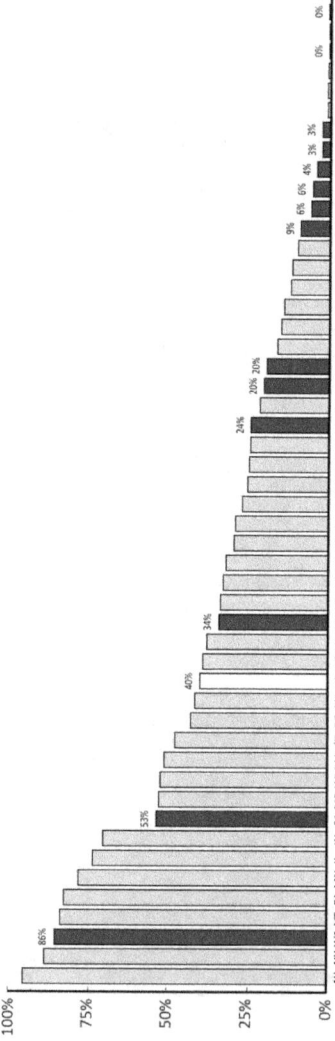

Figure 2.6 Total expenditures for state need-based aid as a percent of total Pell Grants awarded in the state, 2005.

Source: National Center for Public Policy and Higher Education, *Measuring Up 2006*.

Internationally Speaking

Measuring Up provides international comparisons for all 50 states on three measures that are closely aligned with those used to assess state performance in the graded categories. When measuring internationally, the WICHE states vary in college enrollment of the traditional college-age young people, similar to the variability within the region, as mentioned previously. However, the problem lies in the states that largely account for the nation's future population growth among young people. Those "growth" states, including Arizona, California, Nevada, and New Mexico, tend to rank below other OECD nations in enrolling young people in education and training beyond high school.

The underperformance of the WICHE region stands out particularly in the area of college completion. Washington and Wyoming, the best-performing states in the region, fall behind nine other countries and Alaska and Nevada are at the bottom of all international competitors in the total number of undergraduate-level degrees and certificates awarded per 100 students enrolled.

Furthermore, the western states face a serious challenge of closing the generation gap in postsecondary attainment and keeping pace with progress in other nations. The educational level of the young population (aged 25–34) is lower than that of older adults (aged 25–64) and surpassed by the young peers in other countries. In 10 of 15 WICHE states (Alaska, Arizona, California, Colorado, Hawaii, Idaho, Nevada, New Mexico, Oregon, and Washington), the college degree attainment rate by young adults is lower than that of older adults. In only five states (Montana, North Dakota, South Dakota, Utah, and Wyoming)—all of which are mediocre as compared with the best states—did young adults match or improve on the degree attainment rates of older adults.

A Roadmap for Policy Change—Understand the Challenge First

The primary goal of this chapter was to assess the WICHE member states in several key higher education areas drawn from the *Measuring Up* report cards. In preparing students for college in the K-12 education or in enrolling students in college, the overall state scores show a mixed picture, suggesting that the WICHE states may be more dissimilar than alike. The affordability and completion categories are a different story. In college affordability, the states' scores tend to split between the top and the bottom ends of the spectrum, while the problem of poor college completion rates are running through nearly all states in the region. Measuring internationally, even the best states in the West fall behind many other OECD nations in degree completion; so do the "growth" states, such as Arizona, California, Nevada, and New Mexico, which largely account for the nation's future population growth.

To drill down the data further and perhaps present a roadmap for future policy change in the region, we identified three specific areas of concern, as defined by the majority of states not having improved over the past decade and still trailing other states. Apparently, all three areas listed below are closely tied to college accessibility, the topic on which the WICHE states will require renewed policy attention because despite the reform long advocated, little progress has been made:

- The poor and declining success rates in on-time high school graduation and immediate transition to college;
- The stalled enrollment rates among traditional college-age young people (aged 18–24); and
- The lack of focus on low-income students in the state financial aid programs.

As suggested by the trend analysis, the current challenge facing western higher education is twofold: the poor and declining status of college accessibility as well as the poor degree completion rates. This means that they must address how to raise the attainment of population by advancing both access and completion at the same time. In other words, the goal of "college access *and* success" should be understood as one paired goal, rather than what appears to be the pendulum of policy priority in some recent policy proposals.

For decades, college access has been on the forefront of state and federal-level policymaking, but the policy focus is now increasingly shifted toward college completion. In fact, the state legislators in the West have increased their focus on data, accountability, productivity, and college completion in recent years (WICHE, 2012), but the focus on accessibility does not appear in their higher education legislative activity lately. This new development can undercut, implicitly or explicitly, state support for greater accessibility for historically underserved populations in the states. Apparently, providing greater access to higher education is meaningless if no one completes, and improving completion at the cost of reduced access will equally undermine the nation's attainment goals and further impair the educationally disadvantaged students. In this light, there is early evidence of increasingly unsatisfactory progress occurring in higher education as a result of misalignments between the accessibility and the chance for success.

There have been shifts in postsecondary enrollment from four-year to two-year institutions among low-income students, as defined by the Pell Grant recipients. The Pell recipients have been increasingly concentrated in community colleges or for-profit institutions, while the share of Pell recipients enrolling in four-year institutions has dropped by half to 39 percent since 1980 (*Postsecondary Education Opportunity*, 2011). The federal spending for Pell grants has doubled in recent years, allowing for the largest one-year increase in the program's history with the maximum award reaching an all-time high. Nonetheless, the sole focus on access can become an invisible trap for lower-income students if access to higher education continues to segregate, with disadvantaged classes increasingly absorbed by resources-deficient community colleges or pricey for-profit schools, both of which are typically associated with lower degree completion rates, indebtedness, or other poor outcomes.

Accessibility to higher education is still an imperative for the WICHE states, as evidenced by our analysis of the state report cards. This is why the aforementioned disturbing national trend has important implications as they continue the work on accessibility. More and more low-income students in the region may be given access to postsecondary education. However, policies must ensure that increased accessibility serve diverse populations equitably and warrant successful completion and other positive learning outcomes for all who qualify. Without drastically improving the pathways to a quality credential especially among the growing numbers of disadvantaged students in the region, its chronic problem of low college completion is likely to further worsen as a consequence of expanded but inequitable access to higher education.

As we look to the impending demographic changes, the western region is of particular importance in meeting the nation's demand for a strong workforce. For the first time in American history, the younger generation is not significantly more educated than its parents' generation. Further, racial/ethnic minority groups, including Hispanics, actually saw a decline in younger generation's educational attainment relative to their older peers (Ryu, 2010). Given the geographic concentration of rapidly growing Hispanic population combined with the chronic educational attainment disparities in the region, there is no doubt that the educational success of the West is critical to the nation's global competitiveness. To achieve this, US higher education must begin with careful consideration of the new normal—college access *and* success.

Appendix

The State of Western States

A Summary of Individual State Higher Education Report Cards

1. Alaska

Alaska's college enrollment rate is low; and among those who do enroll, many drop out and fail to complete the degree. The result is the lowest degree completion rate in the country. The state has received straight "Fs" in college completion throughout all four editions of report cards. Its poor college enrollment and completion scores are partly due to the issues related to academic preparation and college affordability.

Alaska has not kept up with other states in accelerating students' academic preparation for college. The state particularly needs to get more students to take advantage of the Advanced Placement test program, an effective avenue to college access and success. College costs have risen in Alaska, and the fact that the state provides very little financial aid to low-income students surely is a contributing factor in college affordability problems. Alaska is one of the least affordable states in the WICHE region.

2. Arizona

Arizona ranks second lowest in the region in getting students college-ready. As compared with other states, it enrolls a fairly large proportion of working-age adults (aged 25–49) in college. Among young people, however, college enrollment rate is low, with less than one-half of high school graduates enrolling in college immediately after high school.

Only one-in-two students complete the bachelor's degree within six years of enrolling, placing the state's score below the national average. Arizona needs to do more to help students complete the degree once they enroll in college.

College education in Arizona has become less affordable over the past decade: a year of education at two- or four-year public colleges or universities, which enroll 70 percent of the state's students, amounts to one-quarter to one-third of family income on average, after financial aid is taken into account. Since the state makes no financial aid commitment for needy students in spite of rapidly rising public tuition, college education has become more burdensome particularly for low-income families. Not surprisingly, Arizona is one of the most unaffordable states in the West to pay for college.

3. CALIFORNIA

Despite its mediocre performance in K-12 education, California achieved relatively high college enrollment levels for both young and older adults, primarily through the lower priced community college system. However, the state's problem lies in low success rates of completing degrees and certificates. Nearly all states in the region are struggling with low completion rates, but California ranks in the bottom one-half of the western states. A recent policy report has warned that the sole focus on "access," as has historically been the case in California, would undermine the student's chance of actually completing the degree (Shulock and Moore, 2007).

Because of the state's high-living costs and low-income level of the neediest families in the state, the low community college tuition policy alone is not adequate to resolve the college affordability issues for California.

4. COLORADO

Colorado reaps high economic and social benefits from a highly educated population, primarily by importing them from other states rather than through "home-grown" human capital. Only four out of every ten ninth graders finish high school on time and enroll in college without delay. Given the growth of racial minorities in the state—mostly Latinos—one of the challenges facing the state is to close one of the largest race-induced educational gaps in the nation. Currently, 17 percent of minorities are enrolled in college, as opposed to 40 percent of whites among 18–24 year olds.

Over the past decade, college costs have increased sharply in public four-year colleges, where the majority of state residents enroll. Currently, a year of education at the public four-year college consumes 27 percent of family income on average, after financial aid is counted. The state does not offer sufficient financial assistance to low-income students: it matches only 34 cents for every federal dollar spent for the needy students. A major change has recently occurred in financing of higher education in Colorado. Many concerned educators and policymakers, both within and outside of the state, are anxious to see if the new voucher system, called the College Opportunity Fund, will help or further dampen college affordability in Colorado.

5. HAWAII

Hawaii ranks very low in all performance areas measured, and in fact it is one of the poorest-performing states in the WICHE region. The state ranks low not only in current performance but also in terms of improvement over time. Over more than a decade no progress has been made to the already mediocre academic record of secondary students in the state. And student achievement gaps add to the problem. Although a very small proportion of students are proficient in math (18% of eighth graders), the proficiency level is even lower among low-income students (7% of low-income eighth graders).

Perhaps the most disturbing finding concerning Hawaii is large declines—the second largest in the nation—in both the high school graduation and the college-going rates among young people. In the early 1990s these rates were both above the national rate, but have fallen below it since. About 35 percent of ninth-grade students do not finish high school in four years, while 49 percent do not enroll in college immediately after high school.

Hawaii has maintained college tuition at a low level relative to other states; however, it lacks a focus on student financial aid that targets low-income students who would still have unmet financial needs despite low tuition. It has only a small and declining need-based aid program. Hawaii has dropped in total aid investment since the early 1990s, from $1 million to $0.78 million, 1992–2005, in inflation-adjusted dollars.

6. Idaho

Taking the right curriculum during high school increases the chance of enrolling in and completing college. However, a very small proportion of students in Idaho take upper-level math and science courses during high school. Idaho's students get further behind in their chance for college success due to their low participation in and poor scores on the Advanced Placement tests.

Over the past decade, Idaho has lost ground in its already low college participation rate among young and working-age adults. Both high school graduation rates in four years and college-going rates of high school graduates have declined. As a result, the college enrollment rate is now below the national average rate. College participation is influenced by race as well as family wealth. Among young people aged 18–24, Whites enroll in college at three times the rate of Hispanics/Latinos in the state. And 41 percent of young people from high-income families attend college, as compared to 27 percent of their counterparts with low-income backgrounds.

Idaho's colleges and universities need to do more to help students finish college programs. Among those who start at a four-year institution, public or private, only 44 percent of them complete the bachelor's degree within six years of enrolling. This rate is among the lowest in the country.

College tuition charges in Idaho are more affordable relative to other parts of the country; yet, when compared to the family income of state residents, a year at the public four-year colleges—where the majority of state residents enroll—would cost almost one-third of the annual income for the poorest 40 percent of families in the state. The lack of state support for the poor has contributed to the affordability problem. Since the early 1990s, the state has reversed the focus from need-based aid toward non-need based financial aid. Currently, nonneed-based aid constitutes 70 percent of the total $7 million aid investment that Idaho makes. By comparison, it only spends three cents for every federal Pell Grant dollar in support of needy students.

7. Montana

Despite its fair academic performance at K-12 level in general, very few high school students in Montana take and score well enough to qualify for college credits on the Advanced Placement tests. Over the past decade, Montana has lost ground in college enrollment. Among young adults, high school completion rates in four years have dropped, lowering the chance for college by age 19. The college enrollment of the traditional college-age group, aged 18–24, has also declined. The state has always been among the bottom states in college participation among working-age adults, aged 25–49.

College costs have grown faster than family ability to pay in Montana. The cost increase was particularly steep in public four-year colleges where the majority of state residents enroll. There is very little state financial aid for low-income students and families whose earning power is lower compared to the low-income population in other states. In 2004, families in the bottom income quintile earned $10,000 on average in Montana, which makes it one of the bottom 10 states in terms of the income level of poor families.

Although most students are enrolled in four-year colleges and universities, a very low proportion of them obtain the bachelor's degree in six years (43%), which is below the national average rate. Montana also trails other states in developing a strong workforce through college education and training. It does not reap the economic benefits of college education, measured as personal income increases associated with postsecondary education.

8. Nevada

As one of the poorest-performing states in the region and the country, Nevada has serious challenges not only in academic preparation and college participation but also in completion. Nevada does well relative to other states in enrolling working-age adults (aged 25–49) in postsecondary education and training, but young adults are enrolling in college at one of the lowest rates in the nation. The chances of enrolling in college by age 19 are a mere 28 percent, the nation's lowest rate. In addition, the number of degrees and certificates produced per student enrolled is the second lowest after Alaska.

Following the nationwide trend, Nevada has also seen college cost increases over the past decade, with current costs at public four-year colleges taking 28 percent of family income on average. The state investment in need-based aid remains low.

9. New Mexico

New Mexico ranks second lowest in the nation and lowest in the region in academic preparation for college. This adversely affects the state's performance in other areas, such as college participation and degree completion. New Mexico is among the bottom three states in the nation in terms of college completion rates.

It should be noted that New Mexico received the top grade in college participation in 2006, primarily because a large proportion of working-age adults (aged 25–49) are enrolled in college. However, the state has much work to do to educate its young population. The chances of enrolling in college by age 19 (a measure for college-going rates among young people) remain very low. In fact, this proportion has declined over the past decade, primarily due to a drop in on-time high school completion rates.

10. North Dakota

North Dakota boasts one of the top high school completion rates among the traditional college-age youth. Once students enter college, however, the educational pipeline becomes leaky, resulting in low rates of persistence and degree completion. The labor market return for college degrees (measured as earning premium associated with college degree) appears weak, as compared with other states in the region.

Three major areas deserve policy attention. First is a very small proportion (16%) of eighth graders taking algebra. This proportion is below the already mediocre national average of 22 percent. Algebra is the entry course of the college-bound academic curriculum and college admissions and placement tests are largely focused on algebraic concepts, according to a recent analysis (Achieve, 2007). North Dakota also needs to improve on the National Assessment of Educational Progress on writing and college entrance exams.

Second, college participation among working-age adults is low. It may be due in part to the fact that the college degree does not translate into a high earnings premium in the North Dakota labor market.

Third, there has been little change to the state's policy toward student financial aid for low-income students. North Dakota relies on state four-year colleges and universities to educate most of its residents and with little financial support offered, low-income students and working poor adults are more likely to find college education beyond their reach. North Dakota's higher education system is among the most unaffordable in the region.

11. Oregon

Oregon struggles with its leaky educational pipeline problems from secondary school through college completion. The state ranks in the bottom one-half of the region in all areas measured; in affordability, it is the second lowest performer in the West.

Although a fair proportion of students appear proficient in mathematics, there is much more room for improvement in taking upper-level mathematics and science courses and particularly the Advanced Placement tests. While the high school completion rate has been flat over the past decade, the college-going rate has declined among high school graduates and currently falls below the national rate.

Public four-year and two-year colleges and universities together serve over 80 percent of students in the state. Community colleges experience student dropouts at a rate almost twice that of the four-year institutions. As for four-year institutions, even though they retain students better during the first year, only a little more than 50 percent of students eventually graduate with a degree.

Oregon is among the states that have seen the sharpest increase in college costs over the past 10 years. Attending a public institution now costs about one-third of annual family income (after aid is taken into account), and the state financial aid program targeting low-income students has not kept pace with rising tuition.

12. SOUTH DAKOTA

South Dakota has made strides in secondary school student achievement and college participation. It has enrolled more students in rigorous courses and the Advanced Placement programs. The state has also increased the proportion of young people holding a high school credential. However, it still trails most states in terms of student performance in college entrance exams and Advanced Placement tests. And the proportion of students finishing high school on time has dropped over the past decade. The good news is that high school graduates go onto college at a higher rate than they did a decade ago.

The bulk of students is enrolled in four-year public institutions, where the net costs as a share of family income grew from 17 percent to 27 percent during the last decade. Historically, South Dakota has made little or no aid available to low-income students. While the state ranks in the bottom one-third in the region on college affordability, it must address the issues related to student persistence and degree completion. About one-third of students on four-year campuses do not return in their second year and less than one-half of students complete the program with a degree within six years of enrolling.

13. UTAH

Utah has shown some impressive academic performance at the K-12 level, such as 75 percent of high school students taking upper-level math courses, the highest rate in the nation. On the other hand, it can improve student proficiency in writing, reading, or college entrance exams. On the whole, however, Utah is the best performer in the West and the second best in the nation in terms of academic preparation for college.

Because of the religious missions that many Mormon students undertake during their late teens or early twenties, it is difficult to assess accurately college enrollment and persistence rate for traditional college-age youth. Nonetheless, given strong academic achievement demonstrated prior to college, the success rate during college seems lacking. In fact, Utah ranks in the middle in both college enrollment and completion. Low college participation is pervasive among the older population as well. Although we know that the more educated, the more likely to pursue further learning, a low percentage of adults (aged 25–49) is seeking some kind of postsecondary education. The state has not translated the benefits of strong academic preparation into better college participation and completion for young people.

As of 2006, Utah was one of only a few states that has held college costs at the level comparable to a decade ago. It offers little or no financial aid to low-income students, but tuition increases have been kept minimal, making the state's higher education system one of the most affordable in the nation. However, by 2008, the college affordability in Utah deteriorated, and it ended up receiving an F in this category.

14. Washington

Substantial progress was made over the past decade in terms of college-readiness, as indicated by improvements on the college entrance exams and Advanced Placement tests. Nevertheless, Washington still falls behind many top-performing states. The state has seen a drop in on-time high school completion. Traditional college-age young adults enroll in college at a rate below the national average and this participation rate has been flat since the early 1990s. This is also true for working-age adults (aged 25–49) who appear less likely to enroll in a postsecondary program than their counterparts elsewhere.

More than one-half of college students in the state are enrolled at a community college. However, only 55 percent of first-year students return in the second year. Nevertheless, Washington's four-year institutions compare well with their peers in other states on the retention and the bachelor's degree completion rates.

Washington leads the West in completing the college degree and ranks second best in the country. Nevertheless, Washington has experienced one of the fastest growing college costs in the nation over the past decade; at community colleges net costs as a share of family income have increased from 19 percent to 27 percent after considering financial aid. The good news is that the state has increased need-based financial aid substantially during the same period; while the tuition growth has outpaced the increase in financial aid, not to mention the growth in family income. Therefore, it is not surprising that Washington received an F in the Affordability category in 2008.

As seen in California or Colorado, Washington enjoys high economic and social benefits from a highly educated population due to an influx of talented people educated out-of-state. However, without investing in the development of educational capital in its own state, Washington's continued economic prosperity may be at risk.

15. Wyoming

Although Wyoming has made some progress in secondary school performance, the outcomes are still far from the best. Most notably, the state has lost ground in the high school graduation rate in four years. However, among those who graduate on time, more of them go onto college immediately after high school than did students a decade ago.

Because those who made it to college are among the academically select few, the state is less likely to see a high dropout rate or a low degree completion rate. Wyoming thus performs very well in both persistence and degree completion and it has made strides in these areas over the past ten years.

Considering that high school completion has been a damaging bottleneck in the state's educational pipeline, Wyoming must meet the educational need of young people who failed to finish high school on time. In addition to preparing them academically, it needs to provide financial assistance for them to pursue college education. Currently, the state offers no financial aid program for low-income students.

References

Achieve, Inc. *Aligned Expectations? A Closer Look at College Admissions and Placement Tests.* Washington, DC: Achieve, Inc., 2007.

Goldin, C., and L. Katz. *The Race between Education and Technology: The Evolution of U.S. Educational Wage Differentials, 1890 to 2005.* Cambridge, MA: The President and Fellows of Harvard College, 2008.

National Center for Higher Education Management Systems (NCHEMS). *As America Becomes More Diverse: The Impact of State Higher Education Inequality.* Available at: www.higheredinfo.org, 2005.

National Center for Public Policy and Higher Education. *Measuring Up 2006* through *2008: The National and State Report Cards for Higher Education.* San Jose, CA, 2006.

Organisation for Economic Co-operation and Development. *Education at a Glance.* Paris, France: Organisation for Economic Co-operation and Development, 2011.

"Pell Grant Shares of Undergraduate Enrollments at 4-Year and 2-Year Institutions," *Postsecondary Education Opportunity,* No. 228, 2011.

Ryu, M. *Minorities in Higher Education 2010.* Washington, DC: American Council on Education, 2010.

Shulock, N., and C. Moore. *Rules of the Game—How State Policy Creates Barriers to Degree Completion and Impedes Student Success in the California Community Colleges.* Sacramento: California State University at Sacramento, Institute for Higher Education Leadership and Policy, 2007.

Western Interstate Commission for Higher Education (WICHE). *Knocking at the College Door: Projections of High School Graduates.* Boulder, CO: Western Interstate Commission for Higher Education, 2012a.

———. *Policy Insights; New Approaches to the New Normal: Recapping 2012 Higher Education Legislative Activity in the West.* Boulder, CO: Western Interstate Commission for Higher Education, 2012b.

3

THE FEDERAL GOVERNMENT, RESEARCH FUNDING, AND WESTERN HIGHER EDUCATION POLICY

David A. Longanecker

The federal efforts in higher education and the development of higher education have traditionally been more in sync in the West than in other sectors of the country (Longanecker, 2013). In great part this was simply a function of serendipity. The federal government's first foray into higher education, the Morrill Act of 1862, which deeded land to the states to support the creation of universities, and the subsequent companion Hatch Act of 1887, which provided federal funds to develop agricultural experiment stations and support agricultural research, occurred at the same time that the region was being settled and western states were coming into being. It was natural that the development of public higher education dominated the western landscape and that the resources and direction from the Morrill and Hatch Acts became imbedded in the region's land-grant colleges that emerged from that federal act. Similarly, the next major federal thrust into higher education, the Servicemen's Readjustment Act of 1944, more commonly referred to as the G. I. Bill, came along at the same time as the great migration to the West (particularly to California) that followed the end of World War II. As before, the benefit of a federal program had a greater shaping influence on the West than on other regions, fueling a substantial expansion of enrollment in public education. Interestingly, little of this expansion came from new institutions but rather from the expansion of the missions in existing public institutions. The main exception to this was the creation of institutions in established and emerging metropolitan areas that had not previously been well served in higher education, including Sacramento State College (1947), Los Angeles State College (1947), and Long Beach State College (1949) in California, and Portland State College (1946) in Oregon.

Yet not all of the connections between the federal government and the evolution of Western higher education were accidental. The massive expansion of the federal role in expanding educational opportunity via student financial assistance (grants, loans, and college work-study) as part of the Great Society programs of the 1960s were matched in the West by intentional state policies to capitalize on these federal efforts. The most significant of these efforts was the expansion of community colleges. The 1960 California Master Plan provided the rationale and frugal funding strategy for this in California and also served as the model for other western states, creating a tiered system in which most students would attend less expensive community colleges, with only academically meritorious students attending more expensive flagship universities. In the research domain, western politicians, such as US Senator Warren Magnuson of Washington, assured that emerging federal research and development funds flowed into their state's universities, including institutions in Alaska, Arizona, California, Colorado, Hawaii, and North Dakota. Regardless of political persuasion, federal politicians from the West capitalized on these new funds to advance universities in their region. In addition, the development of energy and natural resources of the West (particularly oil, gas, hydroelectricity, and nuclear energy) helped to bolster the unusually close link between the West and the increasing federal engagement in higher education.

Where We Are Today—The Federal/Western Research Policy Nexus at the Beginning of a New Century

The twenty-first century is bringing fresh changes in federal policy regarding higher education, and it is not clear whether the West's uniquely advantaged "federal connection" will persist. Prognosticating about what the future holds is risky business. Some existing policies, past practices, and current trends, however, stand as portents of what the relationship between western higher education and the federal government might become. In the near term, for example, it is likely that higher education may experience a bifurcation of federal support for higher education.

On the one hand, federal support for research, though often perceived as in decline by the academic community, appears to be holding its own. The perception that it is declining has been fostered by four factors. First, while research support has not dropped in terms of actual dollars, it has been declining as a share of national gross domestic product. In addition, federal funding for university research has been declining as a share of overall federal research and development, a larger share of which now goes to nonacademic research. Second, more universities have been vying for the same pot of funds. While some institutions have fared exceptionally well, others have seen their research support decline. Third, those institutions that benefited from federal research domains that have experienced declines—such as earmarked funding for research, which has been virtually eliminated—have without doubt experienced reduced funding. Finally, the US share of the global investment in research and development has declined as other developed and developing countries, particularly many of the newly competitive global powers in Asia, have increased substantially their investments in research and development. In absolute terms, however, the federal commitment to university-based basic research, applied research, and general research and development remains relatively steady at approximately $30 billion, fluctuating modestly depending on both federal budget circumstances and political inclinations (National Science Foundation, 2010).

This maintenance of support has occurred despite the financial distress visited upon the federal budget by two recessions in close proximity. In 1998, Congress authorized doubling federal research and development funding for the National Institutes of Health. This ambitious agenda was based on an assumption that the economic growth that the United States had experienced in the 1990s would persist into the future. And despite the recession of the early 2000s, this ambitious commitment was maintained until completed on the planned five-year timeline in 2003. While health research received special attention and ample funding, other areas of federal research suffered. By 2009 federal research funding had declined by 9.1 percent below the high point in funding in 2004 (National Science Foundation, 2010). Nevertheless, the advent of "the great recession" of 2008 actually proved to be a boon for academic research: a large share of the funds provided through the American Recovery and Reinvestment Act (ARRA) of 2009 were provided for academic research and development, resulting in substantial increases in 2010 and 2011. Those funds expired, however, with culmination of the ARRA in 2012, creating the appearance of funding reductions.

Looking forward, it is not clear whether the disproportionate success of western institutions in competing for federal research and development funding will continue. For one thing it is not clear that the significant focus on reducing the US budget deficit and containing taxes will allow for a federal budget sufficient to sustain current levels of federal research and development. Furthermore, the anti-intellectualism reflected in some corners of modern American politics could militate against support for such activities.

Less populated western states have begun experiencing mixed results in securing research funding in recent years. Until the late 1970s, many institutions in less populated states fared less well in federal research funding, because they simply did not have the critical mass of research infrastructure to compete with the larger and better-funded major private universities and public flagship institutions in more populous states. To rectify this, in 1979 the federal government established a program within the National Science Foundation, the Experimental Program to Stimulate Competitive Research (EPSCoR), which has helped western states with smaller populations a great deal. Since its inception, EPSCoR has become part of a National Research Initiative, which in FY2013 provided one-half a billion dollars annually in grants, spread among 28 states and 3 territories, including 9 of the 15 western states: Alaska, Hawaii, Idaho, Montana, Nevada, New Mexico, North Dakota, South Dakota, and Wyoming (National Science Foundation).

Many frontier state universities in the West also benefited substantially from research funds garnered as earmarks in appropriations by influential federal legislators. In 2010, 7 of the top 25 institutions in receipt of earmarked federal funds were western universities—University of North Dakota, North Dakota State, University of Hawaii, Utah State, New Mexico Tech, University of Utah, and Montana State—only 2 of which (Hawaii and Utah) otherwise fall within the top 50 federally funded research institutions in the country. These seven institutions received nearly 10 percent of the total amount provided in earmarks that year (Lederman, 2010). However, the era of earmarks appears to have come to an end. No resources for earmarks were provided in the FY2011 or 2012 federal budget, and the political climate seems to suggest that such funding will not be available in the future. Certainly, those institutions that benefited from this largess will miss this noncompetitively granted federal research funding.

The newest thrust of the federal funding for universities, the ARRA that provided billions of dollars of funding to shore up depleted state budgets in 2010 and 2011 was a short-term fix only. These funds helped states "weather the storm" and gave them time to adjust to what became termed "the new normal": a fiscal environment with long-term lower revenue streams than were available in the go-go years at the close of the last century. Now that this funding has expired, there have been calls, particularly from the American Association of Universities, which represents the most highly regarded universities in the county, to focus what limited federal resources are available in research and development on a few premiere universities, where the "best" research is conducted. All of which is to say that the future of federal funding for research and development is not clear, and the strong presence of the West in this arena may well be at risk.

THE FEDERAL/WESTERN EDUCATION POLICY NEXUS REGARDING ACCESS

The story is similar with respect to federal programs that support student access to higher education, which has been a major federal thrust since the Higher Education Act was adopted in 1965. Since the turn of the century, funding for federal student assistance has skyrocketed, from combined federal budget costs in 1999 of approximately $10 billion to more than $50 billion in 2010 (College Board, 2011). That increase suggests exceptional support for this form of federal involvement—but it is not the whole picture. A major portion of the increase resulted in the establishment during the last years of the last century of a federal tax credit for higher education expenses. This program has become quite popular with middle-class Americans (most of the benefits accrue to middle-income families), so much so that this tax benefit was protected in the American Taxpayer Relief Act of 2012, which extended the authorization of this benefit for five years. Current public policy, however, could still put this tuition tax credit at risk. Given the federal government's primary responsibility in student financial assistance—to assure affordability to the most financially needy students—when push comes to shove, programs for the middle class, despite their popularity, could well be in jeopardy. Indeed many of the policy positions being proposed by think tanks and others propose eliminating this program and using the "savings" to invest more in programs like the Federal Pell Grant Program, which focus resources more on the poor. In addition, many of the policy solutions being suggested for reducing the federal budget and the deficit involve major changes to the tax code, almost all of which suggest reducing or eliminating tax credits, such as this federal credit for tuition and fee expenses.

The other major factor causing the substantial increase in federal student aid during the first decade of the new century was a jump in the costs of the Pell Grant Program, which provides foundation grant assistance to poor students. Federal appropriations for the Pell Grant Program in fiscal year 1999 were $7.7 billion. By fiscal year 2012, this appropriation had increased to $36.1 billion for several reasons. Congress and the executive branch (under both President George W. Bush and President Barack Obama) committed to significantly increasing the size of the Pell Grant to provide more assistance to students from families with assessed financial need. From 1999 to 2011, the maximum Pell Grant increased from $3,125 to $5,550 (US Department of Education, "2011–2012 Federal Pell Grant Program Statistics"). This 78 percent increase in grant size, when applied only to the previous pool of recipients, however, accounts for just one-fifth of the overall 369 percent increase in program costs. The remaining 80 percent comes from an exceptional increase in the size of the recipient pool (WICHE, 2010). From 1999 to 2011, the number of Pell Grant recipients increased from 3.8 million to 9.1 million students. The increased unemployment and underemployment resulting from the two recent recessions, which created a new class of needy students eligible for financial aid, is only one reason. Much less understood is the fact that a seriously flawed formula on which the Pell Grant Program is based has simply made a whole slew of students who were not previously eligible, because they were not "needy" enough, look like they are needy now, even though their circumstances have not changed in the least.

These factors have created a spiral in Pell Grant costs that simply cannot be sustained, and federal policymakers are looking for ways in which costs can be contained, if not reduced. Some policymakers are trying to find ways that will enhance the likelihood that grant recipients will succeed in their studies, as recent research has shown that a disproportionate share of Pell Grant recipients never complete their education. Others are simply focused on finding ways to cut costs.

This dilemma is not unique to the federal government. States have also faced challenges in how to respond to an increased demand for financial aid, both because of rising costs facing students and because many families have seen their incomes severely reduced by the dual recessions of recent years and have lost the capacity to fund their children's education.

The federal government could benefit from looking at some of the innovations in financial aid being adopted by states, particularly in the West.

One of the most creative responses is the "shared responsibility" program developed by Oregon in 2007. Oregon faced many of the problems currently facing the Pell Grant Program. Demand for aid was increasing, state resources were constrained, and the old state financial aid grant program had no pizzazz, in part because the original student aid philosophy no longer garnered broad public support. After conducting research on what the public would support, an advisory group created by the governor developed the shared responsibility plan. The plan begins by expecting the student, as the principal beneficiary of the education being received, to contribute what he or she reasonably can; the parents, as the guardian of the student, to contribute what they can; the federal government to contribute whatever it will; and the state to fill in the gap, because everyone else is tapped out. And, by the way, the student can provide their contribution via work, borrowing, savings, or receipt of a scholarship, so there are incentives for the student to be engaged both academically and financially. It is a modern, rational approach that gained support from moderates and conservatives, because they could understand it and agree with it.

The state of Washington has pursued two different new approaches to meeting the financial aid needs of students. Washington has always been a leader in state financial assistance, but tough budget times and rampant tuition increases have challenged the efficacy of the state's highly regarded programs. In response, the state has shored up its standard need-based program by requiring institutions that impose high tuition increases on state residents to assure that these increases do not erode financial access for the neediest students. In addition, the state has created a public-private partnership program to garner scholarship aid for students willing to major in the much needed science, technology, engineering, and math (STEM) fields of study.

In addition, a number of states, most notably Oklahoma through its "Oklahoma Promise Scholarship" and Indiana through its "Twenty-first Century Scholars" program have begun programs that commit future resources to middle and high school students who, in return, commit to preparing well for college. These programs are based on clear and profound research demonstrating that students who enter college well prepared, whether they get high grades or not, complete college (US Department of Education, 2006).

Absent reform, the Federal Pell Grant Program could be seriously at risk—and not for the first time. The program has a history of fits and spurts. In the decade from 1986–1987 to 1996–1997, for example, the maximum Pell Grant increased only from $2,100 to $2,470, losing nearly 18 percent of its inflation-adjusted value. By 2002–2003, however, the maximum Pell Grant had increased to $4,000, bringing the inflation-adjusted value to virtually the same level it had been in 1986–1987. Then funding languished for this program again, with the maximum award being held virtually constant (at $4,050) through 2006/2007, at which time it was increased substantially over the ensuing four years to $5,550.

The federal student loan program, the third largest federal student aid program, has also faced increased federal scrutiny. Originally established as a bank-based program that relied on local financial institutions to provide the student loan capital—with the federal government subsidizing and guaranteeing the loans to make it attractive for banks to participate—the program has since evolved into a federally financed initiative managed by private servicing companies. These are much less expensive to run, thanks to the elimination of the substantial subsidies required to entice private lenders. The program, which began as a $1 billion enterprise in the late 1970s, now provides more than $90 billion in student loan capital annually. While the costs of this program were reduced substantially by shifting from private- to public-sector financing, subsidies to students and defaults continue to present a substantial cost to the government. The widespread use of these loans almost certainly requires a continued federal involvement in providing them, despite common conservative political dogma.

Federal policy and investment in student financial assistance is likely to change significantly in the future. One major reason: The government is cracking down on defaults, not only on student defaulters but also on the institutions in which a disproportionate share of student borrowers end up defaulting. New, income-contingent repayment schemes have been implemented to make student debt repayment less onerous on borrowers and more secure for the federal government. Yet major discussions continue with respect to whether these loans are too highly subsidized and too risky for federal involvement.

The title of a major 2008 report from The College Board, *Rethinking Financial Aid,* captures the policy environment at both the federal and state levels—one in which many policymakers have come to believe that financial aid needs to be reinvented. The philosophy and strategies of the past neither achieved their objectives nor are they well suited to changes in demographics and finances facing policymakers now and in the future. This is especially true in the West. It will be essential, therefore, for the federal government and western policy actions to continue to be in sync as we move forward.

That is particularly true now, as we face a future scarcity of funds for higher education. There simply are not sufficient resources at the federal level to support increased support for federal higher education programs, even if there were greater interest in doing so. Within the education sphere, reform of elementary and secondary education has taken front stage. Elsewhere, the rapid growth in defense-related costs associated with our incursions throughout the world, costs of federally provided medical care, and payments on the federal debt will also constrain federal spending for discretionary domestic funding programs, such as those that support higher education.

The Evolving Federal/Western Policy Thrust

Despite the obvious fiscal constraints that exist today, the federal government's expressed interest in and concern about American higher education have certainly been heightened in recent years. Indeed, the government has dedicated considerable attention to higher education, both within the executive and legislative branches.

Former US Education Secretary Margaret Spellings, who served during the later years of the George W. Bush administration, sponsored a Commission on the Future of Higher Education, which issued its final report, *A Test of Leadership, Charting the Future of U.S. Higher Education*, in 2006. While the commission had the potential of focusing national attention on the importance of higher education to the future economic vitality of the United States, it became consumed by and infatuated with a narrower focus: improving the efficiency and effectiveness of higher education. Efficiency and effectiveness are certainly legitimate and important areas for both federal and state government, but the dogged attention given to these concerns by a national commission had the effect of ignoring the much greater and more pressing issue facing the country and American higher education: how our nation will sustain economic competitiveness in the global economic community now and in the future, an environment in which the United States is already losing ground.

Congress, in a prolonged process of reauthorizing the Higher Education Act, followed a similar track, culminating in the renaming of the act and the revising of the federal role in the Higher Education Accountability Act of 2008. The 2008 act focuses mostly on how to contain the costs of college and the costs of federal programs, particularly expensive student loan programs. President Barack Obama blended this focus on accountability with a major thrust on relevance in federal education policy, particularly with respect to job creation. His initiatives have worked to increase the number of college graduates, in support of the nation's workforce needs, with a focus on achieving this by increasing college graduation rates and reducing equity gaps in completion between students of color and others. The Obama initiatives have focused heavily on community colleges, both because these institutions have weaker completion rates and because they serve the largest number of traditionally disadvantaged students.

These are excellent steps. During President Obama's tenure, however, the Department of Education has also focused a great deal on the trees rather than the forest. It has been consumed by regulatory changes intended to improve the performance of higher education institutions, including rules and regulations related to state authorization of institutions to operate. It has also focused on a host of other issues, including the consequences for institutions with high-loan default rates; what time and effort qualify a student for an academic credit; and whether students enter gainful employment upon leaving institutions. These are without doubt important issues, particularly with respect to the fiscal integrity of federal programs. However, they do not address the most fundamental problems facing America and American higher education. This could prove extremely dangerous for the nation and for the western region in particular. In the president's 2013 State of the Union address, however, he focused substantial attention on the need for the nation to increase its success in both the education and research missions of higher education. He focused specifically on the need to revamp the quality assurance processes in higher education and to begin adopting new technology based approaches to deliver education in order to provide "more, better, faster." What is not clear, however, particularly given the exceptional fiscal constraints facing the federal government, is whether this vision for the future will be reflected in more than rhetoric at the federal level.

THE EMERGING FEDERAL/WESTERN POLICY DISCONNECT—RHETORIC OUT OF SYNC WITH REALITY

There appears to be a disconnect between what our public policy espouses and what state and federal governments are willing to support. Without doubt, the general philosophy of our society toward higher education is that we need to move toward not just a more egalitarian perspective but also an "essentialist" model: Americans believe that higher education is essential for most individuals if our country is to succeed in the new global economy and if we are to enjoy "the good life." Polls show that almost all parents, be they rich or poor, believe that their children must go to college and expect that they will do so. Furthermore, increasingly, adults are continuing their own higher education as lifelong learners.

Other countries have followed the American lead and have radically expanded access to higher education—so much so that in 2011, 15 nations exceeded the United States in the share of the young adult population that had completed a college-level degree program (Organisation for Economic Co-operation and Development, 2011). This presents a unique challenge for the western United States, which trails the rest of the country in the share of its population receiving a college education. There are many ways to look at the statistics that reflect this, but virtually all confirm this trend. For example, all 11 of the states in which the share of young adults (25–34 years old) with a college degree is below the share of older adults (45–64 years old) with a degree are western states (NCHEMS, "American Community Survey," 2009).

Essentially, the West is becoming less well-educated as the rest of the world is becoming better educated. In the United States in 2002, only about 39 percent of those students who were ninth graders four years earlier finished high school "on time" and enrolled in college the following year. Only 18 percent completed college within six years. As startling as those statistics are, they are worse for the West. Only 37 percent of western ninth graders finished high school in four years and immediately entered college, and just 16 percent earned a degree within six years (NCHEMS, "American Community Survey," 2009). That is not the whole story, of course. Many students eventually complete high school and go on to college—and about twice as many as our original "fast-track" cohort earn a degree. However, the fact remains that the United States is falling behind many other countries, and the West lags behind the rest of the United States.

So, the West moves into the future from a disadvantaged position. Indeed, the future presents a much greater challenge for many of the western states than it does for the rest of the nation. The two states with the most rapidly growing rates of high school graduates are in the West—Arizona and Nevada. A number of other western states—including Colorado, Idaho, and Utah—also face substantial growth in the demand for higher education. And while the growth in percentage terms is no longer as high for California, the absolute numbers remain daunting, simply because of the size of the state.

An increasing number of these new students will come from communities of color, particularly Hispanic communities, which western higher education traditionally has not served well. Already the majority of high school graduates in the West belong to racial or ethnic minorities. During the decade from 2008 to 2018, the number of white high school graduates in the West will decline by 17 percent, while the number of Hispanic high school graduates will increase by 29 percent (WICHE, 2008).

Given that the federal government is not inclined to boost funding for higher education, the West is unlikely to receive enough federal assistance to even match today's "per student" support, let alone enough to adequately serve the increasing number of disadvantaged students. Federal programs that are formula-driven—such as campus- and state-based student grant programs—already work against the West, because they "grandfather in" institutional and state shares, thus favoring historical rather than emerging enrollment patterns. This is a problem for the West, where a disproportionate share of the nation's growth—in recent years and projected—is occurring.

The luster of the mid-twentieth century's efforts to support higher education has dimmed, but the demands of the twenty-first century's global economy require a more highly educated citizenry if the nation and the region are to compete economically and sustain a just society. The United States could easily be headed for a substantial shift in its position in the world with respect to the comparative levels of education and to the quality of life that education allows.

This is true for the West, as well. Already, educational achievement levels in some western states, such as Arizona, Nevada, and New Mexico, align most closely with those of OECD's lower-performing nations. Consider Nevada and Arizona, the nation's most rapidly growing states. Only two-thirds of 18–24-year-old Nevadans have a high school diploma, the lowest rate in the country; Arizona ranks only slightly ahead of Nevada, with 69 percent of its young adult population having earned a high school diploma (NCHEMS, 2005). The collision of demographic growth and distressed educational performance certainly bodes ill for these two states and potentially for the West as a whole.

The West could face exceptional challenges in the years to come and may receive small assistance from a federal government that currently has no comprehensive plan for addressing our nation's postsecondary educational deficiencies. While the West must do as much as possible to take advantage of all federal assistance that is available, it must also develop its own ways of addressing the huge economic and demographic challenges it faces. It is unlikely that the federal government will be there to help in a significant way.

The consequences to the nation as a whole—and to the ability of the federal government to serve this country well in the future—are not insignificant. If the West finds a way to provide the education that its citizens need and deserve, the entire nation's economic and social vitality will benefit. On the other hand, if the West is unable to adequately provide these educational services, the nation as a whole will suffer. As the West goes, so will go the rest—with or without federal support.

References

College Board. *Trends in Student Aid 2011*. Retrieved from www.collegeboard.org/student_aid_2011.pdf, 2011.

———. "Rethinking Student Aid Report Creates Policy Path to Simplify Student Aid and Make Finance Options Obvious Much Earlier in Life." Retrieved from www.collegeboard.org, in September 2008.

Goodchild, L. F., R. W. Jonsen, P. Limerick, and D. A. Longanecker, eds. *Higher Education in the American West: Regional History and State Contexts*. Higher Education and Society series. New York, NY: Palgrave Macmillan, 2014.

Lederman, D. "Analysis: Congressional Earmarks to Colleges $2 Billion." *Inside Higher Education*, April 29, 2010.

Longanecker, D. A. "The Federal Government and Western Higher Education." In L. F. Goodchild, R. W. Jonsen, P. Limerick, D. A. Longanecker (eds.), *Higher Education in the American West: Regional History and State Contexts*. Higher Education and Society series. New York: Palgrave Macmillan, 2014.

National Center for Higher Education Management Systems (NCHEMS). "American Community Survey, 2009." Retrieved from www.higheredinfo.org/dbrowser/index.php?measure=93.

———. "American Community Survey Educational Attainment by Degree-Level and Age-Group, 2009." Retrieved from www.higheredinfo.org/dbrowser/index.php?submeasure=232&year=2011&level=nation&mode=graph&state=0.

———. "American Community Survey Educational Attainment by Degree-Level and Age-Group, 2005." Retrieved from www.higheredinfo.org/dbrowser/index.php?submeasure=232&year=2011&level=nation&mode=graph&state=0.

National Science Foundation. "Academic Research and Development," Chapter 5, in *Science and Engineering Indicators: 2010*. Retrieved from www.nsf.gov/statistics/seind10/c5/c53.htm.

———. Office of Experimental Program to Stimulate Competitive Research—see section on criteria for eligibility. Retrieved from www.nsf.gov/epscor/.

Organisation for Economic Co-operation and Development. *Education at a Glance 2011*, OECD. Retrieved from www.oecd/education/highereducationandadultlearning/48631550.pdf, 2011.

US Department of Education. Retrieved from www.ed.gov/about/overview/budget/history, in December 2012.

———. "Table 1: Federal Pell Grant Program: Summary Statistic for CrossYear Reference (Parts 1–5)." Retrieved from www.2.ed.gov/finaid/prof/resources/data/pell-2010–11/pelleoy-2010–11.html, in December 2012.

———. *The Toolbox Revisited*, February 2006. Retrieved from http://www2.ed.gov/rschstat/research/pubs/toolboxrevisit/index.html, in December 2012.

———. *A Test of Leadership, Charting the Future of U.S. Higher Education*. USDOE, 2006.

Western Interstate Commission for Higher Education (WICHE). "Affordability: Table 28: Distribution of Federal Pell Grants by State, 1995–96 to 2009–10." In *WICHE Regional Factbook for Higher Education in the West: Policy Indicators for Higher Education*, analysis, 2010. Retrieved from www.wiche.edu/factbook.

———. *Knocking on the College Door: Projections of High School Graduates by State and Race/Ethnicity 1992–2022*. Boulder, CO: WICHE, 2008.

4

STATE POLICY LEADERSHIP IN THE PUBLIC INTEREST

IS ANYONE AT HOME?

Aims C. McGuinness Jr.

INTRODUCTION

State leaders increasingly recognize that higher education is the key to the future quality of life of their state's population and the ability of the state to compete in the global knowledge economy. The reality, however, is that state coordinating and governing structures established for an earlier time do not always have the capacity to provide the necessary policy leadership in the new environment. This chapter reviews the changing expectations for state policy leadership and the implications of these changes for states with a focus in particular on the western states.

CHANGING EXPECTATIONS

A fundamental change has taken place over the past decade regarding the state role in higher education. Historically, states have focused on the financing and governance of public institutions. This remains an important function, but state leaders are increasingly emphasizing the contributions of higher education to a broader "public agenda," best illustrated by the issues raised by the national report card, *Measuring Up* (National Center for Public Policy and Higher Education, 2000, 2002, 2004, 2006, and 2008):

- The scores on *Preparation* raise questions about the effectiveness of P/K-12 reform: standards, assessment, curriculum and course-taking patterns, secondary school retention and completion, as well as alignment of K-12 standards with requirements for college-level work or employment in a twenty-first-century workforce.
- The scores on *Participation* raise questions about differences in college-going rates among different groups (e.g., race, ethnicity, gender, and

income) and the state's regions, about relationships with the adequacy of preparation and affordability, and about disparities in the availability of postsecondary services among the state's regions (e.g., the regional availability of community college services).
- The scores on *Affordability* raise questions about the overall relationship of student financing policy (tuition and student aid) to incomes of the state's families and students, and about the interrelationship among tuition policy, student aid policy, and state appropriations for higher education.
- The scores on *Completion* raise questions related to the adequacy of preparation and affordability as well as incentives and accountability requirements for institutional performance. Initiatives to improve retention and completion and the proportion of a state's population completing a degree require articulation and coordination between education levels and an environment that focuses on student success rather than institutional status.
- The scores on *Benefits* raise questions related to state strategies to raise education attainment and improve the quality of the state's workforce and improve the civic participation and quality of life of the state's population.

In recent years, the focus of the public agenda at the national and state levels has intensified and the emphasis increasingly is on restoring the nation's global competitiveness in the educational attainment of its population. Driving this change is President Obama's goal that the United States should have the highest proportion of students graduating from college in the world by 2020 (see, The White House, http://www.whitehouse.gov/issues/education). The Lumina Foundation's "Big Goal" to increase the percentage of Americans with high-quality degrees and credentials to 60 percent by the year 2025 is also having an impact (Lumina Foundation, 2012). The change is reflected in the strategic plans of western states. The State of Oregon has established a "40–40–20" plan to improve educational attainment over a 10 to 15 year period. The goals to attain are:

- Forty percent of Oregonians earning a four-year degree or more—currently 29.2 percent (Lumina Foundation, 2012).
- Another 40 percent earning an associate's degree or post-high-school certificate—currently 26.9 percent (Oregon University System, 2011).
- The remaining 20 percent earning a high school diploma or equivalent (10.9% of Oregonians do not have a high school diploma today), and ready to enter the workforce (Oregon University System, 2011).

Based on the recommendations of a 2010 Governor's Excellence Commission, Utah has adopted a similarly ambitious goal of increasing the educational attainment of the population ages 25 to 64 with a higher education degree or credential to 66 percent by 2020 (Utah Board of Regents, 2010).

These goals are not "higher education" goals *per se* but concern the status and performance of the state's population and education system as a whole. They require policy decisions that cut across higher education sectors, across levels of education from pre-kindergarten through lifelong learning (P-20) and link with state economic development and innovation strategies across other public policy domains. And they are distinctly different from issues that traditionally concern institutional leaders: issues about institutional mission and the basic capacity to accomplish that mission (faculty resources, programs, facilities, and other assets). At the state level, the new agenda requires a shift away from transition concerns about unnecessary program duplication to policies that spur collaboration across sectors to achieve state goals. Within higher education, the emphasis has shifted from access to a greater concern for retention and degree completion. Spurred by initiatives of the National Governors' Association and national foundation–funded projects, such as Complete College America, the push is to accelerate completion of degrees and certificates within institutions as well as through improved collaboration across the system (see, "Complete College America," from http://www.completecollege.org/).

Changes in the Basic Assumptions

These changed expectations require state higher education coordinating boards to give less emphasis to the traditional functions of coordinating *institutions* and more attention to using the policy levers of regulation, accountability, and finance to stimulate institutional response to state priorities. Similarly, governing boards for state university and college systems must balance their internal governing responsibilities with increased attention to policy leadership related to a public agenda. The changes in the underlying assumptions about the state role in higher education are summarized in figure 4.1[1].

The Challenge of Change: National Overview

The process of change from previous state roles has been slow and difficult for many states. In the early 1990s, the overall picture of state capacity was bleak. State decision-making structures were seemingly unable to make the transition to new missions and modes of operation. Governors focused on short-term agendas or immediate budget crises. Legislatures were unable to sustain attention to long-term change agendas, because of legislative turnover, short-term agendas, intensified interest-group pressures, and lack of core staff capability focused on the "public interest" perspective on higher education. There was no venue within most legislative processes to link a strategic agenda with strategic financing policy or broader issues related to the future of the state's economy and the quality of life of its population.

In states with state-level governing boards (consolidated systems as well as multicampus universities; see Appendix A), the state boards often focused

A shift from:	To:
Focus on primarily providers and serving as "owner-operators" public institutions the principal means of serving public purposes.	Focus on clients (students/learners, employers, and governments) and utilization of the capacity of multiple as providers to serve public purposes.
Centralized control and regulation through tightly defined institutional missions, financial accountability, and retrospective reporting.	Decentralized management using policy tools to stimulate desired response (e.g., incentives, performance funding, consumer information).
Financing policies focused primarily on institutional subsidy and on the adequacy of institutional financing	Financing policies designed to "enter the market on behalf of the public" and to channel competitive forces toward public purposes
Accountability focused on institutional performance	Accountability focused on public priorities: the impact of higher education on the education attainment and performance of the state's population and the competitiveness of the state's economy

Figure 4.1 Changes in underlying assumptions about the state role in higher education.
Source: McGuinness, Jr., A. C., *Reflections on Postsecondary Education Governance Changes*. Denver, CO: Education Commission of the States, July 2002; available at: http://wwwecs.org/clearinghouse/31/02/3102.htm.

primarily on *internal* institutional concerns and often functioned as vertically organized, closed systems designed to protect the institutions from competition for students and resources from other providers. States emphasized one-size-fits-all policies that run counter to strategies to address the unique needs of each region of a state. The boards were often challenged by weaknesses in the quality of board and system leadership.

In coordinating-board states, the state boards often remained mired in regulatory practices, shaped by the statutory mandates of the 1970s and 1980s. They continued to focus primarily on *coordinating public institutions* and not on leading a public agenda and were politicized through appointments of both board members and staff. Many were experiencing an accelerating turnover of senior staff leadership and had significant deficits in terms of core information and analytic capabilities (especially those necessary for leading a public agenda as summarized above). State structures and politics continued to create barriers to collaboration between and among sectors to address common, crosscutting issues (e.g., "picket-fence" relationships among segments resulting in competing, uncoordinated services within each region of a state). The state budget crisis led states to cut state agency staffs and, in several cases, eliminate state higher education agencies.

State policies were *not* aligned with a public agenda—in fact, they were not aligned with any long-term agenda. The picture was one of splintered decision-making organized around specific programs or sectors, financing policy characterized by short-term agendas and driven by the most immediate fiscal crisis, fragmentation (e.g., state appropriations, student aid, and tuition policy), and disincentives for performance and collaboration. At the same time, regulatory policies mired in state bureaucratic processes did little to achieve efficiencies and often hindered the capacity of the higher education system to respond to public priorities, such as human resources, purchasing, and capital financing.

Promising Developments

Fortunately, a few states made efforts to counter these generally negative trends. Among the early developments, several states recognized the need to adopt major reforms in the late 1990s and early 2000s and led the nation in implementing new approaches to not only state leadership but also related policies of finance and accountability. Among the more far-reaching early developments were:

- The Kentucky Postsecondary Education Reform Act of 1996, leading to a sustained campaign to raise the education attainment of the state's population to the national average by 2020 (Kentucky Council on Postsecondary Education).
- The North Dakota Education Roundtable, which engaged the state's business, political, civic, and education leaders in multiyear strategy to link higher education to the state's future economy and quality of life (North Dakota University System).
- The Texas Higher Education Coordinating Board's *Closing the Gaps* initiative aimed at achieving significant advanced in enrollments, degree production, quality, and research competitiveness by 2015 (Texas Higher Education Coordinating Board).

Each of these states:

- Focused on a long-term public agenda linking higher education to the future of the state's quality of life and economy,
- Linked financing policy and accountability to the public agenda, and
- Pursued balanced strategies emphasizing both *capacity building* and *capacity utilization*.

The severe economic conditions in the early 2000s reinforced by the recommendations of several national projects and reports spurred other states to act. The National Collaborative for Higher Education Policy (2003–2006), funded by the Pew Charitable Trusts, worked with five states (Missouri, Rhode Island, Virginia, Washington, and West Virginia) to test a model for developing a public agenda. The project report, *Setting a Public Agenda for Higher Education in the States: Lessons Learned from the National Collaborative for Higher Education Policy*, served as an important guide to other states as they seek to change state policies (Davies, 2006a).

Recognizing the challenge of dramatically increasing the education attainment of the population, the National Center for Public Policy and Higher Education in 2005 published a policy statement, "The Need for State Policy Leadership," which called on states to strengthen their capacity for this critical function (National Center for Public Policy and Higher Education, 2005). In the policy brief, the National Center recognized that the specific organizational approaches would differ across states, but emphasized that sustained policy leadership in higher education must include, among other points, a broad-based public entity with a clear charge to increase the state's educational attainment and prepare citizens for the workforce and capacity and responsibility for articulating and monitoring state performance objectives for higher education that are supported by the key leaders in the state. Objectives should be specific and measurable, including quantifiable goals for college preparation, access, participation, retention, graduation, and responsiveness to other state needs.

Other reports in the early 2000s underscored the need for states to shape long-term goals in terms of the education attainment of the state's population and global competitiveness of the state's economy and to redefine the terms of higher education accountability. These included the 2005 report of the National Commission on Accountability in Higher Education, *Accountability for Better Results: A National Imperative for Higher Education*, and the National Conference of State Legislatures' 2006 Blue Ribbon Commission on Higher Education report, *Transforming Higher Education: National Imperative— State Responsibility*.

As indicated earlier, President Obama's goal to increase the nation's educational attainment, reports from the National Governors' Association, and foundation initiatives, such as Lumina's "Big Goal," as well as the Bill and Melinda Gates Foundation and other foundations' support for *Complete College America*, accelerated the attention to these issues.

More recent leaders of this change were: Ohio with the *Strategic Plan for Higher Education 2008–2017* (University System of Ohio, 2010);[2] the Tennessee Complete College Act of 2010 (State of Tennessee, 2010); and the Indiana strategic plan, *Reaching Higher, Achieving More* (Indiana Commission for Higher Education, 2012).

The Great Recession and the political divisions since 2008 have only exacerbated challenges that developed during the prior decade. Unfortunately, the negative forces working against state-level policy leadership continued to take a toll. Among the early leaders, Kentucky and Texas, were able to sustain attention to long-term goals. However, political change in North Dakota distracted the state from the promising earlier developments. Changes in the state's political leadership stalled the promising developments in Ohio.

As the nation emerged from the recession, there were signs of renewed attention to a "public agenda" in at least some states. In some cases, these were a continuation of earlier reforms. Table 4.1 lists a range of state higher

Table 4.1 Examples of state higher education reforms, 1996–2013

States	Goals	Governance	Regulation	Finance Policy	Accountability
Mississippi and Maine	Devised in context of funding model development, no statewide consensus	No change	No change	Performance funding	Only in context of funding model
Illinois	Public agenda—broad consensus	No change	No change	Minimal performance funding	Annual report
Montana	Goals established for "success" agenda	No change; increased attention to community colleges within system	No change	Performance funding linked to increased degree completion under development	New accountability reporting
Virginia	Goals established	No change	Deregulation in return for attention to state goals	Performance funding linked to increased degree completion under development	Accountability for contributing to state goals; simplification of earlier (2004) accountability requirements
Nevada	Goals devised with limited involvement	No change	Institutions given tuition authority	Performance funding—some investment in research capacity	No history
Louisiana	Goals devised with limited involvement	Creation of a community college system	Admissions requirements at 4-year institutions raised Articulation & transfer	Performance funding Significant investment in community colleges	In context of funding model
Texas	Clearly articulated Widely accepted Sustained over 14 years	No change	College and career readiness standards Articulation & transfer	Incentive funding for completion. Major investment in research universities	Annual report

Continued

Table 4.1 Continued

States	Goals	Governance	Regulation	Finance Policy	Accountability
Oregon	Aggressive goal in statute	Major changes Oregon Education Investment Board, Higher Education Coordinating Commission, and institutional boards	Compacts	No new money; moving to funding model that integrates appropriations tuition student aid	Tied to compacts
Indiana	Goals developed by Indiana Commission for Higher Education	Creation of a community college system	Little change	Performance funding	Annual report
Tennessee	Goals devised with broad involvement—general requirements in statute	Created a community college system Made student financial aid agency a part of Tennessee Higher Education Commission	P-12 alignment Articulation & transfer	100% performance funding closely linked to goals	Tied to funding model
Kentucky	Clearly articulated Widely accepted Sustained across changes in education and political leadership	Creation of CC system Strengthened mission distinctions Strengthened statewide coordination	Articulation & transfer P-12 alignment	Investment Trust funds established to build capacity aligned with goals	Annual report

Source: NCHEMS, "Laying the Groundwork: SUNY Investment Fund for Regional Development," presentation to Presidents' Council, State University of New York, Albany, May 21, 2013.

education reforms from 1996 to 2013, illustrating how the states have used key policy tools to effect change:

- Establishing and gaining broad consensus on long-term goals and related metrics,
- Changing governance,
- Changing regulation (either establishing new regulations or deregulating),
- Aligning finance policy with goals through performance funding, and
- Establishing new accountability requirements.

The states in table 4.1 are listed in a sequence from relatively simple reforms focused on only one or two policy tools, to the most comprehensive reforms.

Developments in the Western States

The 15 states comprising the Western Interstate Commission for Higher Education (WICHE) face varied challenges in responding to the call for increased capacity for policy leadership. More states in the West have statewide governing boards and therefore, as discussed earlier, do not have a coordinating entity charged with responsibility for shaping and leading a public agenda for the whole state. Out of the 15 western states, 11 have statewide governing boards with authority and responsibility limited primarily to governing the public institutions within their jurisdiction (as displayed in Appendix B). This compares to the national picture of one-half the states with state coordinating boards and the other half with state governing boards. The 11 western governing board states are: Alaska,[3] Arizona, California, Hawaii, Idaho, Montana, Nevada, North Dakota, South Dakota, Utah, and Wyoming. The addition of California and the deletion of Oregon from this category of governing board states are striking changes. In 2011, the Governor of California eliminated state funding for the California Postsecondary Education Commission. At the time of this writing, discussions were underway about forming a new entity but no decisions had been made (California Legislative Analyst's Office, 2012). The state boards in Alaska, Hawaii, Idaho, Montana, Nevada, North Dakota, and South Dakota govern essentially all the public degree-granting postsecondary institutions in their states. Oregon established a new P-20 policy entity, the Oregon Education Investment Board and a new Higher Education Coordinating Commission.[4] The state boards in Arizona and Wyoming govern only the public universities, while the community colleges are locally governed.

In spite of the structural challenges facing western states, several have made significant progress, providing policy leadership on behalf of a public agenda in their states. Although their primary responsibility is to govern the institutions within their jurisdiction, several governing boards have demonstrated that they also can provide the leadership, either directly or in collaboration with others, in shaping a public agenda for the whole state. This shift is reflected in the board- and system-planning documents, board minutes, and in the actions of state political leaders. The Board of Regents of the Montana University System developed a strategic plan for 2006–2010, recently updated in December 2011, which reflects many of the themes of a public agenda in terms of goals for raising the education attainment of the state's population and linking higher education to the state's economic future (Montana University System, 2008). The Nevada System of Higher Education has made significant strides in establishing long-term goals and developing a new performance funding model aligned with these goals. The Utah Board of Regent's planning and policies are aligned with the state's "66%" goal noted earlier. The University of Hawaii System's *Performance Measures, 2011* emphasized the link between higher education and the future of the state's educational attainment, quality of life, and economy (University of Hawaii System, 2011).

The statewide higher education coordinating entities in western states have all been challenged in the past decade. As a result, these states have had difficulty developing and sustaining long-term reforms. Early in the 2000s, New Mexico abolished its coordinating commission and established a cabinet-level Secretary of Higher Education. California eliminated the California Postsecondary Commission (CPEC). This change left California with no effective means for establishing statewide goals and related metrics and shaping policies to narrow the growing gaps in the educational attainment of its population. The change resulted from concerns expressed for more than a decade about the effectiveness of CPEC and were precipitated by the state's budget crisis. As of the writing of this chapter, the California State Legislature was debating several alternatives for establishing a new statewide entity to provide the policy leadership that the Legislative Analyst's Office and others see as an essential means to address statewide and intersegmental issues facing the state. In 2011, Washington State eliminated the Washington Higher Education Coordinating Board (HECB), effective July 1, 2012, but replaced the board with The Washington State Achievement Council. The new entity has a stronger emphasis on improving the state's educational attainment, but will have more streamlined powers and functions than the previous HECB.[5] The state's universities used their political influence to abolish the HECB in part because they saw the board as an obstacle to their efforts to gain greater authority to raise tuition. The Steering Committee established to design a replacement, however, recognized the need for an entity focused on a long-term agenda to improve the state's educational attainment and to strip away some of the "barnacles" that had hindered the performance of the HECB. It remains to be seen whether the new entity will have the authority and influence to carry out the intended functions.

The Colorado Commission on Higher Education faced several challenges but has emerged as a stronger and more effective leadership entity. In 2012, a Higher Education Strategic Planning Committee developed a strategic plan for Colorado higher education, *The Degree Dividend: Building Our Economy and Preserving Our Quality of Life* (Colorado Higher Education Strategy Planning Steering Committee, 2010). With this report as a foundation, the Colorado Commission on Higher Education is moving ahead with implementation strategies focused on narrowing gaps in educational attainment, improving productivity, changes in finance policy, and other issues raised by the Higher Education Strategic Planning Steering Committee report.

The changes underway in Oregon are perhaps the most far-reaching in the West. As noted above, the state's 40–40–20 goals are the most aggressive in the nation in shaping a P-20 agenda for improving the educational attainment of a state's population. The Oregon Education Investment Board (OEIB) is charged with leading the state toward these goals, using strategic finance policy and accountability as the principal policy tools to leverage change. Recognizing the need for an entity to focus specifically on the contributions of postsecondary education to the statewide goals, Oregon in 2010 established the Higher Education Coordinating Commission (HECC) which functions within the overall jurisdiction of the OEIB. At the time of this writing, Oregon was debating a proposal to establish local governing boards for the University of Oregon and Portland State University and potentially at Oregon State University, leaving the other public institutions within the governing authority of a significantly diminished Oregon University System. At the same time, the authority of the HECC would be increased, and it would assume the responsibility for state student financial assistance and overseeing the community colleges, currently under the State Board of Education.

A major challenge in all western states will be to sustain attention to a long-term, crosscutting agenda over changes in political leadership and severe budget constraints facing the states and the nation. In spite of the turmoil in several of the states, there is a clear trend in the West, of states establishing long-term goals to increase the educational attainment of the states' populations and implementing performance funding models and accountability requirements that have the potential of moving the systems toward these goals.

PREREQUISITES FOR POLICY LEADERSHIP IN THE PUBLIC INTEREST

From the experience in working with states on major higher education reform initiatives and a review of the states that have achieved improved performance on the indicators, such as those in *Measuring Up*, several characteristics emerge as prerequisites for state capacity to pursue a consistent, long-term agenda in the public interest (Davies, 2006b). The emphasis is purposely on a cluster of "characteristics"—not on specific "governance" alternatives. Alternatives for any state would have to be shaped in terms of its unique history and culture. The states that lead the nation in improving the life-chances of their citizens and improving their quality of life and economies through higher education will be states that:

- Pursue a consistent, year-by-year, step-by-step public agenda over a 10 to 15 year period, an agenda focused on narrowing gaps in performance in comparison to other states on key indicators of public priorities (e.g., pursuit of a "public agenda" reflected in a strategic plan or other policy documents focused on the education attainment and performance or quality of life of the state's population) and the state's economic competitiveness.
- Align policy with the long-term public agenda:
  - Leadership and decision-making structures;
  - Financing policy (including performance funding and student financial aid);
  - Regulatory policy; and
  - Standards, assessment, and accountability.
- Establish a venue (a board, agency or other entity) with authority/capacity to:
  - Lead, nurture, manage, and sustain attention to the public agenda over a multiyear period—across changes in political leadership and economic conditions;
  - Gain consensus around and commitment to the public agenda among the state's political, business, and civic leaders, as well as the higher education community;
  - Maintain a stance of—and sustain a reputation for—independent, nonpartisan leadership and objective analysis in the public interest;
  - Focus primarily on *capacity utilization* (on aligning the state's higher education capacity with the public agenda) more than *capacity building*—that is, on developing the capacity of public institutions and other providers;
  - Develop and oversee the implementation of financing policy linked to the public agenda;
  - Maintain public accountability systems, including supporting information and analytic capacity, for monitoring:
    - Progress on the public agenda, and
    - Performance in relationship to the public agenda at the regional and institutional levels.
  - Engage the state's political business and civic leaders and higher education community in an annual dialogue and monitoring of progress on the public agenda.
- Recognize the potential contribution of all the state's education institutions and providers (public and private), not only the state's public institutions, to the public agenda.
- Pursue systemic strategies to advance the public agenda:
  - Linking higher education to improvement at all education levels (P-16/20);
  - Linking education policy to other policy areas (e.g., economic development, health and criminal justice); and

- Ensuring integrated policy formulation in critical areas, such as:
  - Student aid, institutional subsidy and tuition/fee policy, and
  - Alignment of standards and assessments between secondary education and higher education.
- Provide consistent support (through the quality of board appointments, board training and other means) of effective *institutional governance*:
  - Ensuring that institutional planning, resource allocation, and accountability are linked to both institutional missions and the public agenda, and
  - Providing for institutional management flexibility and responsiveness within the framework of statewide policy and accountability.
- Provide incentives for collaboration and partnerships between institutions and between institutions and schools, business, and other entities, to achieve improvements in performance consistent with the public agenda.
- Differentiate solutions to respond to the unique needs of different regions and population groups within the state (avoiding one-size-fits-all solutions) within the framework of statewide goals and policy.

CONCLUSION

Sustaining attention to the public/societal purposes of higher education in the turbulent times of the next decade and beyond will require fundamental improvements in the state-level capacity to lead change in the public interest. As summarized above, an increasing number of states are changing the traditional roles of state boards and finding other means to develop their capacity for policy leadership. Several western states are taking the lead in shaping bold public agendas to increase the education attainment of their populations, increase degree production to globally competitive levels, and link higher education to the states' global economic competitiveness. New thinking is needed about the ways that states can shape decision-making structures and policies designed explicitly for new missions and functions.

Appendix A

Classification of State Higher Education Structures

Appendix B displays all states, the District of Columbia, and Puerto Rico according to three broad categories: states with consolidated governing boards, states with coordinating boards, and states with higher education service agencies. The figure organizes states according to the extent of the formal authority of the board or agency for academic policy and budget. Reading from left to right, the boards/agencies in the states on the left have more formal authority in these policy domains that those to the right. Consolidated governing boards have broad authority for both academic and budget-related policy for the institutions under their authority. The states with coordinating boards/agencies are divided according to those with regulatory boards/agencies with program approval authority and those with advisory board/agencies with only program review authority. Within these two categories, the states are grouped according to the board/agency's authority in the budget process.

- Twenty-one states plus the District of Columbia and Puerto Rico are consolidated governing board states. These states organize all public higher education under one or two statewide governing boards. None of these states has established a statewide coordinating agency with significant academic policy or budgetary authority between the governing board and state government. Nine of these states organize all public higher education under a single governing board. The other 12 states have two boards: most often a board for universities and a board for community colleges and/or technical colleges. In several of these states, the second board is a coordinating board for community and/or technical colleges.
- Twenty-three states are coordinating board/agency states.
  ○ Twenty-two of these states have regulatory coordinating boards with academic program approval authority. Fifteen of these boards have significant budgetary authority, six have limited budget authority, and one has no role in the budgetary process.
  ○ Two states have advisory boards with no program approval authority and only limited program review authority. The New Mexico Department of Higher Education has important authority in the budget process whereas the authority of the California Postsecondary Commission in the budget process is limited.
- Five states (Alaska, Delaware, Minnesota, New Hampshire, and Pennsylvania) and the District of Columbia and Puerto Rico have state

higher education service agencies that carry out functions such as administration of student assistance, licensure and approval of nonpublic degree-granting institutions, administration of federal and state categorical programs, and data collection and analysis. These agencies generally do not have significant roles in either program approval or review or the budget process for the higher education system as a whole. The agencies in Alaska, Minnesota, and New Hampshire, as well as the District of Columbia and Puerto Rico, are in entities with one or two statewide consolidated governing boards.

- Two states (Michigan and Vermont) have no statutory statewide higher education agency. The Michigan State Board of Education has constitutional authority for overall planning and coordination of the state's education system, but because of the constitutional autonomy of the state universities and local governance of community colleges, the Michigan board does not function as a statewide higher education coordinating agency. The Michigan board is the licensing authority for nondegree vocational-technical education and proprietary institutions and approves charters for private degree-granting. In Vermont, the Vermont Higher Education Council is a nonstatutory, voluntary-planning entity.
- Five states (Florida, Idaho, Michigan, New York, and Pennsylvania) have state boards with formal legal authority for all levels of education (early childhood education through higher education). Nevertheless, the formal authority of these boards for higher education varies significantly. Only in Idaho does the state board have governing authority for the state higher education institutions. In Florida, New York, and Pennsylvania, the state boards have authority related to higher education, but the authority is for coordination, not governance. In New York, the Board of Regents has no authority in the budget process. In Pennsylvania, the authority related to higher education of the State Board of Education and Secretary of Education is limited and the Pennsylvania Department of Education functions more as a service/regulatory agency than a statewide coordinating agency. As indicated above, the Michigan State Board of Education does not function as a statewide coordinating agency for higher education and has only limited authority related to higher education.

APPENDIX B

AUTHORITY OF STATE BOARDS AND AGENCIES OF HIGHER EDUCATION, 2008

States with Statewide Consolidated Governing Boards and No Coordinating Board (except as noted *)		Regulatory Coordinating Boards and Agencies Boards with Program Approval Authority			Advisory Boards/Agency Boards with No Program Approval Authority—Only Authority to Review and make Recommendations on Academic Programs		Higher Education Service Agencies	No State Higher Education Board or Agency
One Board for All Public Institutions	Two Boards Encompassing All Public Institutions	Consolidated or Aggregated Budget (f)	Budget Review and Recommendation (f)	No Statutory Budget Role	Consolidated or Aggregated Budget (f)	Budget Review and Recommendation (f)	No Statutory Budget or Program Review or Approval Roles	
Alaska (b)	Arizona (m)	Alabama	Connecticut	New York (a)	New Mexico (h)	California (o)	Alaska (b)*	Michigan (a) (g)
Hawaii	Florida (a) (l)	Arkansas	Nebraska				Delaware	Vermont (k)
Idaho (a)	Georgia (n)	Colorado	New Jersey				Minnesota (b)*	
Kansas (d)	Iowa (c)	Indiana	Texas				New Hampshire (b) (c)*	
Montana	Maine (n) (e)	Illinois	Virginia				Pennsylvania (a) (i)	
Nevada	Massachusetts (j)	Kentucky	Washington				DC (b)*	
North Dakota	Minnesota (g)*	Louisiana					Puerto Rico (b)*	
Rhode Island	Mississippi (c)	Maryland						
South Dakota	New Hampshire (b) (n)*	Missouri						
DC (b)*	North Carolina (n)	Ohio						
Puerto Rico (b)*	Oregon (c)	Oklahoma						
	Utah (n)	South Carolina						
	Vermont (k)*	Tennessee						
	Wisconsin (n)	West Virginia						
	Wyoming (c)							
States = 9, and DC and Puerto Rico)	States = 12, plus 3* (MN, NH and VT)	States = 14	States = 6	States = 1	States = 2	States = 2	States = 2, plus 3* and DC and Puerto Rico	States = 2

Notes: States listed in more than one column are noted with an asterisk (*) with the total number of duplicates at the bottom of the column.

(a) State board/agency responsible for all levels of education (P/K-16/20). State boards/agencies in Florida, New York, and Pennsylvania have coordinating, not governing, authority for public institutions. State board in Idaho has governing authority.

(b) State has both consolidated governing board(s) and coordinating or planning/service agency.

(c) One of the two boards is a statewide coordinating body for community colleges and/or postsecondary technical institutions.

(d) Kansas Board of Regents is a consolidated governing board for universities and coordinating board for locally governed community colleges and Washburn University.

(e) Maine Maritime Academy is the only public institution with its own governing board outside a system.

(f) Several states, for example, Texas Coordinating Board for Higher Education, develop the formulae for allocation of state appropriations and/or make recommendations for overall system funding but do not review and/or make recommendations on individual institutional budgets.

(g) Michigan State Board of Education has constitutional authority for overall planning and coordination of the state's education system, but because of the constitutional autonomy of the state universities and local governance of community colleges, the state board does not function as a statewide higher education coordinating agency. State Board is the licensing authority for nondegree vocational-technical education and proprietary institutions and approves charters for private degree-granting institutions within the state.

(h) The New Mexico entity is a cabinet-level department headed by a Secretary of Higher Education. The department has authority to review, adjust and approve public university budgets prior to submission to the department of finance and administration and limited authority primarily to review and study but not to take formal action to approve academic programs or other institutional decisions.

(i) Pennsylvania State Board of Education's program approval authority is limited to specific areas (e.g., teacher education). Board also must approve new campuses or sites. Department of Education has budget responsibility for community colleges and regulatory responsibilities regarding for-profit institutions.

(j) State-level governing boards in Massachusetts include the Board of Trustees, University of Massachusetts, and the Board of Higher Education for other public institutions including community colleges. The latter board is also the coordinating board for whole public system.

(k) Vermont has no statutory planning/coordinating entity. Vermont Higher Education Council is voluntary.

(l) Florida State Board of Education has responsibility for policy direction and coordination of state's education system, P-20. Constitutional amendment passed in November, 2002, created a Board of Governors for Universities, but the State Board of Education retains overall responsibility for policy coordination for all education. State Board of Education, through a chancellor for community colleges, coordinates locally governed community colleges.

(m) State law enacted in 2002 eliminated most powers of the Arizona State Board of Directors of Community Colleges except for data collection and preparing an annual report.

(n) The two boards in these states include a statewide governing board for universities and a statewide governing board for community colleges and/or technical institutions.

(o) Authority of the California Postsecondary Education Commission related to budgets is limited response to requests from the Governor and General Assembly for review and recommendations of budget requests of the segments (Community Colleges, California State University, and the University of California)

Source: Aims C. McGuinness Jr., National Center for Higher Education Management Systems, updated October, 2008.

Notes

1. For discussion of changes in role of government see McGuinness, A. C. "A Conceptual and Analytic Framework for Review of National Regulatory Policies and Practices in Higher Education." Paper prepared for the Organisation for Economic Co-operation and Development (OECD), February 17, 2006 (EDU/EC/2006).
2. University System of Ohio (2007). *Strategic Plan for Higher Education 2008–2017.* Note: with the change state leadership in 2010, the strategic plan is no longer available on the website of the University System of Ohio.
3. The Alaska Commission on Postsecondary Education has authority for coordinating development of comprehensive plans for the orderly development of public and private postsecondary education but historically has not been seen as the venue for statewide policy leadership on higher education issues.
4. Oregon 76th Legislative Assembly, 2012 Regular Session, Senate Bill 1538.
5. Washington State Legislature, 62nd Regular Session, Engrossed Second Substitute, HB 2483.

References

California Legislative Analyst's Office. "Improving Higher Education Oversight," 2012. Retrieved from www.lao.ca.gov.

Colorado Higher Education Strategy Planning Steering Committee. "The Degree Dividend," 2010. Retrieved from http://highered.colorado.gov/Publications/General/StrategicPlanning/Meetings/Resources/strategicplan_final_nov0410.pdf.

Davies, G. K. *Setting a Public Agenda for Higher Education in the States: Lessons Learned from the National Collaborative for Higher Education Policy.* San Jose, CA: NCPPHE, December, 2006a.

———. *Setting a Public Agenda for Higher Education in the States: Lessons Learned from the National Collaborative for Higher Education Policy.* National Center for Public Policy and Higher Education, December, 2006b. Retrieved from www.highereducation.org/reports/public_agenda/.

Indiana Commission for Higher Education. *Reaching Higher, Achieving More,* 2012. Retrieved from www.in.gov/che/files/2012_RHAM_3_21_12.pdf.

Kentucky Council on Postsecondary Education. *Reform Legislation & Related Reports.* Retrieved from www.cpe.ky.gov/planning/legislation/.

Lumina Foundation. "Lumina's Strategic Direction: The Big Goal." Retrieved from www.luminafoundation.org/goal_2025/goal2.html.

McGuinness, A. C. "A Conceptual and Analytic Framework for Review of National Regulatory Policies and Practices in Higher Education." Paper prepared for the Organisation for Economic Co-operation and Development, February 17, 2006.

Montana University System. *Montana Board of Regents Strategic Plan, 2008.* Retrieved from www. mus.edu/data/strategic_plan.asp.

National Center for Public Policy and Higher Education (NCPPHE). *Measuring Up: The State-by-State Report Card for Higher Education.* San Jose, CA: NCPPHE, 2000, 2002, 2004, 2006, and 2008.

———. "State Capacity for Higher Education Policy." A Special Supplement to *National Crosstalk,* July 2005.

National Commission on Accountability in Higher Education. *Accountability for Better Results: A National Imperative for Higher Education*. Boulder, CO: State Higher Education Executive Officers, March 10, 2005.

National Council of State Legislatures. Blue Ribbon Commission on Higher Education. *Transforming Higher Education: National Imperative—State Responsibility*. Denver, CO: National Conference of State Legislatures, November 27, 2006.

North Dakota University System. *Roundtable on Higher Education*. Retrieved from www.ndus.nodak.edu/reports/default.asp?ID=355.

Oregon University System. *2011 Legislative Brief: Educational Attainment in Oregon, Moving Toward 40-40-20*, 2011. Retrieved from www.ous.edu/sites/default/files/dept/govrel/files/2011IB40-40-20.pdf.

Texas Higher Education Coordinating Board. *Closing the Gaps*. Retrieved from www.thecb.state.tx.us/closingthegaps/.

State of Tennessee. "The Tennessee Complete College Act," 2010. Retrieved from http://tn.gov/thec/complete_college_tn/ccta_summary.html.

University of Hawaii System. *Performance Measures, 2011: Serving the State of Hawai'i*. Retrieved from www.hawaii.edu/ovppp/uhplan/PM11.pdf.

University System of Ohio. *Strategic Plan for Higher Education 2008–2017*, 2007.

Utah Board of Regents. "Education Panel Sets Ambitious Goal for Higher Education," October 13, 2010. Retrieved from www.higheredutah.org/education-panel-sets-ambitious-goal-for-higher-education/.

5

HIGHER EDUCATION FINANCE POLICY IN THE WESTERN STATES[*]

Dennis P. Jones

As in all states, higher education finance policy in the Western Interstate Commission for Higher Education (WICHE) states is shaped by numerous forces: deeply held values about the importance of higher education to society, changes in population, the distribution of that population, the accumulation of decisions over many decades that have determined the shape of the higher education system in the state, state-level decisions about tax policies, the priorities for the expenditure of public funds, and the impacts of changes in the global economy. While there are clearly many differences across the western states, there also are some common threads that run through them. For example, all of the western states are heavily dependent on public colleges and universities as the providers of postsecondary education opportunities; none of these states has a large share of their undergraduate students enrolled in private institutions, as shown in figure 5.1. Even in the states with the highest proportion of private college enrollments, nearly three out of four undergraduates are enrolled in a public college or university.

All of the western states espouse the importance of higher education and some have a highly educated citizenry, but, interestingly, most find themselves below the national average in the proportion of recent high school graduates going on to college, and almost one-half the states are at the very low end of participations rates (see figure 5.2).

Until recently, the western states have pretty uniformly emphasized low tuition as the means of ensuring access to educational opportunity. Only Wyoming has a constitutional provision requiring that tuitions be kept low, but the other states have historically had public policies built around philosophies of relatively low tuition. The economic problems that bedeviled most states at the turn of the millennium created circumstances in which pragmatism overruled philosophy, and tuitions were increased in many of the western states, in some instances significantly. This has reached the point in four states—Colorado, Montana, South Dakota, and Oregon—where students contribute more than the state to the general operating revenues of public colleges and universities. Even so, in the majority of the WICHE

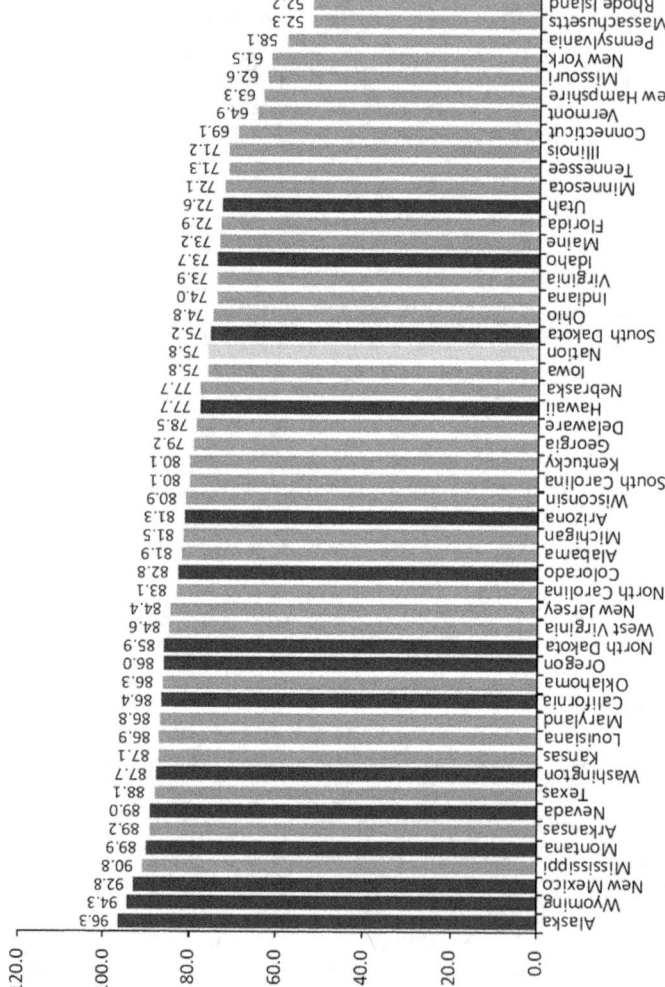

Figure 5.1 Percent of total undergraduate headcount in the public sector, Fall 2010.

Note: Figures aggregated form postsecondary Title IV degree-granting institutions. The following institutions primarily serve out-of-state students online and are excluded from their respective state results but included in the National total; University of Phoenix Online (AZ), Western International University (AZ), Ashford University (IA), Kaplan University (IA), Colorado Technical University Online (CO), and American Public University (WV).

Source: NCES, IPEDS Fall 2010 Enrollment File (Early Release).

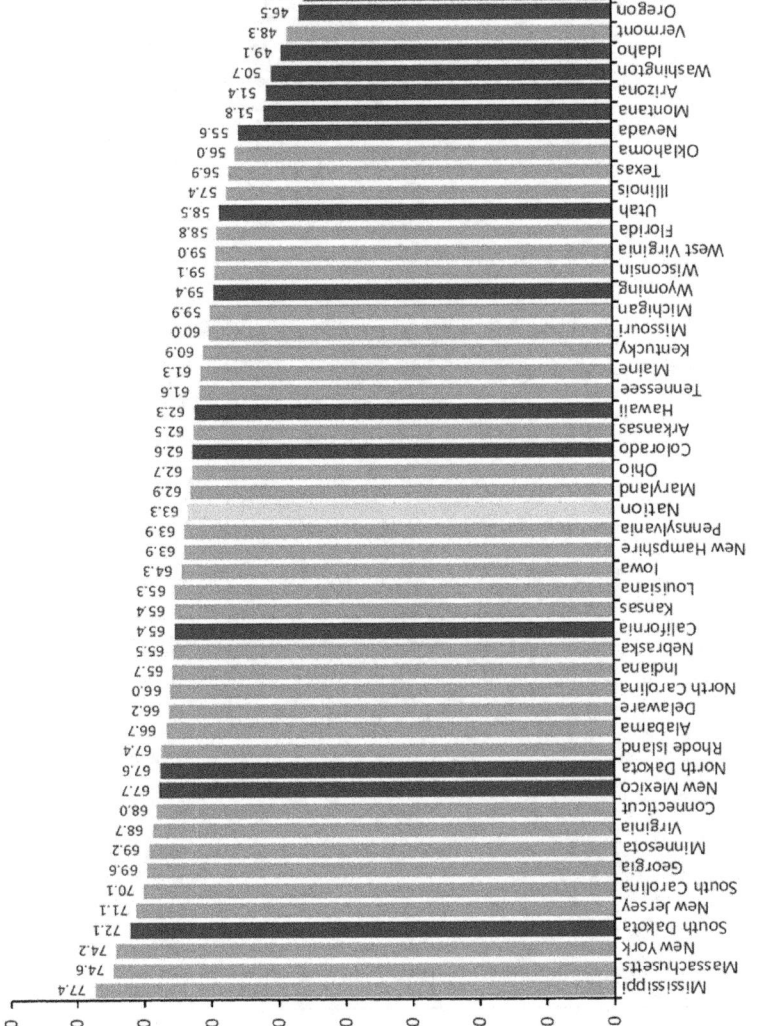

Figure 5.2 Percent of high school graduates going directly to college, Fall 2008.

Source: SHEEO.

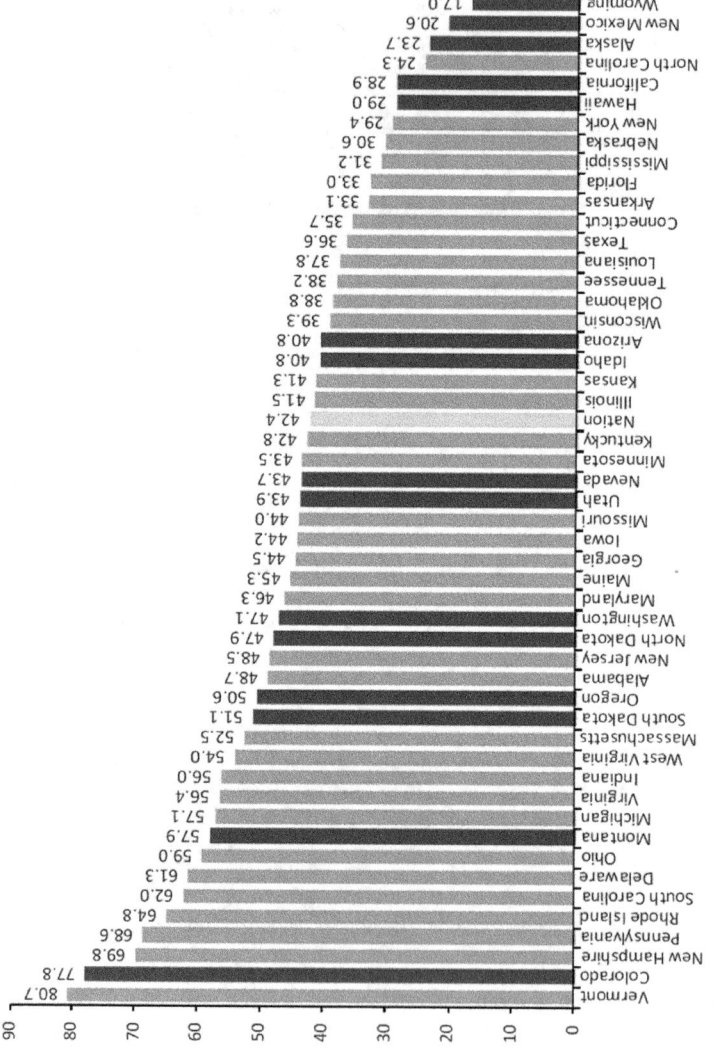

Figure 5.3 Family share of funding for public higher education, FY 2010.
Source: SHEEO SHEF.

states, students and their families continue to bear a relatively smaller share of overall educational costs (see figure 5.3).

The WICHE states uniformly have tax structures that bode ill for the future. All 15 of the WICHE states have projected long-term deficits in their budgets, according to analyses performed by the Rockefeller Institute of Government for the National Center for Higher Education Management Systems (NCHEMS; Jones, 2006). A finance policy expert at the Rockefeller Institute notes that:

> Western states have resolved conflicting [tax policy] goals in very different ways from most other states. Three of the five states without broad-based sales taxes are in the West (Alaska, Montana, and Oregon). Five of the nine states without a broad-based income tax are in the West (Alaska, Nevada, South Dakota, Washington, and Wyoming). Alaska is one of only two states with no sales tax or income tax. Washington relies disproportionately on the sales tax, and several other Western states rely very heavily on this tax. Alaska and Wyoming rely extremely heavily on taxes on natural resources, and New Mexico and North Dakota rely considerably on similar taxes. For these and other reasons, one recent analysis labeled Western states' tax structures as "wobbly."
>
> Western states practice direct democracy far more routinely than other states. Combined with strong anti-tax sentiment, this has lead to considerable constraints on Western states' revenue-raising ability, in the form of initiatives and referenda (as well as occasional legislatively enacted statutes) that limit taxes and spending, and that require legislative supermajority votes to raise taxes. These constraints are particularly strong in Colorado, Oregon, and California but are widespread in some form throughout the region.
>
> The combination of these factors will cause most Western states to face projected budget gaps in the next five to 10 years—with the gaps likely being largest in the states that do not have income taxes, or that rely on them least. Western states will face considerable pressure to bring revenue structures and spending policies into line. (Boyd, 2003, p. 5)

Although the western states have features affecting higher education finance policy in common, they also are facing some very different circumstances with regard to both economics and demographics.

Many of the western states were among those most affected by the bursting of the housing bubble that fostered the recession that started in the first decade of the twenty-first century. States like Arizona, California, Colorado, and Nevada that lost large numbers of construction jobs were particularly hard hit and sustained large decreases in state revenues (and accompanying large increases in the costs of their social support safety nets). At the other end of the spectrum is North Dakota that saw a large increase in state revenues resulting from greatly increased oil and gas production. The West experienced both the worst and the best of broader economic forces.

The extremes regarding demographic change are found in these same states. In the period until 2018, Nevada is projected to face what can be labeled only as explosive growth in the number of high school graduates, more than doubling the potential number of college enrollees in 14 years ending at that time. Substantial growth is also projected for Arizona, California, and Washington. At the other extreme is North Dakota, which is expected to see a decrease of almost 25 percent in the number of high school graduates over this same period of time. Other states (Montana and Wyoming, for example) are also expected to experience decreases in their college-age population (WICHE, 2003). The states with the largest economic challenges will also have the greatest demographic challenges.

As a result of these wildly differing circumstances, the western states will be faced with different sets of postsecondary education issues. Financing policies will have to evolve in ways responsive to these diverse issues.

In the high-growth states, demand will substantially exceed available institutional capacity. Policies will have to be fashioned in ways designed to finance growth and accommodate demand. The constraints imposed by the tax structures in most of these states will inevitably create ever-increasing demands for efficiencies and pressures for limiting demands on the public purse. The problems faced by the high-growth states will be exacerbated by the different demographic characteristics of the large numbers of potential new students. They will be less proficient in English, less well prepared academically, and from poorer families (thus less able to contribute financially to their own educations). In addition, all high-growth states also have large numbers of young adults (those in their 20s and 30s) who have not completed high school.

Given the importance of education beyond high school as preparation for employment, the provision of adult literacy and basic workplace skills training will be an increasing priority. All of these factors will complicate the formulation of financing policy that yields adequate levels of funding for institutions while simultaneously keeping education affordable to both students and taxpayers.

In those states with declining student populations, the issues will be those of sustaining institutions in the face of waning enrollments. With declining student numbers, state policymakers will be hard-pressed to maintain higher education funding, especially in the face of increasing demands for other services (such as health care). The future of higher education in some of these states may hinge on the willingness and ability of institutions to assume new roles in service to their states—contributing in more focused ways to expanding and diversifying the states' economies, for example. In the absence of the capacity and willingness to provide a wider range of services to their surrounding regions, the calls for institutional closure or consolidation likely will increase.

THE OPTIONS

There are relatively few options in this environment:

1. *Reduce levels of service to the point where demand is capped at the level of affordable supply.* This will be a difficult and politically risky policy to

choose. While it has been implemented implicitly and over short periods of time (in California, e.g., during the economic downturn of the 1990s and again in 2009–2011 when many thousands of students were denied meaningful access to college), it is hard to conceive of western states employing this option over an extended period. There are too many economic and social downsides for states that educate fewer rather than more of their citizens.

2. *Increase taxes to provide the additional resources needed for states to support higher education in the ways they have in the past.* Theoretically, this is a legitimate option, but it is an unlikely one. The orientation in the West is to cut taxes, not raise them—at least at the state level. The "direct democracy" that allows (in some cases, requires) tax policy to be determined by a vote of the people has made it very difficult to increase rates of broad-based state taxes, such as sales and income taxes. In recent years, only Nevada has taken this unpopular step. Tax increases, if they are to be accomplished at all, are more easily achieved at the local level. A minority of the western states have local taxing districts that support institutions of higher education, and then only in the community college sector.

3. *Find more cost-effective ways of doing business.* This is not really an option; rather, it is an imperative in almost all states. Economics will force change; the question is whether or not the changes will be made in ways that yield true efficiencies, while preserving access and quality. This will require fundamental changes, the kinds that colleges and universities have resisted. In some states—like Arizona, California, and Nevada—even far-reaching changes cannot possibly yield savings sufficient to offset increases in demand. Substantial amounts of new resources will be required.

4. *Change strategies for financing higher education.* In reality, there have been changes to financing policy occurring for the past decade as students have been asked to shoulder an increasing share of the cost of their educations. This phenomenon has not been universal throughout the West; until very recently, several states—Hawaii, California (especially the community colleges), and New Mexico—have managed to adhere to their policies of low tuition. Most other states have, year by year, effectively backed into a change of policy without explicitly deciding to do so. They have allowed (in some cases, encouraged) tuitions to rise as a way of plugging the gap left when state appropriations could not keep pace with expanding resource requirements. In 2011, both California and Hawaii succumbed to the fiscal realities and substantially increased tuition levels. More increases are clearly likely in the future. In this regard, western states are becoming more like the rest of the country. However, they are doing so without attention to the broader array of policy tools and actions necessary to ensure that the goals of access, affordability, and quality get equal billing with that of adequate funding for institutions.

THE POLICY FUTURE IN THE WESTERN STATES

The collision of economic realities and demographic change will create a need to reexamine higher education financing policy in most of the western states. In the high-growth states, policy will have to change in ways designed to generate the revenues needed to expand capacity and accommodate growth. In the states faced with decreasing numbers of college-age citizens, policy will have to change to promote attention to a broader set of statewide goals (such as economic development) and prevent a pernicious degradation of institutions that leave them without the resources necessary to effectively serve any mission, old or new. All states will be faced with the need to redress problems of deferred maintenance on facilities built to accommodate the baby-boom generation and now in need of serious renewal and renovation in order to serve the sons and daughters of that generation.

This reexamination must inevitably start with the choices illustrated in figure 5.4. This diagram indicates that the states' choices affecting the financing of higher education are comprised of four decisions that in theory are closely interrelated but in practice seldom are. These four decisions are:

1. *The share of the state budget devoted to higher education.*

Higher education's share of the budget has been declining steadily in most states for at least a decade. This does not necessarily mean that higher education has been receiving less money (although this was the case in several instances during the economic downturn that began in 2000 and again in

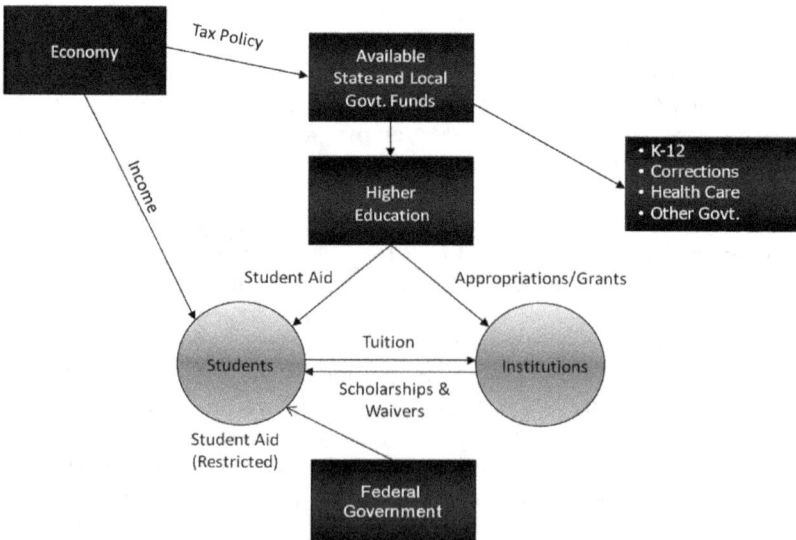

Figure 5.4 The decision space for state funding of higher education.

2008). Rather, it indicates that there are competitors for state funds that have been given higher priority by state legislatures in recent years. Chief among these are Medicaid and K-12 education. Certainly, funding for higher education could be increased if it received a higher priority vis-à-vis programs that represent competing claims on the public purse.

Data indicate that a change in this condition is unlikely in the near term. Analyses performed for NCHEMS by the Rockefeller Institute of Government at the State University of New York indicate that in only Utah, Nevada, Delaware, Texas, Arizona, Georgia, and Idaho do state demographics create circumstances in which the need for higher education services will increase faster than the need for other state services. The data in figure 5.5 indicate the relative extent of competition from other state programs.

In these seven states, despite the fact that higher education has a legitimate claim on an increasing share of state funds, increased revenues will not necessarily be realized; the pressure to increase tuition and become more efficient will likely continue unabated. In all other states higher education will have to play defense, fending off claims for needed resources from other state programs. These facts about demand for state resources from other programs coupled with a widespread reluctance to increase state revenues through tax increases suggest that higher education should not count on state government having substantial additional resources to devote to higher education. It is likely that the general level of funding being provided for higher education in most states is the level that will obtain in the future. Strategies more complicated than "more state money for all higher education claimants" will have to be employed if new resources are to be acquired.

2. *The levels of support to be provided by students.*

While state-level decisions about overall levels of resources made available to higher education are unlikely to lead to substantial additional funding from the state treasury, this does not mean that no additional resources will be available to institutions of higher education in WICHE states. As noted earlier, the historical state policies of low tuition as the guarantor of financial accessibility have begun to erode. This erosion is accelerating, although this condition is more a consequence of expedient responses to state funding constraints than well-considered policymaking. In attempts to sustain institutional funding in the face of declining state support, several states have allowed (or encouraged) large tuition increases. As a consequence, many states are backing into a policy that has students paying a larger share of overall institutional funding without accompanying attention to issues of affordability.

Such approaches to tuition policymaking can result, over time, in tuition schedules for public institutions that are inconsistent with broader state priorities (such as affordable access to higher education). It is true that tuition will likely have to increase, but considered policymaking would result in differential tuition levels at different types of institutions—with the differentials determined by such factors as:

- Family income distributions of students enrolled in different types of institutions.
- Student aid resources available to students in different types of institutions.
- The numbers of students enrolled in different types of institutions, especially the numbers of low-income students.

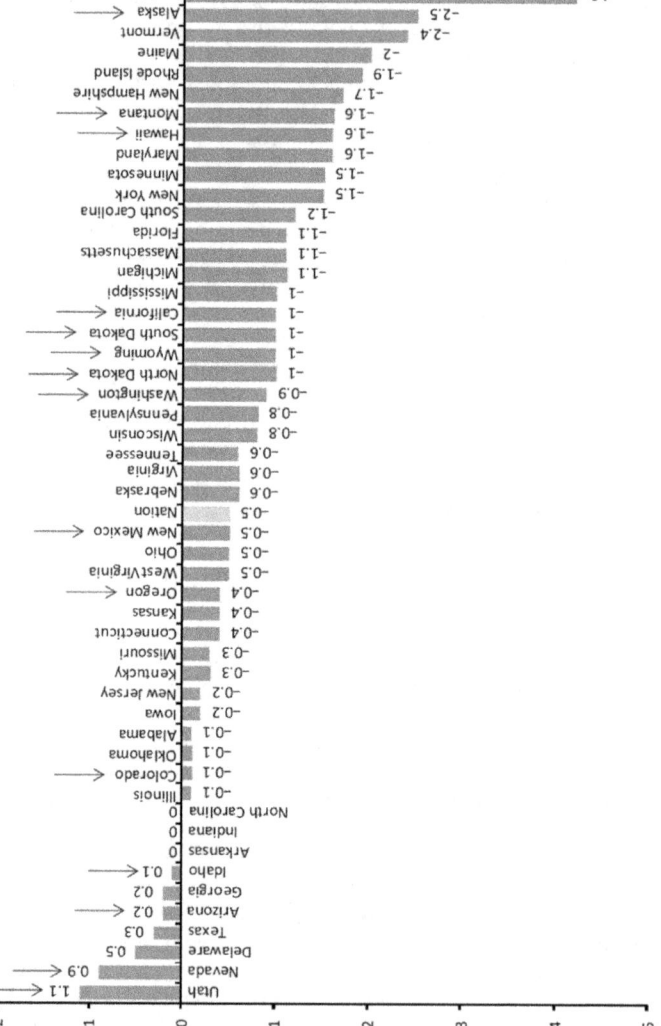

Figure 5.5 Competition for state resources based on projections of service loads.
Source: NCHEMS; Don Boyd (Rockefeller Institute of Government), 2009.

This more sophisticated approach to tuition policies that simultaneously reflects the needs and capabilities of states, students, and institutions will necessarily become an increasingly important component of state higher education finance policy. Heightened attention to this piece of the financing equation will create challenges for many states in the West. It will mean attention to policies that in many cases have been delegated to institutions and their boards creating the need for coordinated policymaking between institutional governing boards and state policymakers. This will require practices quite different from those that have historically been employed. Equally important, it will generate the need for certain kinds of information that has not been a primary ingredient in state-level decision making, for example, the numbers of students from different economic backgrounds enrolled in the different institutions in the state, measures of affordability based on these data, and the resources that institutions are using to make college affordable. In short, state decision makers will have to become as sophisticated about understanding students' ability to pay as they have been about understanding the financial needs of institutions and the capacity of the state to address those needs.

3. *The distribution of state funds between allocations to institutions and allocations to student financial aid.*

When a state decides the share (or amount) of its budget that is to be directed toward higher education, its decision making regarding the financing of higher education is not complete. Two additional sets of decisions remain. The first is the distribution of the total allocated funds between support for institutions on the one hand and support for students (i.e., student financial aid) on the other. In most western states, this decision has historically tilted heavily toward the institutions. As shown in figure 5.6, several of the WICHE states have no financial aid programs, and only six—California, Colorado, Nevada, New Mexico, Oregon, and Washington—devote more than 5 percent of their state appropriations for higher education to student aid programs.

This is consistent with the approach embraced in most western states of addressing the affordability of higher education by keeping tuition low. However, this approach is falling victim to philosophies (and/or fiscal realities) that result in tuition charges that are escalating and doing so rapidly in some instances. Figure 5.7 reveals that tuition costs at four-year institutions are relatively low in the WICHE states, but figure 5.8 indicates that tuition fees at two-year colleges are higher than the national average in many western states. If affordability is to be sustained, more of the WICHE states will have to confront the need to provide additional student aid support, while increasing the share of the state higher education appropriation devoted to this purpose. They will also have to confront the necessity of establishing differential tuition policies for different types of institutions.

Treating the policy decisions concerning funding for institutions, funding for student aid, and tuition changes as an integrated package is becoming ever more important. The overall objective will have to provide adequate support to institutions, while ensuring affordability from the perspectives of both the state and students. There is no single right way to accomplish this objective; states have accomplished these purposes in different ways. However, unless WICHE states reverse trends and fund institutions in ways that decrease dependence on

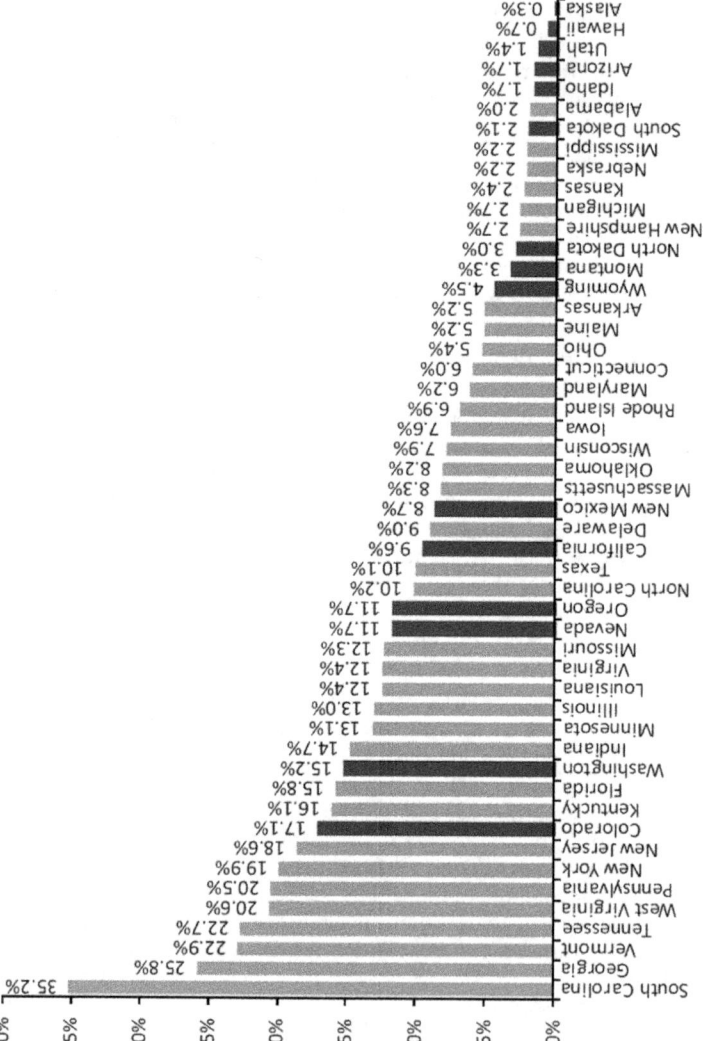

Figure 5.6 Total state grant expenditures as a percentage of appropriation of tax funds for higher education operating expenses by state, 2009–2010.

Source: National Association of State Student Aid and Grant Programs (NASSGAP) Annual Survey, 2009–10.

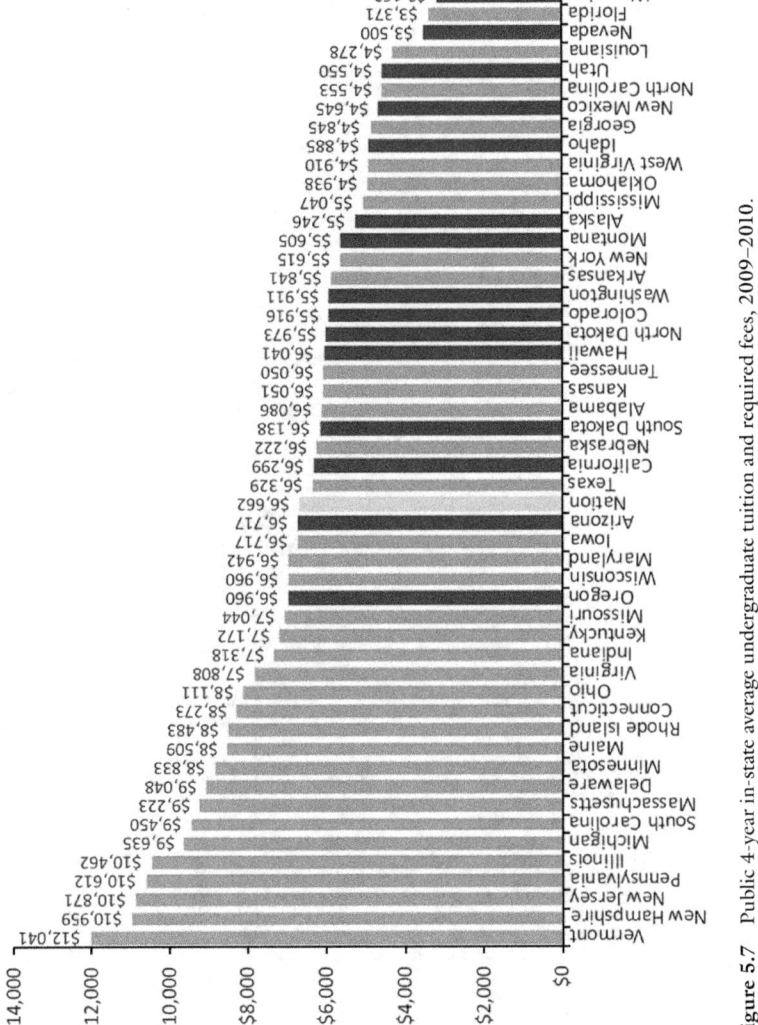

Figure 5.7 Public 4-year in-state average undergraduate tuition and required fees, 2009–2010.

Source: NCES, IPEDS 2009–10 Institutional Characteristics File; ic2009_ay Final Release Data File. NCES, IPEDS 2009-10 Instructional Activity File; efia2010 Final Release Data File.

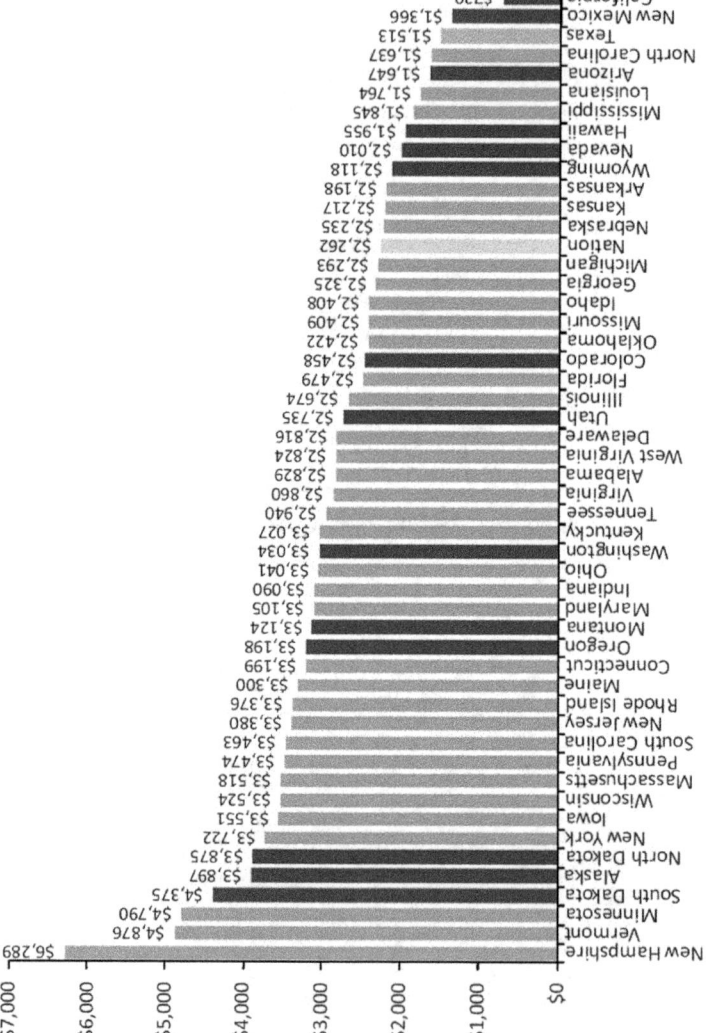

Figure 5.8 Public 2-year in-state average undergraduate tuition and required fees, 2009–2010.

Note: State figures are weighted averages based on reported institution-level charges and undergraduate FTE enrollment.

Source: NCES, IPEDS 2009–10 Institutional Characteristics File; ic2009_ay Final Release Data File. NCES, IPEDS 2009–10 Instructional Activity File; efia2010 Final Release Data File.

tuition revenues, their approaches to financing policy will have to become more inclusive of all components of the financing framework. Tuition and financial aid policy will have to be considered in conjunction with institutional funding decisions in ways that have not been the norm in the western states.

4. *The methods employed to distribute resources.*

State decisions about financing higher education extend beyond how much is to be distributed to institutions and student aid to consideration of how the pools of resources are divided among the intended recipients. Figure 5.9 summarizes the array of choices.

This simple diagram draws attention to the fact that how resources are distributed is (or should be) determined by state priorities. One key purpose is sustaining public institutions as viable and productive enterprises—maintaining institutional capacity. In addition, however, states have an interest in having these public institutions serve purposes of particular importance to the state and its citizens, such as:

- Contributing to the improvement of K-12 education.
- Enhancing the state's human capital—increasing the skills, knowledge, and education attainment of the state's adult population.
- Contributing to the economic development of the state.

The ground rules that govern the ways in which resources are distributed can create incentives or disincentives for students and institutions to align their actions with these priorities. Requiring students to take a rigorous curriculum creates incentives for high school reform and can improve the preparation of secondary school graduates. Ensuring availability of need-based aid can remove barriers to college participation and ultimately increase the number of college graduates. The list of examples could be extended considerably. The purpose here, however, is not to illustrate all the possibilities but to make the point that financing policy extends to allocation methodology and intention as well as allocation amounts.

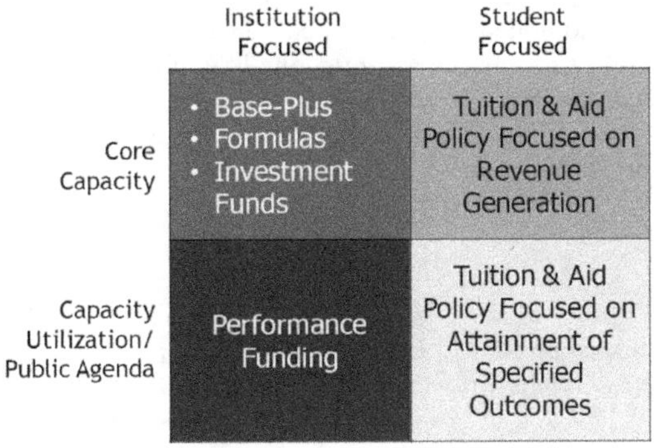

	Institution Focused	Student Focused
Core Capacity	• Base-Plus • Formulas • Investment Funds	Tuition & Aid Policy Focused on Revenue Generation
Capacity Utilization/ Public Agenda	Performance Funding	Tuition & Aid Policy Focused on Attainment of Specified Outcomes

Figure 5.9 Finance policy—the options.

Source: Adapted from figures in "Financing in Sync: Aligning Fiscal Policy with State Objectives," in "Policies in Sync: Appropriations, Tuition, and Financial Aid for Higher Education," Western Interstate Commission for Higher Education, 2003.

Summary

In this brief chapter, an effort has been made to make the case that higher education financing policy in most western states will have to change to meet a new set of demographic and economic realities. Specifically, policymaking will have to expand beyond determining the amount of state funds to be provided to colleges and universities and the methods of equitable distribution to include:

- Determining shares to be borne by students at different types of institutions and appropriate levels of tuition and fees at different types of institutions.
- Allocations of funds for student financial aid and the criteria for distribution.
- Ways in which state funds can be allocated to enhance the likelihood that critical state priorities will be pursued and achieved.

Most states are poorly equipped to make policy effectively in this broader context. This has not been their experience. Further, the supporting infrastructure is often not in place. This is particularly true of an infrastructure needed to provide decision information about the economic barriers faced by students at different institutions within a state.

In this more complex environment, states have little choice but to gain the necessary expertise in financial policymaking. The future of the states and their citizens may well depend in large part on how well policymakers learn and apply these lessons.

Note

*The student-related data for this chapter were taken from the Integrated Postsecondary Education Data System (IPEDS); the finance data from State Higher Education Finance, a publication of the State Higher Education Executive Officers (SHEEO) with data compiled from an annual SHEEO survey; the data about competition for state funds from work commissioned by the National Center for Higher Education Management Systems (NCHEMS) and conducted by Donald Boyd; and the state student aid data from the annual survey of the National Association of State Student Grant and Aid Programs (NASSGAP).

References

Boyd, D. *Are Western States' Tax Structures Adequate?* Boulder, CO: Western Interstate Commission for Higher Education, 2003.

Jones, D. "State Shortfalls Projected to Continue Despite Economic Gains." In P. Callan (ed.), *Policy Alert*. San Jose, CA: National Center for Public Policy and Higher Education, February, 2006.

Western Interstate Commission for Higher Education (WICHE). *Knocking at the College Door: Projections of High School Graduates by State, Income, and Race/Ethnicity, 1988–2018*. Boulder, CO: Western Interstate Commission for Higher Education, 2003.

6

Public Financing of Higher Education in the Western States

Changing Patterns in State Appropriations and Tuition Revenues

*Charles S. Lenth, Kathleen J. Zaback,
Andrew M. Carlson, and Allison C. Bell**

Introduction

Across the nation demands are growing for a variety of publicly funded services, while nearly all states are facing tightening budgetary constraints. Pervasive, long-term structural imbalances between the costs of these services and the resources available to support current service levels are exacerbated when variable economic conditions create high unemployment and erode tax revenues, while temporarily increasing demand for many public services.

More directly than many components of state budgets, public funding for higher education is affected by both longer-term structural imbalances and by the severity of recession-related disruptions in the balance between current revenues and service demands. Some observers may see this as an unavoidable, even necessary transition that will force higher education to replace public funding with other sources and to find fundamentally different and more efficient modes of education delivery. We do not agree, at least not without a much more careful analysis of the shifting patterns of financing higher education and of the consequences of different patterns of public support. We believe that the squeeze on public funding for higher education from many causes and in nearly all states needs close examination. Further, we believe that the resulting cost-shifting to students and parents poses a severe risk of potential underinvestment in higher education by individuals, particularly those most affected and underserved by higher education, and society as a whole.

To assist closer examination of these issues in the West, this chapter provides a picture of changing patterns in core funding for higher education—a picture built around graphs intended to inform understanding of these changes and prompt additional analysis of both incremental effects and longer-term consequences. Are western states jeopardizing the broad human capital development needed by job seekers and employers alike to recover from currently high rates of unemployment and low rates of business investment? Are western states underinvesting in higher education research, infrastructure, and the generation of new knowledge? Will current levels of public investment limit the long-term capabilities of the West, its populations, and its economy to compete and thrive in an increasingly global environment? Can enrollments in higher education continue to grow when the costs of higher education for students and families continue to climb as fast as or faster than other sectors of the economy? These are difficult and debatable questions—questions needing careful attention.

The West (defined here as the 15 US states that are members of the Western Interstate Commission for Higher Education, or WICHE) is a particularly interesting and important region in which to examine how patterns in financial support for higher education are changing over time. Our analysis uses the financial indicators developed by the State Higher Education Executive Officers (SHEEO) association to examine core sources of support for higher education over a 32-year period, from 1980 to 2012. We use a long and somewhat unusual time period to make use of all the available time-series data in the State Higher Education Finance (SHEF) data base.

We begin with a description of SHEF, including the data, sources, and analytic methods on which this relatively new set of higher education financing indicators is based. We then use these indicators to look at the western states as a region in comparison to the United States as a whole, followed by a closer look at the West and at western states individually. We close with some observations about the challenges facing higher education funding and with a hope that this analysis will contribute to broader public understanding of the issues raised and the consequences of decisions being made with respect to financial support for higher education in the nation and the western states in particular.

Origins and Development of the SHEF Report

Higher education financing is complex. Various forms of governmental support along with revenue from a variety of other sources are combined and used by institutions to provide a mix of educational and ancillary services. Both the revenue streams and the educational services vary across states and institutions. At public colleges and universities, funding (often called "subsidies") from state and local governments provides financial support for broadening access to higher education and maintaining the breadth and quality of education programs. Appropriations to institutions are supplemented by revenue from tuition and fees paid by students and families to support what are broadly defined as "Education and General" (E&G) expenditures, which is the primary source of revenue supporting instructional costs and related academic services in public institutions. While some federal programs may offset part of the tuition costs for students and encourage higher enrollment, federal funding support for institutional E&G expenditures is primarily indirect.

States shape and adapt this basic approach to financing higher education in light of their particular needs, policy preferences, budgetary constraints, and other factors. Western states share some characteristics, such as historical reliance on public institutions, to provide broad access and comparatively low or moderate tuition levels (or as they are called in some western states, education "fees"). But western states also vary substantially in their higher education structures and governance, in their mix of public and private institutions, and in their reliance on tuition revenue as a source of funding. Such complexity and variation make it difficult to analyze and compare higher education funding across states, even within a single region such as the West. Too often, however, this complexity becomes an excuse for not analyzing underlying patterns and trends and not dealing with the resulting consequences.

Reliable measures or "indicators" are needed to determine the extent of public funding for core educational services, how funding levels compare across states on a per student basis, the balance between public funding and student charges, and how these and other variables in financing higher education are changing over time. To help meet this need for core financial indicators and reliable comparisons, SHEEO produces an annual report, *State Higher Education Finance (SHEF)*, that helps states and others examine trends in core support for higher education in their own states, over time and in comparison to other states. The SHEF report and the databases and analytic framework underlying it provide the core financial indicators to assist in addressing questions such as:

- What are the components of state and local government funding available to public institutions, private institutions, student financial aid, research and specialized programs, and other higher education programs or services in each state?
- How much revenue is generated through tuition and fees at public institutions to help support education programs, net of financial aid and other restricted purposes?
- What "student load" (or total credit-hour enrollment) is being served by the education programs and services using the revenues available to public institutions?
- How do these core higher education financial and service indicators change over time, across states, and in relation to external factors such as inflation rates and economic recessions?

Each year since 2004, SHEEO has made available on its website (www.sheeo.org) an annual update of the SHEF report, based on a survey of SHEEO members, to collect information on all sources of public support for higher education in each state. For years prior to the annual SHEEO finance survey, SHEF uses data adapted from an earlier survey established by Kent Halstead, who created a report on state finance for higher education and a database that extends from the early 1970s to the late 1990s.

Using these sources SHEF provides foundational "reference points" for state higher education financing that are useful to decision makers, understandable to nonexpert audiences, as comparable as possible across different contexts, and demonstrative of longer-term trends as well as shorter-term changes in funding for higher education.

Since 2010 SHEF also has functioned in conjunction with the *Grapevine* survey of state appropriations to higher education, established in 1962 by M. M. Chambers and maintained by his successors, Edward Hines and then James Palmer, at Illinois State University. Beginning in 2010 the collection of *Grapevine* state appropriations data and SHEF core financial indicator data was combined into a single annual survey instrument and collection cycle. While the state appropriations data is collected by SHEEO, the analysis and reporting of the data continue to be undertaken by the Center for the Study of Education Policy at Illinois State University, which issues a separate report in January of each year. The SHEF report, published annually by SHEEO in February/March, reports the revenues available and other financing indicators through the most recently completed fiscal year. Together, the annual SHEF report containing higher education revenue data for the most recently completed fiscal year and the *Grapevine* report containing appropriations data for the current fiscal year provide a set of reasonably current and comprehensive financial indicators for higher education in each state and the nation as a whole.

The core SHEF financial indicators include the following:

- *SHEF State and Local Support* consists of all state tax appropriations and local tax support plus additional nontax funds, including revenue from lottery receipts, royalty revenue, and state-funded endowments. It also includes funds appropriated to other state agencies that support costs attributable to higher education: for example, staff and faculty retirement benefits provided through centralized state or system-wide agencies.
- *SHEF Educational Appropriations* are the subset of total State and Local Support that supports the operating expenses of public higher education. This category excludes funding identified for support of research and agriculture extension, for high-cost medical education programs, and for independent (private, nonprofit) colleges and universities in the state, including state-funded financial aid to their students. Because these components of higher education funding are earmarked for these purposes, they are excluded in calculating Educational Appropriations (and in the FTE calculations, as defined below).
- *SHEF Net Tuition Revenue* is the share of total instruction-supporting revenue at public institutions collected from students and their families,

including some proportion that may have come through federal financial aid grants to students to pay their tuition charges. Net Tuition Revenue is calculated from estimated "gross" tuition revenue, less any amounts for state and institutional financial aid, tuition waivers, or discounts. This indicator reflects tuition- and fee-derived revenue available to public higher education institutions for support of education and general expenditures, although the decisions about how this revenue is used are ultimately shaped by the receiving institution.[1] It is important to note that SHEF Net Tuition Revenue is not the same as the tuition rate charged or the net cost paid by individual students even when calculated on a per student basis. In addition to being a calculated amount, Net Tuition Revenue includes revenue derived from students who pay different rates (resident/nonresident, undergraduate/graduate programs, etc.).

- *SHEF Total Educational Revenue* is the sum of Educational Appropriations and Net Tuition Revenue (as defined above) and is used as the primary indicator of the total support available to public institutions to support general instruction and related expenditures (E&G). This is by far the largest of the standard expenditure categories at most public regional or state universities and community colleges. At research universities, where financing is required for many activities in addition to instruction, this will be a smaller proportion of total institutional revenue. Only a small proportion of public institutions have access to significant revenue from federal research funding, gifts, endowments, or other sources, and generally very little of this is used to support instructional costs.
- *Full-Time-Equivalent Enrollment (FTE)* is an indicator of total enrollment or enrollment "load" calculated on the basis of total student credit hours (excluding noncredit courses) divided by the number of credits typically taken by students attending full-time for a full academic year. This simplified, commonly used metric facilitates comparison of enrollment levels across states and over time, and allows analysis and comparison of categories of financial support across states and institutions on a uniform, per student (FTE) basis.

In order to improve comparability across these core financial indicators, the SHEF report employs three adjustments: (1) a Cost of Living Adjustment (COLA) to account for cost of living differences across states; (2) an Enrollment Mix Index (EMI) to adjust for differences in the mix of enrollments across types of institutions within states; and (3) the Higher Education Cost Adjustment (HECA) to adjust for inflation over time. Descriptions of these data adjustment protocols are provided in the full SHEF report and on the SHEEO website at www.sheeo.org.

In the following sections, we look first at trends and growth rates in overall higher education enrollment in the nation and then in the western states as a region and western states individually. Following this, we use the basic

SHEF indicators for the nation, the region, and each western state in order to address the following questions:

- How has total State and Local Support (the public "subsidy") for higher education changed in relation to enrollment in the 32-year period, 1980–2012?
- To what extent has Net Tuition Revenue (the "student share") increased as a proportion of Total Educational Revenue, particularly in comparison to state and local government funding?
- Has the combination of government support and tuition revenue kept pace with growth in enrollment?
- Have funding trends been predictable over time or disrupted by external factors such as economic recessions?

Thirty Years of Enrollment Growth: Context and Comparisons

In the 30 years between 1980 and 2010, full-time-equivalent enrollment in American public higher education increased by 66 percent. This increase in overall enrollment substantially exceeded the growth in total US population, which increased 36 percent during the same period. In simple comparative terms, enrollment grew 1.8 times more rapidly than population. In the western states, between 1980 and 2010, FTE enrollment in public higher education increased by 72 percent, while total population in these states increased by 65 percent.

Figure 6.1 shows the growth in public institution FTE enrollment and population by state for the period 1980–2010. As is apparent, both the rate of increase in enrollment and the relationship to population growth vary significantly across the region. FTE enrollment increases vary from a low of 31 percent in Hawaii to a high of 255 percent in Nevada, and the ratio of population growth to enrollment growth varies substantially across the states. Any patterns or trends appear to be more state-specific than region-wide.

The levels of higher education participation and educational attainment also vary across western states. Table 6.1 provides two indicators of attainment and participation: the proportion of adults (individuals age 25 or older) with at least an associate's degree; and the proportion of adults (individuals age 18 or older) currently enrolled in college at any level.

The West as a region has only a slightly higher attainment rate than the nation as a whole—37.4 percent compared to 35.8 percent. Attainment rates vary from a high of 44.2 percent in Colorado to a low of 28.8 percent in Nevada. Similarly, the percentage of adults over age 18 in the WICHE region enrolled in college or graduate school is slightly higher than the national average. Three states—Utah, California, and North Dakota—are above the regional average, with more than 13 percent of Utah's adults enrolled in some type of higher education in 2010. Nevada has the lowest

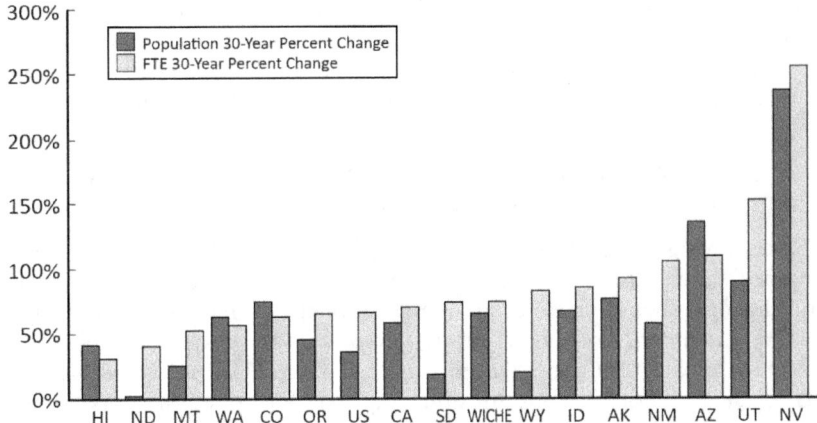

Figure 6.1 Percent change FTE enrollment growth and population, 1980–2010.
Source: SHEEO SHEF, U.S. Census Bureau.

Table 6.1 Attainment and participation rates 2010 western states, western region, and nation

State	Attainment Rate, Associate's Degree and Higher, Adults 25+ (%)	College or Graduate School Enrollment Rate, Adults Age 18+ (%)
Alaska	36.10	9.40
Arizona	34.00	9.90
California	37.70	11.20
Colorado	44.20	10.00
Hawaii	38.70	9.60
Idaho	32.70	9.90
Montana	36.70	9.10
Nevada	28.80	8.00
New Mexico	32.00	10.10
North Dakota	39.30	11.10
Oregon	36.60	9.50
South Dakota	36.30	9.10
Utah	38.30	13.20
Washington	40.50	9.00
Wyoming	34.80	8.90
WICHE States	37.43	10.48
United States	35.80	9.90

Source: US Census Bureau, 2010 American Community Survey.

rate with only 8 percent of adults over the age of 18 enrolled in college or graduate school.

While these intraregional state differences are considerable, it is worth noting that only 5 of 15 Western states are below the national average in adult degree attainment, but 10 of the 15 are at or below the national average in terms of current college enrollment rates. While many factors may contribute to this, differences in the indicators of enrollment and participation should prompt questions about whether current policies and levels of funding will meet the education and training needs of states with rapidly changing economies and comparatively high rates of population growth.

Charting Public Support and Tuition Revenue across States and Over Time

Accompanying the annual SHEF report, SHEEO provides a set of charts (dubbed "wave charts" because of the very visible patterns) to illustrate enrollment trends over time, Total Educational Revenue per student, and relative dependence on Net Tuition Revenue. Wave charts that look at a single state over time are adjusted only using the HECA cost adjustment (to adjust indicators to constant dollar values), but no adjustments for the enrollment mix or cost of living differences are made. (This reduces the statistical comparability of individual state wave charts.) While the line graph showing FTE enrollment at public institutions uses a different scale than Total Educational Revenue, the resulting charts visually illustrate relationships between enrollment and funding levels.

The US wave chart, figure 6.2, includes data for all 50 states (Puerto Rico and the District of Columbia are not included in these charts). As shown, Educational Appropriations per FTE decreased from $7,603 in 1980 to $5,906 in 2012, a decline of 22 percent in constant dollar value, with an even steeper drop of 32 percent from the historical high point in 2001. This decrease in per student state and local support takes into account substantial growth in enrollment, with the amounts made available divided across total enrollment of approximately seven million FTE in 1980 compared to more than 11 million FTE in 2012, a change of 69 percent. Net Tuition Revenue, in contrast, increased from $2,009 per FTE student in 1980 to $5,189 in 2012, far more than doubling (158 percent increase) in constant dollar terms. With increased revenue from tuition, Educational Revenue per FTE increased from $9,612 to $11,095 nationally, a 15 percent increase in constant dollar terms over the 32-year period. Perhaps most significant, the proportion of Educational Appropriations derived from student tuition increased from 21 percent of the total in 1980 to 47 percent in 2012.

The "waves" in these figures are caused by a combination of shorter-term factors. Public institution FTE enrollments increased substantially following the national economic recessions in the 1980s, 1990s, and early 2000s and most recently following the 2008 recession, when more students turned to higher education in the face of tight labor markets and higher unemployment rates. This enrollment effect works in conjunction with tighter government budgets to produce a potentially damaging countercyclical funding pattern: Reduced state tax revenues combined with higher enrollments magnify reductions in Educational Revenue per FTE student, even with higher tuition revenues. Several times during the 32-year period Educational Revenues recovered to prerecessional levels within three to four

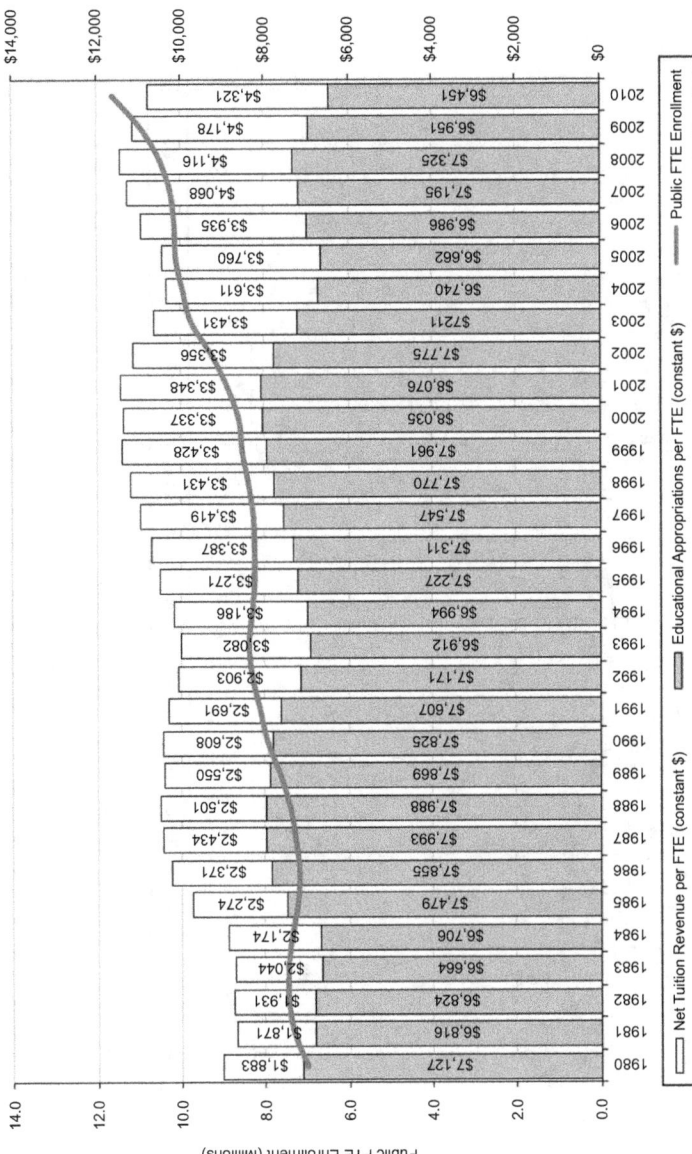

Figure 6.2 Public FTE enrollment, educational appropriations and total educational revenue per FTE, United States—fiscal 1980–2010.

Note: Constant 2010 dollars adjusted by SHEEO Higher Education Cost Adjustment. Educational Appropriations include ARRA funds (HECA).

Source: SHEEO.

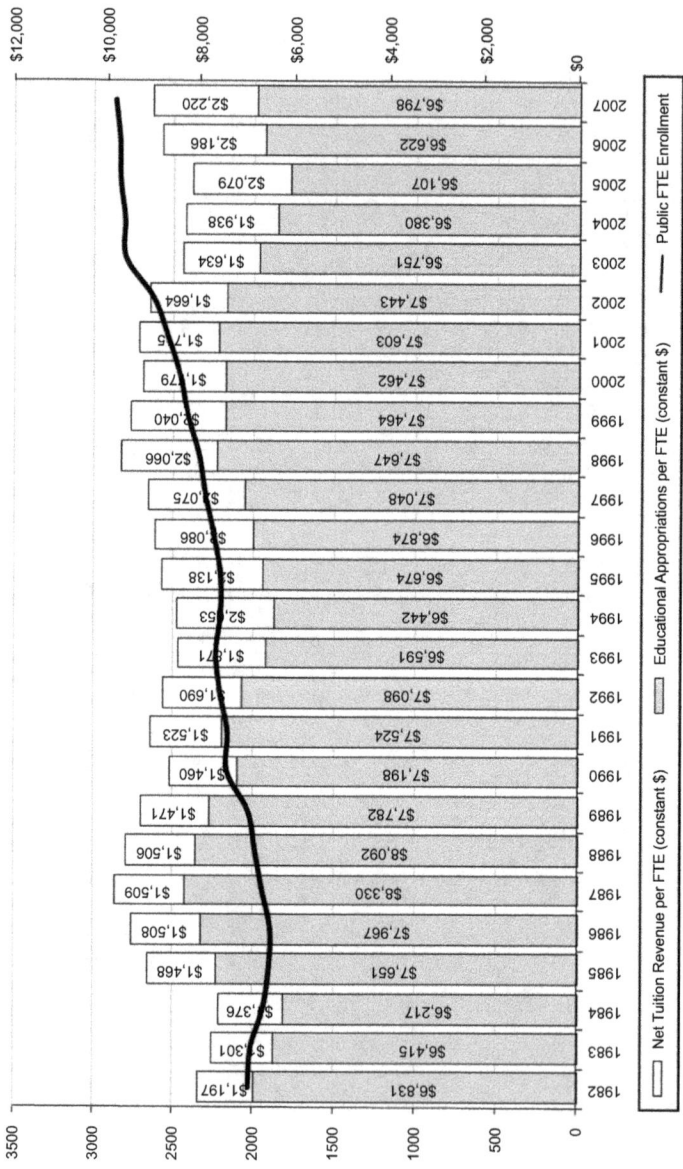

Figure 6.3 Public FTE enrollment, educational appropriations, and total educational revenue per FTE, all WICHE States—fiscal 1982–2007.

Note: Constant 2007 dollars adjusted by SHEEO Higher Education Cost Adjustment (HECA), EMI, and CCLA.

Source: SHEEOSHEF.

years, although clearly this recovery has not yet occurred following the Great Recession of 2008.

The western region (figure 6.3) reveals trends similar to the nation as a whole, with, however, a somewhat different balance between public appropriations and reliance on tuition revenue. Educational Appropriations per FTE were 8 percent higher in the West than in the nation as a whole in 1980, but were essentially the same in 2012. The decrease from $8,280 in 1980 to $5,925 in 2012 reflects higher enrollment growth in the West, as well as lower constant dollar Educational Appropriations. Consistently since 1980 the West has shown comparatively low reliance on tuition revenue as a component of Total Educational Revenue, although the proportion has increased from 18 percent of the total in 1980 in 38 percent in 2012. The combination of lower Educational Appropriations and comparatively lower Net Tuition Revenue per FTE resulted in Educational Revenues per FTE that by 2012 that are significantly (14%) below those of the nation as a whole. One factor contributing to this is the sheer size of California within the region-wide statistics; with California's large community college system and that sector's relatively low tuition rates heavily influencing the region's statistics.

STATE WAVE CHARTS

Within these national and regional patterns, interstate differences are significant. States in the West vary considerably in terms of their public funding for higher education and how the sources and patterns of support are changing. The state-level wave charts presented and discussed below visually display these differences. To simplify yet adequately illustrate the large differences across the West, the 15 states are discussed in three groupings:

1. States where in 2012 Total Educational Appropriations for higher education are now less than $5,000 per FTE—in several states considerably less;
2. States in which Total Educational Appropriations are $5,000–$10,000 per FTE; and
3. States where because of geographic, demographic, economic and other factors Total Educational Appropriations are unusually high.

For each group a short discussion follows the individual state wave charts to point out the similarities and stimulate further discussion of the differences among states within each of these groupings.

In 2012, the six states in the figures below (Arizona, Colorado, Montana, Oregon, South Dakota, and Washington) all provided Educational Appropriations per FTE of less than $5,000. Five of the six states have funded public higher education consistently below the national average since 1980 and have continued to fall increasingly below the national average since the 2008 recession. In terms of Tuition Revenue per FTE, in 1980 four of the six states relied more heavily on tuition than the national average, although for many states the difference was small; in 2012 five of the six were above the national average in the amount and proportion of tuition-generated revenue and the difference had widened. Only Washington was below the national average, with tuition making up 42 percent of Total Education Revenue, compared to 47 percent nationally. Washington's Total Educational Revenue was also 25 percent below the national average in 2012.

When looking at education funding it is important to keep in mind the wide variations in system configurations and institutional types across the West and in enrollment trends (figures displayed in alphabetical order):

- Arizona has three large public universities under the board of regents and numerous community colleges throughout the state, including two large community college systems: Maricopa Community Colleges with ten institutions and numerous centers in the Phoenix area and Pima Community College with six campuses and numerous centers in the Tucson area. Enrollment in Arizona's public institutions has increased steadily, up 109 percent between 1980 and 2010 and it continues to grow, while the state's population increased by 135 percent in this period. Educational Appropriations per student have been close to the national average over the years (figure 6.5), although not quite achieving the "peaks" the nation did in the late 1980s and late 1990s because of Arizona's comparatively rapid enrollment growth. The higher education attainment level in Arizona is slightly below the national average—34 percent of the population over the age of 25 has an associate's degree or higher—while participation levels in Arizona are right at the national average.
- Colorado has 12 public four-year institutions, a community and technical college system with 13 institutions, and 2 locally controlled public community colleges. FTE enrollment in public institutions has increased 65 percent since 1980, while the state's population has increased 74 percent. State coordination is through the Colorado Department of Higher Education and the Colorado Commission on Higher Education. Colorado relies heavily on tuition revenue, with comparatively low levels of state support (see figure 6.7). In 1980 revenue from tuition was 37 percent of Total Educational Revenue at public institutions, compared to 21 percent of the total for the nation and less than 14 percent for the West as a whole. Since 2003, Net Tuition Revenue has exceeded per student Educational Appropriations from state and local sources, increasing to 71 percent of SHEF Total Educational Revenue at public institutions by 2012. The flagship institution has relatively high proportions of out-of-state students, for whom tuition rates are set at "full cost." Colorado has the lowest level of Education Appropriations per FTE in the West and the third lowest nationally. With 10 percent of the population 18 and older enrolled in postsecondary education, Colorado is at the national average; it's above average in educational attainment, with 44 percent of the adult population over 25 holding an associate's degree or higher, due to the continuing in-migration of relatively well-educated adults.

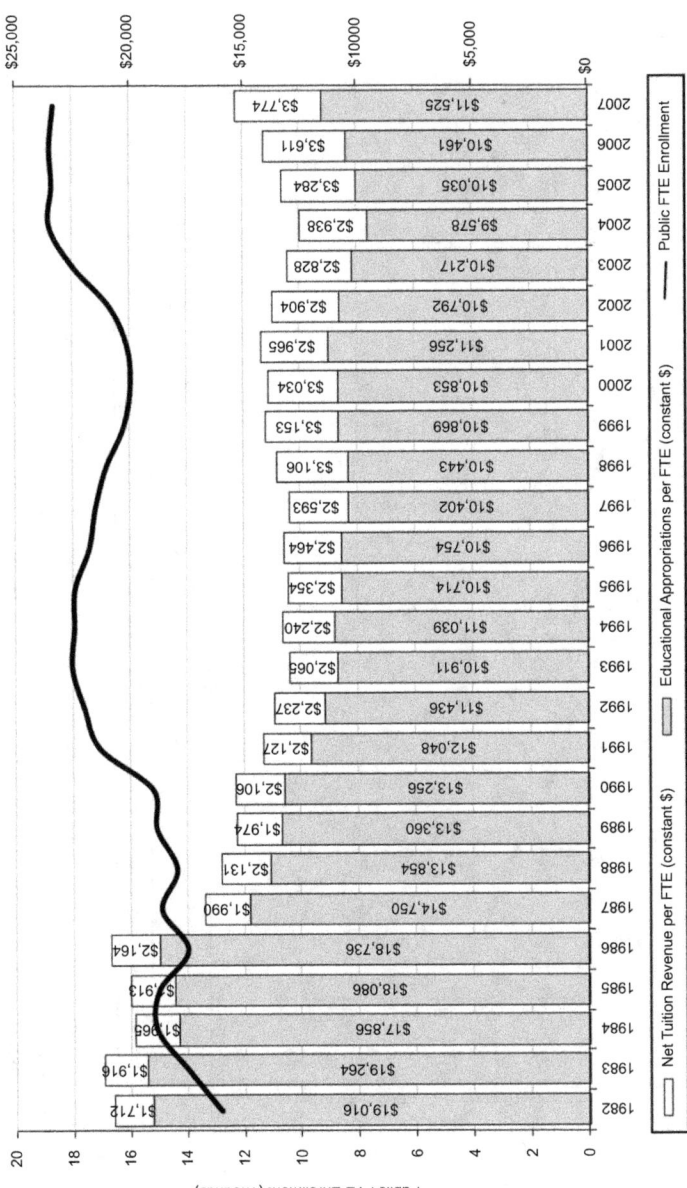

Figure 6.4 Public FTE enrollment, educational appropriations, and total educational revenue per FTE, Alaska—fiscal 1982–2007.

Note: Constant 2007 dollars adjusted by SHEEO Higher Education Cost Adjustment (HECA), EMI, and CCLA.

Source: SHEEOSHEF.

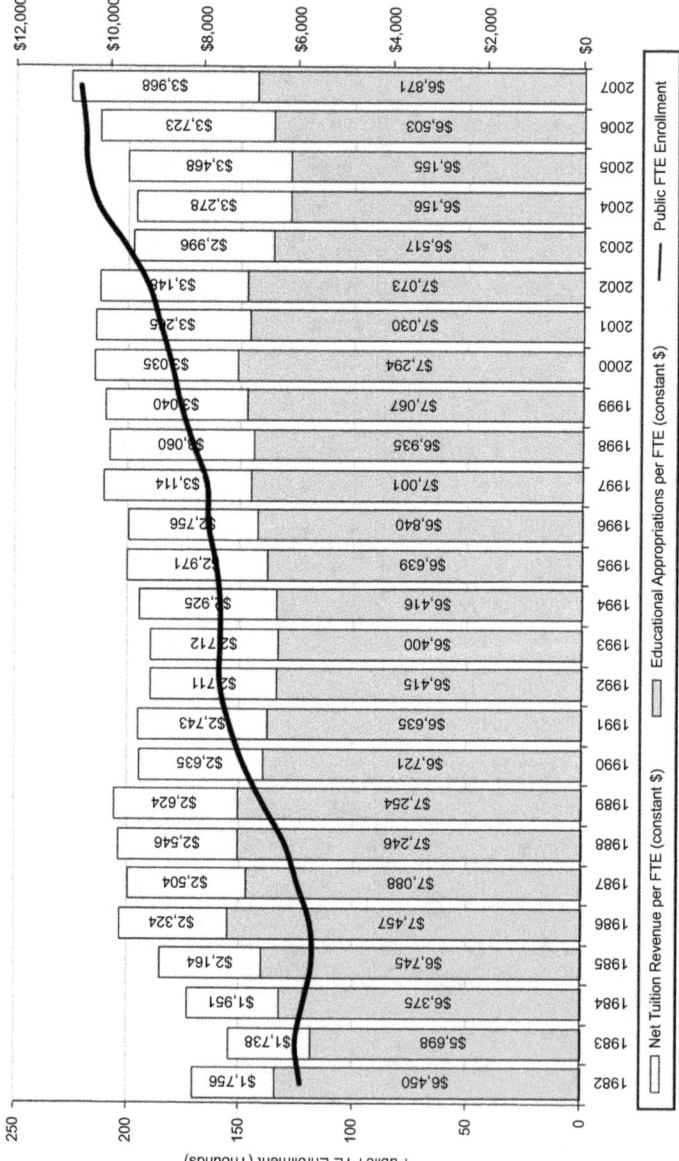

Figure 6.5 Public FTE enrollment, educational appropriations, and total educational revenue per FTE, Arizona—fiscal 1982–2007.

Note: Constant 2007 dollars adjusted by SHEEO Higher Education Cost Adjustment (HECA), EMI, and CCLA.

Source: SHEEOSHEF.

- The Montana University System is composed of four public universities and 12 smaller community colleges. Public institution FTE enrollment increased 53 percent between 1980 and 2010, about double the state's population growth of 26 percent during this period. Montana's wave chart (figure 6.10) is unusual in several respects, with less pronounced countercyclical enrollment waves than the nation as a whole. In inflation-adjusted dollar values, Educational Appropriations per FTE were below the national average and western states average in the early 1980s. While decreasing steadily in subsequent years to about 2003 and since then they have been relatively consistent as Net Tuition Revenue per FTE has risen. Total Educational Revenue per FTE at Montana's public institutions is currently above the regional average, with Tuition Revenue 55 percent of the total. Nine percent of Montana's adult population over 18 is enrolled in postsecondary education, while the proportion of the adult population over 25 with an associate's degree or higher is about 37 percent, both figures slightly below regional averages.
- The Oregon University System is composed of nine public four-year institutions, with 17 locally governed community colleges, coordinated through the Oregon Department of Community Colleges and Workforce Development. Oregon has 35 private institutions as well. The Oregon wave chart (figure 6.14) shows decreasing Educational Appropriations per FTE at public institutions beginning in the late 1980s. From more than $7,000 per FTE student in 1985, Educational Appropriations fell to $5,446 (in constant dollar values) by 2005 and $3,911 in 2012. Net Tuition Revenue per FTE student, in contrast, remained relatively unchanged through the 1980s, approximately doubling over the next 20 years. Also apparent is the sharp increase in FTE enrollment between 2000 and 2003, followed by leveling off and then another spike in 2008 through 2011. Total Educational Revenue per FTE is currently below the national and above the regional averages, with tuition revenue composing more than 50 percent of the total. Educational attainment in Oregon is above the national average but slightly below the regional average: just under 37 percent of adults over 25 have an associate's degree or higher.
- South Dakota, with a small, widely dispersed population of approximately 800,000, has seven four-year institutions and four locally funded and governed technical institutes. The four-year schools are governed and coordinated under the South Dakota Board of Regents. Relatively slow population growth of 18 percent between 1980 and 2010 was far surpassed by an increase in public institution FTE enrollment of 74 percent. The wave chart for South Dakota (figure 6.15) shows a growing reliance on tuition as a component of Total Educational Revenue at public institutions. From 27 percent of the total in 1980, Net Tuition Revenue increased to 63 percent of the total in 2012. Educational Appropriations per FTE fluctuated with economic trends over the 1980s and 1990s and have steadily decreased over the last decade. In most years, Total Educational Revenue per FTE has been slightly above the regional average and is currently above

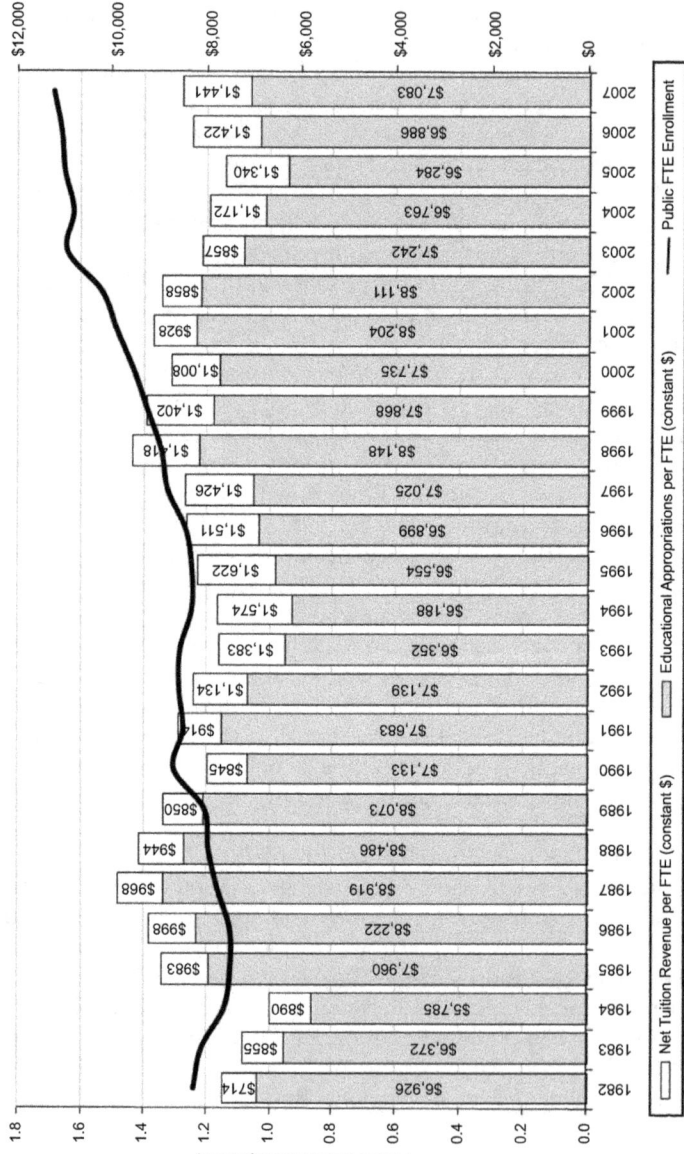

Figure 6.6 Public FTE enrollment, educational appropriations, and total educational revenue per FTE, California—fiscal 1982–2007.

Note: Constant 2007 dollars adjusted by SHEEO Higher Education Cost Adjustment (HECA), EMI, and CCLA.

Source: SHEEOSHEF.

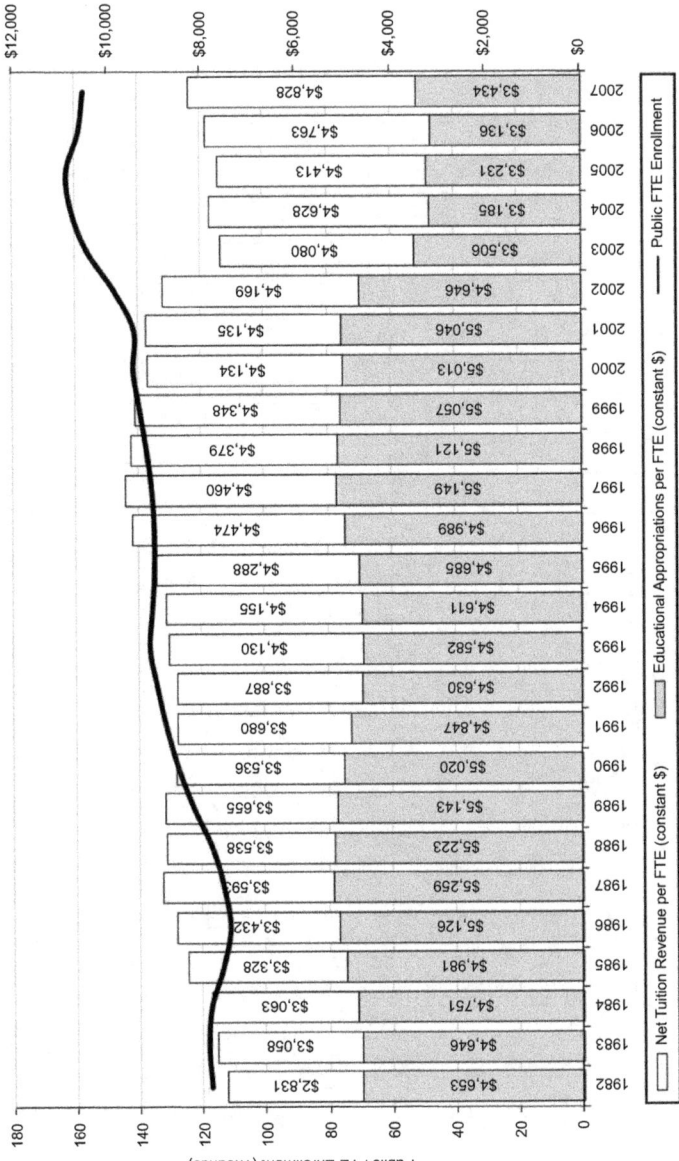

Figure 6.7 Public FTE enrollment, educational appropriations, and total educational revenue per FTE, Colorado—fiscal 1982–2007.

Note: Constant 2007 dollars adjusted by SHEEO Higher Education Cost Adjustment (HECA), EMI, and CCLA.

Source: SHEEOSHEF.

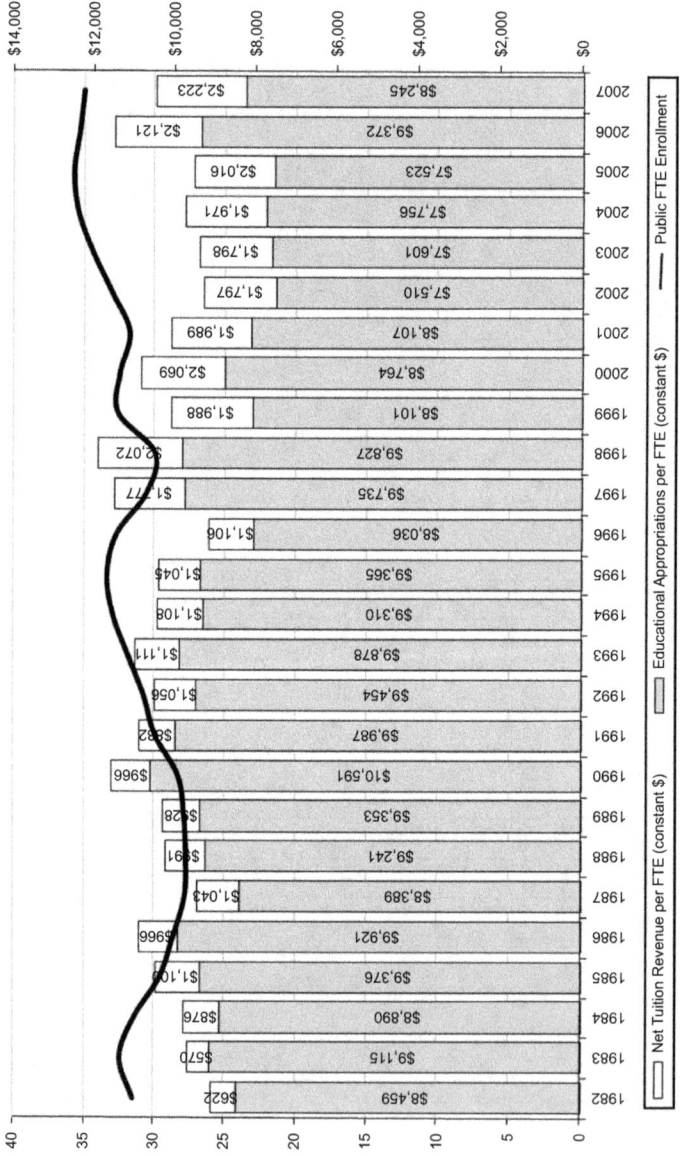

Figure 6.8 Public FTE enrollment, educational appropriations, and total educational revenue per FTE, Hawaii—fiscal 1982–2007.

Note: Constant 2007 dollars adjusted by SHEEO Higher Education Cost Adjustment (HECA), EMI, and CCLA.

Source: SHEEOSHEF.

the national average. Thirty-six percent of South Dakota's adult population (age 25 and over) have an associate's degree or higher, slightly below the regional average. Nine percent of adults were enrolled in some postsecondary education in 2010, below both the regional and national average.

- Washington has nine four-year public institutions and 34 public two-year institutions enrolling more than 250,000 FTE students; enrollments increased nearly 50 percent in the 32-year period. Washington has higher-than-average educational attainment, with more than 40 percent of adults age 25 or older holding at least an associate's degree, compared to the national average of 36 percent and the Western states average of 37 percent. Postsecondary enrollment among adults over 18, at 9 percent, is below both national and regional averages. Washington's Educational Appropriations per FTE reached a high of $9,016 in 1991, decreasing gradually through 2008 and sharply each year since (figure 6.17). Net Tuition Revenue per FTE increased steadily during the 32-year period; for many years it was formally "benchmarked" to a composite of sector-specific public institution rates nationwide. Currently, Net Tuition Revenue per FTE in Washington is well below the national and regional averages.

Six western states—California, Idaho, Nevada, New Mexico, North Dakota, and Utah—currently have Educational Appropriations for public higher education between $5,000 and $10,000 per FTE, and most are near the lower end of this range. Four of the six states also had below-average Net Tuition Revenue in 1980, a number that increased to five below average (all but North Dakota) in 2012.

- California, by far the most populous state, is also atypical in other respects. With nearly 1.6 million FTE students in public institutions and also significant enrollment at large private colleges and universities. California makes up over half of the West's total higher education enrollment. The state's two large multi-institution university systems (the California State University and the University of California systems) together include 35 universities. More than 110 community colleges are distributed throughout the state. Between 1980 and 2010 public institution FTE enrollment increased by 63 percent, compared to a California's population increase of 57 percent. Since 2010 California's FTE enrollment has declined by six percent. Since 2003, Total Education Revenues at public institutions has consistently been lower than average in the West: a total of $8,795 in 2012, compared to a western region average of $9,531 and a national average of $11,095 (see figure 6.6). California relies heavily on comparatively low-tuition community colleges, and Educational Appropriations per FTE have remained somewhat above the national and regional averages. Net Tuition Revenue per FTE has more than tripled since 1980 even when adjusted for inflation, but remains comparatively low. A large difference remains between education fees at the community colleges, which are about one-third the national average, and student charges at the public

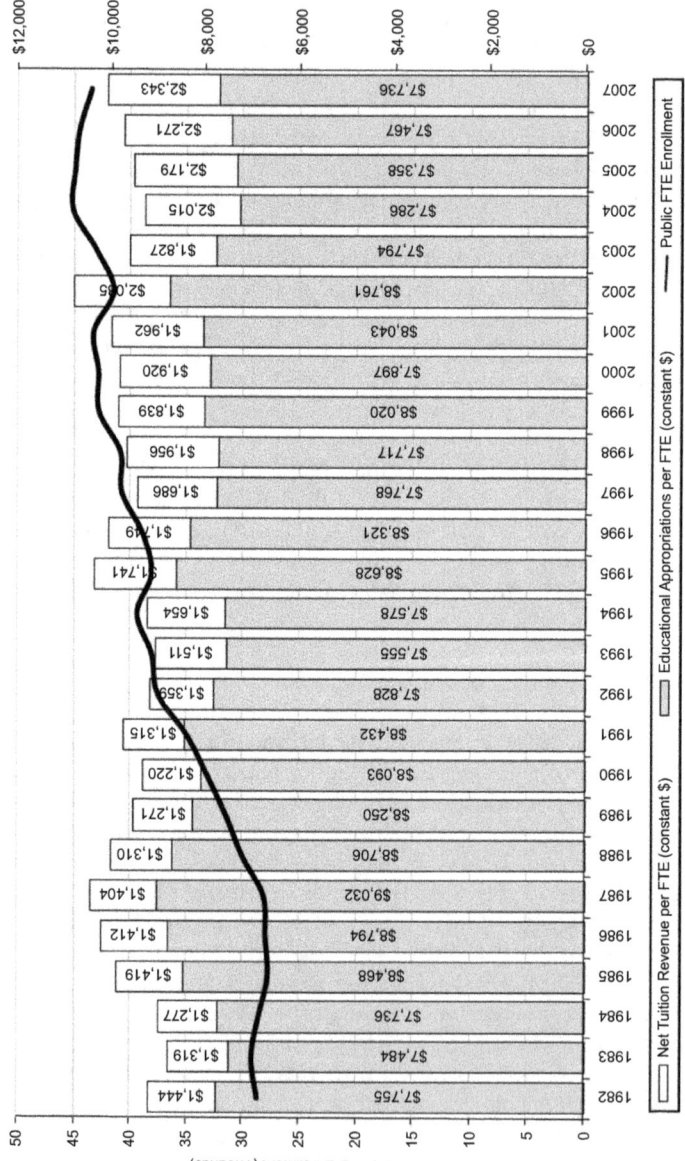

Figure 6.9 Public FTE enrollment, educational appropriations, and total educational revenue per FTE, Idaho—fiscal 1982–2007.

Note: Constant 2007 dollars adjusted by SHEEO Higher Education Cost Adjustment (HECA), EMI, and CCLA.

Source: SHEEOSHEF.

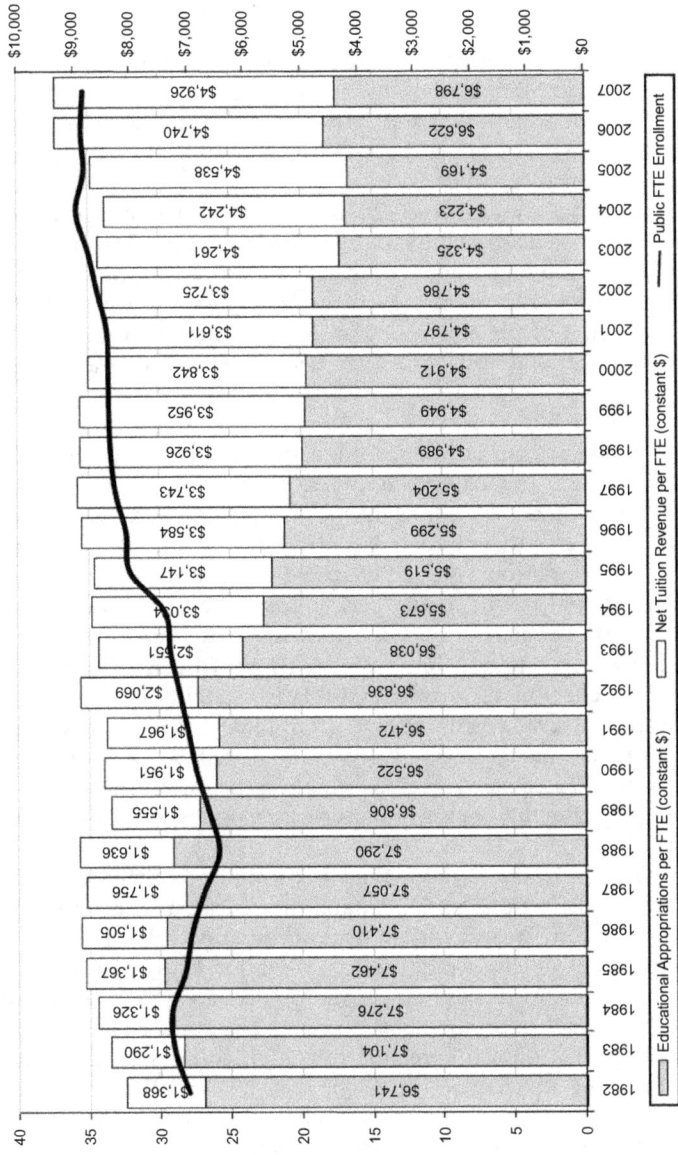

Figure 6.10 Public FTE enrollment, educational appropriations, and total educational revenue per FTE, Montana—fiscal 1982–2007.

Note: Constant 2007 dollars adjusted by SHEEO Higher Education Cost Adjustment (HECA), EMI, and CCLA.

Source: SHEEOSHEF.

universities, which are near the national average. California's postsecondary enrollment rate and educational attainment levels are above the regional and national averages: more than 11 percent of the population 18 years and older were enrolled in postsecondary education in 2010; and more than 37 percent of the adult population over 25 has an associate's degree or higher.

- Idaho has four public universities and three two-year public institutions under a single Idaho State Board of Education. Public FTE enrollment increased steadily between 1980 and 2010 and even more rapidly during the most recent two years, but still totals less than 60,000 FTE students. Educational Appropriations per FTE in Idaho have remained above the regional and national averages until 2010 (figure 6.9), while Net Tuition Revenue has remained below regional and national averages. Postsecondary enrollment among the state's population age 18 and over is approximately 10 percent, just below the regional average and right at the national average. The proportion of the adult population 25 and over with an associate's degree or higher is almost 33 percent, below the regional and national averages.
- Nevada has five public universities and two community colleges, all part of the Nevada System of Higher Education. Public institution FTE enrollment increased 255 percent between 1980 and 2010, while the state's population increased 237 percent. The wave chart for Nevada (figure 6.11) illustrates this rapid and continuing growth in enrollment. Educational Appropriations per FTE stayed relatively consistent with national and regional trends, rising and falling in relation to economic cycles. Net Tuition Revenue per FTE, meanwhile, rose steadily and gradually over the 32-year period but is currently well below the national average. Despite enrollment growth and relative stability in funding for higher education, Nevada's educational attainment level remains below the regional and national averages: 29 percent of the state population over the age of 25 has an associate's degree or higher, the lowest in the region. Postsecondary enrollment among adults over age 18 is also the lowest in the region.
- New Mexico's population of more than two million is served by eight public four-year institutions and 20 public two-year institutions, each with its own governing board, with policy coordination through the New Mexico Department of Higher Education, a cabinet-level agency. Public institution FTE enrollment has more than doubled since 1980, while the state's population increased about 60 percent. The wave chart for New Mexico (figure 6.12) shows comparatively high levels of Educational Appropriations per FTE ($8,550 in 1980 and $7,272 in 2012, in constant dollars), with limited reliance on tuition revenue at public institutions. Net Tuition Revenue per student as a percent of total revenue was one of the lowest in the region at 23 percent. Approximately 10 percent of the state population over age 18 participated in some postsecondary education in 2010, while 32 percent of the adult population over 25 has an associate

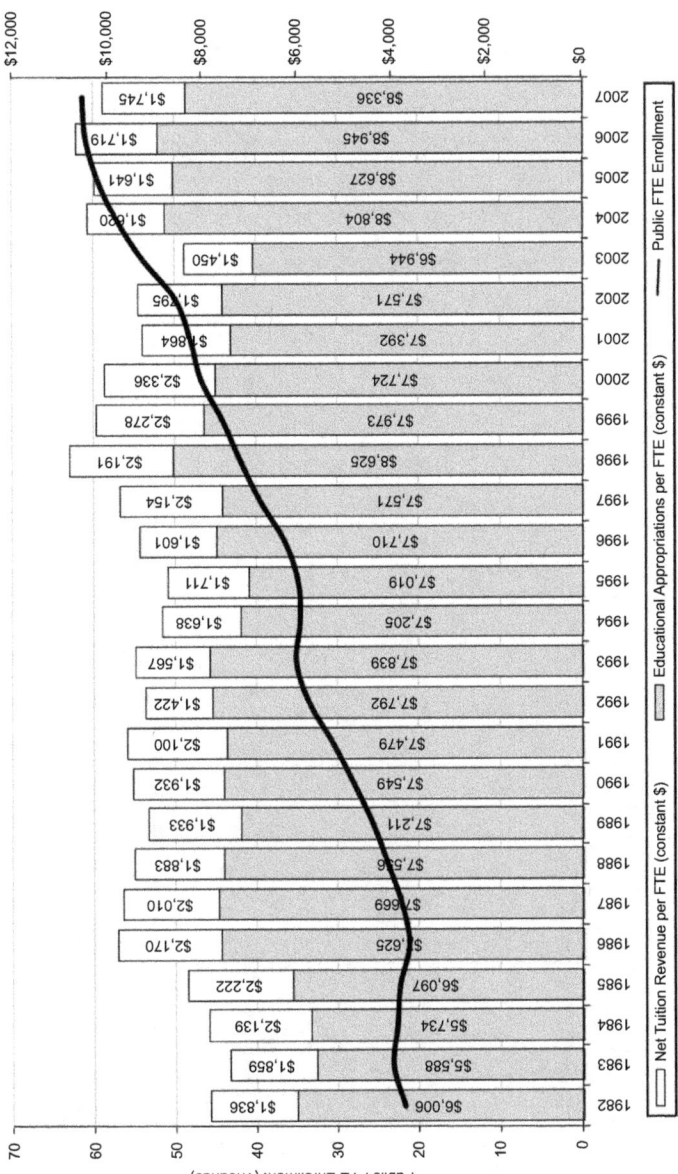

Figure 6.11 Public FTE enrollment, educational appropriations, and total educational revenue per FTE, Nevada—fiscal 1982–2007.

Note: Constant 2007 dollars adjusted by SHEEO Higher Education Cost Adjustment (HECA), EMI, and CCLA.

Source: SHEEOSHEF.

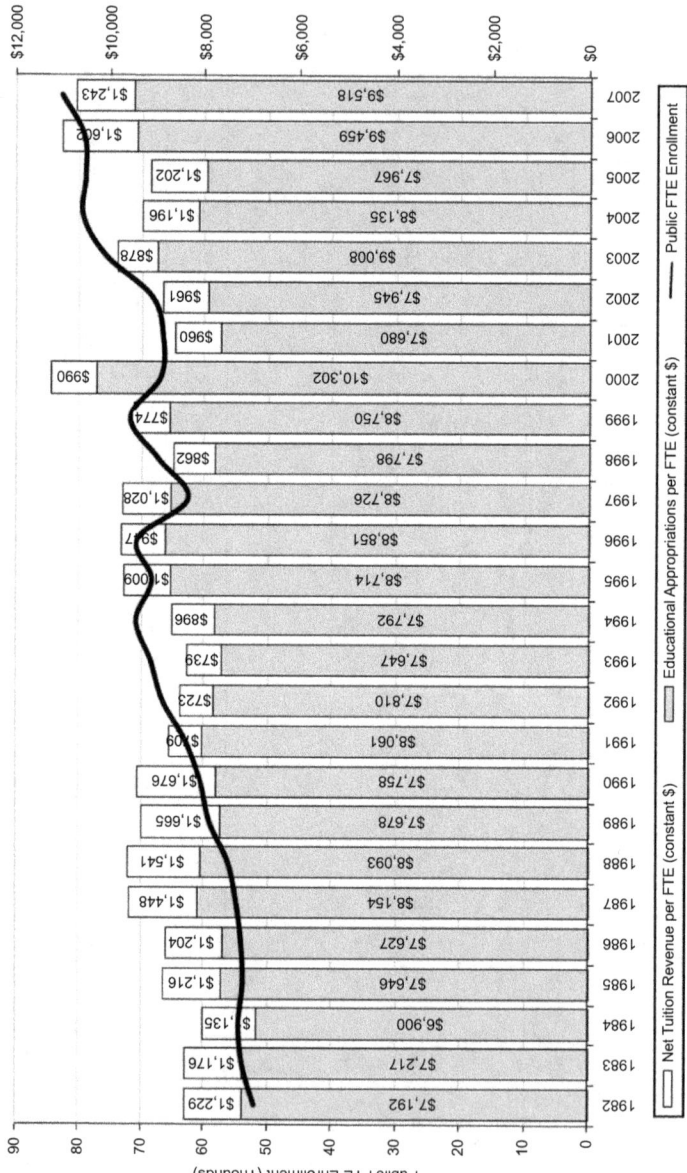

Figure 6.12 Public FTE enrollment, educational appropriations, and total educational revenue per FTE, New Mexico—fiscal 1982–2007.

Note: Constant 2007 dollars adjusted by SHEEO Higher Education Cost Adjustment (HECA), EM, and CCLA.

Source: SHEEOSHEF.

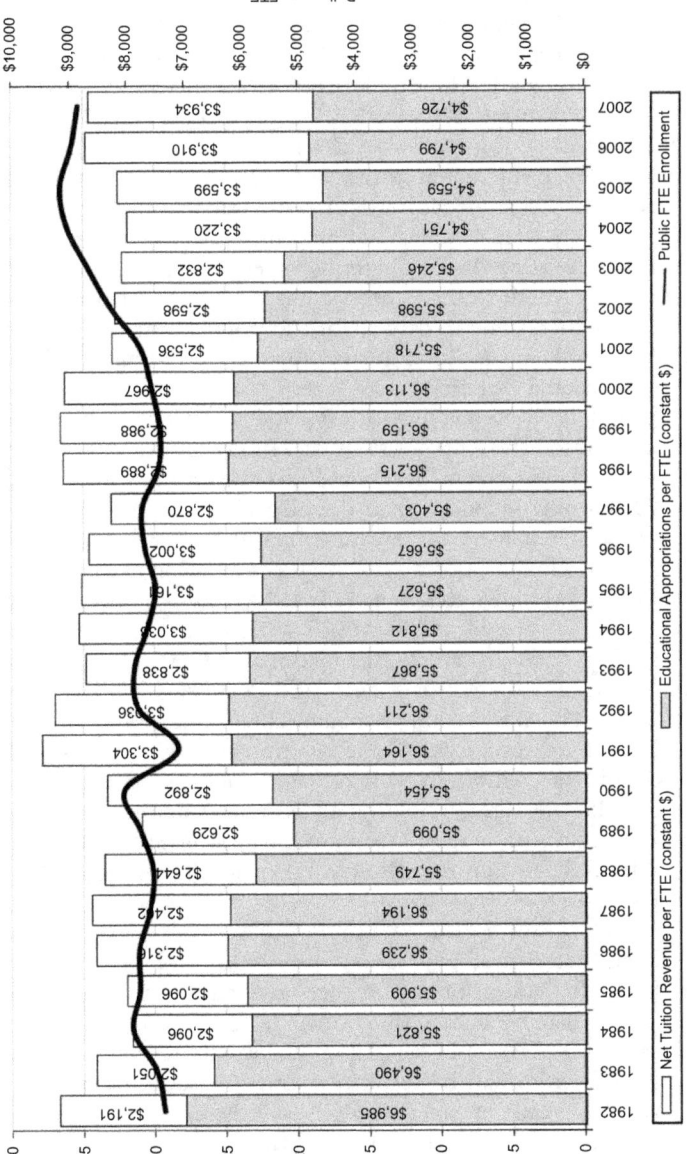

Figure 6.13 Public FTE enrollment, educational appropriations, and total educational revenue per FTE, North Dakota—fiscal 1982–2007.

Note: Constant 2007 dollars adjusted by SHEEO Higher Education Cost Adjustment (HECA), EMI, and CCLA.

Source: SHEEOSHEF.

degree or higher—proportions that are, respectively, higher and lower than national averages.
- North Dakota, with a total population of approximately 700,000, has seven public four-year universities and seven two-year public institutions, all part of the North Dakota University System. Despite slow population growth prior to the recent development of oil and gas resources, North Dakota's FTE enrollment in the public institutions increased unevenly with significant growth from 2000 until 2004 and another spike between 2007 and 2010. As evident in the wave chart (figure 6.13), Educational Appropriations per FTE fluctuated from year to year, with no clear trend. Net Tuition revenue per student, however, increased more than three-fold (even in constant dollar values), composing close to half of Total Educational Revenue since 2005. In terms of educational attainment, almost 40 percent of North Dakota's population 25 and older has an associate's degree or higher, and 11 percent of the population over 18 was enrolled in postsecondary education during 2010. Both figures are above the regional and national averages.
- Utah has seven public four-year institutions and seven public two-year institutions, all part of the Utah System of Higher Education. Utah's population increased 89 percent between 1980 and 2010, while public institution FTE enrollment more than doubled (152% increase) during this 30-year period. Utah also has 20 private institutions serving a significant part (approximately 30%) of the state's higher education needs. Utah's wave chart (figure 6.16) shows increasing reliance on tuition revenue in the public institutions—20 percent of the SHEF Total Educational Revenue in 1980 and 47 percent in 2012—the national average. Educational Appropriations per FTE student have decreased in constant dollar values over the period, with both this component and Total Educational Revenue now below national averages. Educational attainment within Utah's adult population is above the national and regional averages, with more than 38 percent of adults over age 25 holding an associate's degree or higher. The percentage of adults (over age 18) participating in some postsecondary education in 2010 (13%) is significantly above the national average and the highest of any state in the West.

Geographical characteristics, population dispersion, and other factors affect funding for higher education in three western states in unusual ways. Size and population dispersion directly contribute to the cost of delivering higher education in Alaska and Wyoming, while state revenues derived directly and indirectly from natural resource extraction have increased the funding available and, to the extent that high-paying employment is available, perhaps lessened students' need and motivation to seek higher education. The context in Hawaii, while obviously different in geography and population density, has contributed to similarly high per student support in public higher education. These three states have the highest Educational Appropriations per FTE in the nation, and they have been committed to

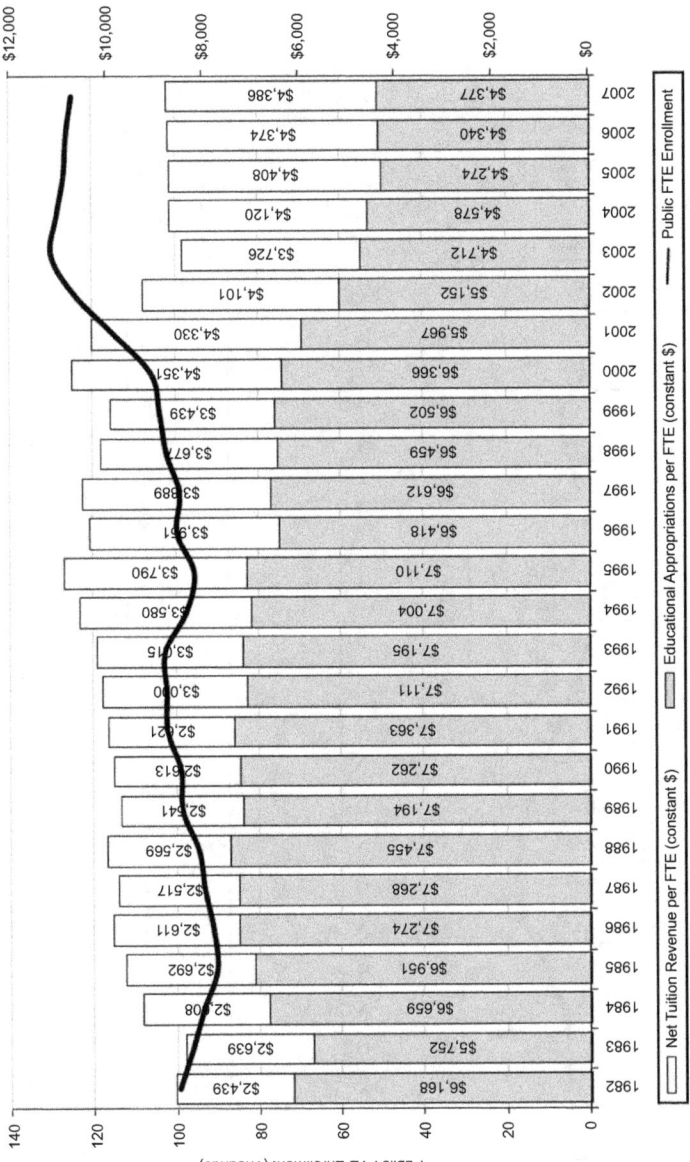

Figure 6.14 Public FTE enrollment, educational appropriations, and total educational revenue per FTE, Oregon—fiscal 1982–2007.

Note: Constant 2007 dollars adjusted by SHEEO Higher Education Cost Adjustment (HECA), EMI, and CCLA.

Source: SHEEOSHEF.

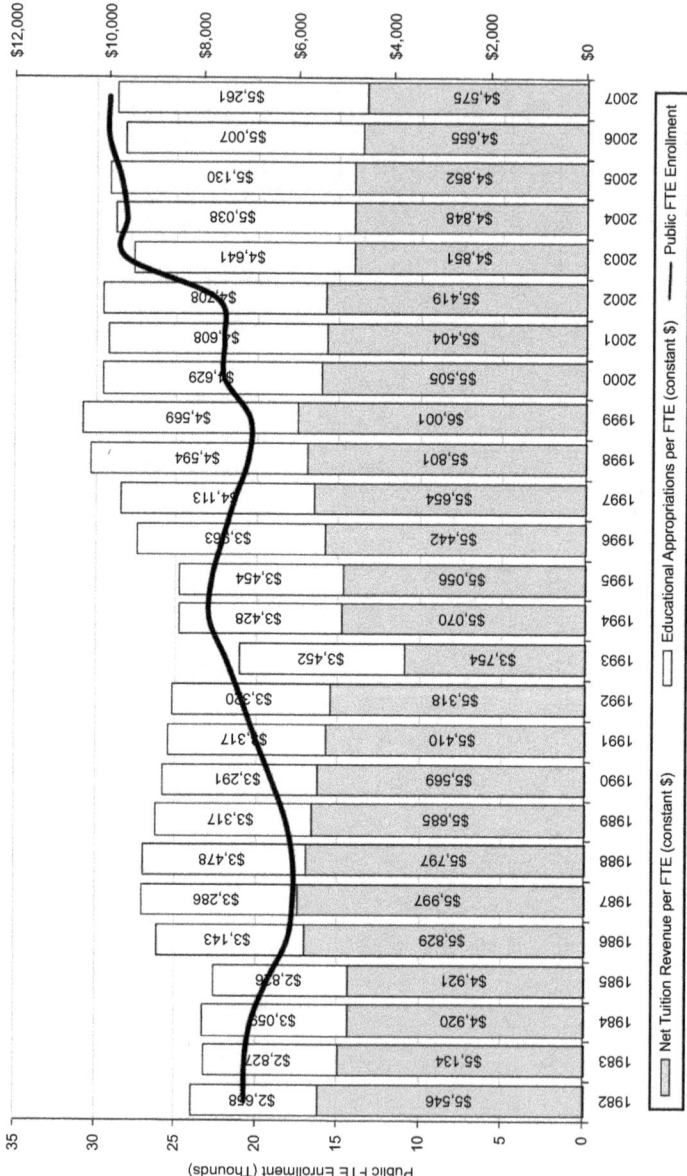

Figure 6.15 Public FTE enrollment, educational appropriations, and total educational revenue per FTE, South Dakota—fiscal 1982–2007.

Note: Constant 2007 dollars adjusted by SHEEO Higher Education Cost Adjustment (HECA), EMI, and CCLA.

Source: SHEEOSHEF.

expanding access and attainment levels in higher education as well as supporting state-focused, university-based research.

- Alaska is distinctive in almost every way: expansive geography, rich natural resources, challenging environments, and extremely dispersed educational needs. The University of Alaska system is composed of three campuses (Anchorage, Fairbanks, and Southeast), with an array of centers or branches and statewide services through online education and extension. The Alaska Commission on Postsecondary Education coordinates state postsecondary services, including a comparatively large state-funded financial aid program. As indicated in figure 6.4, public institution FTE enrollment increased from approximately 10,500 in 1980 to more than 20,000 in 2010 (up 93%), surpassing population growth of 77 percent in the same time period. Educational Appropriations per FTE have historically been high compared to other states, reflecting comparatively low enrollment rates in combination with public funding made possible by high natural resource extraction revenue. State funding for higher education, currently almost $15,000 per FTE student, remains well above the national and regional averages, even though in constant dollars it has decreased significantly in recent years. Net Tuition Revenue, in contrast, is low when compared to public funding, composing less than 10 percent of Total Educational Revenue in 1980 and steadily increasing to 28 percent of the total in 2012. In terms of educational attainment of the state's population, Alaska remains below the regional average but above the national average, with 36 percent of the population over the age of 25 holding an associate's degree or higher. Approximately 9.5 percent of Alaska's adult population over 18 is currently enrolled in higher education, just below the national average.
- Hawaii has four public universities at the four-year level and six two-year campuses, all governed by the University of Hawaii Board of Regents. Public FTE enrollment increased 31 percent from 1980 to 2010, 10 percent lower than the state's population growth of 41 percent during this period. Private nonprofit and for-profit schools and colleges enroll a comparatively large proportion (about one-quarter) of the state's postsecondary students, including significant numbers of out-of-state students. With comparatively low enrollment rates, Educational Appropriations per FTE have been substantially higher than regional or national averages (see figure 6.8), decreasing slowly from an historic high in 1990 and currently more than $10,000 per FTE, compared to less than $6,000 nationally. Historically, tuition at public institutions has been comparatively low, although Net Tuition Revenue per FTE has increased rapidly since 2007–2008. With approximately 9.5 percent of the state's population age 18 and older enrolled in postsecondary education, Hawaii is close to the national average but below the regional average. The proportion of the adult population over 25 with an associate's degree or higher is nearly 39 percent, higher than both the national and regional averages.

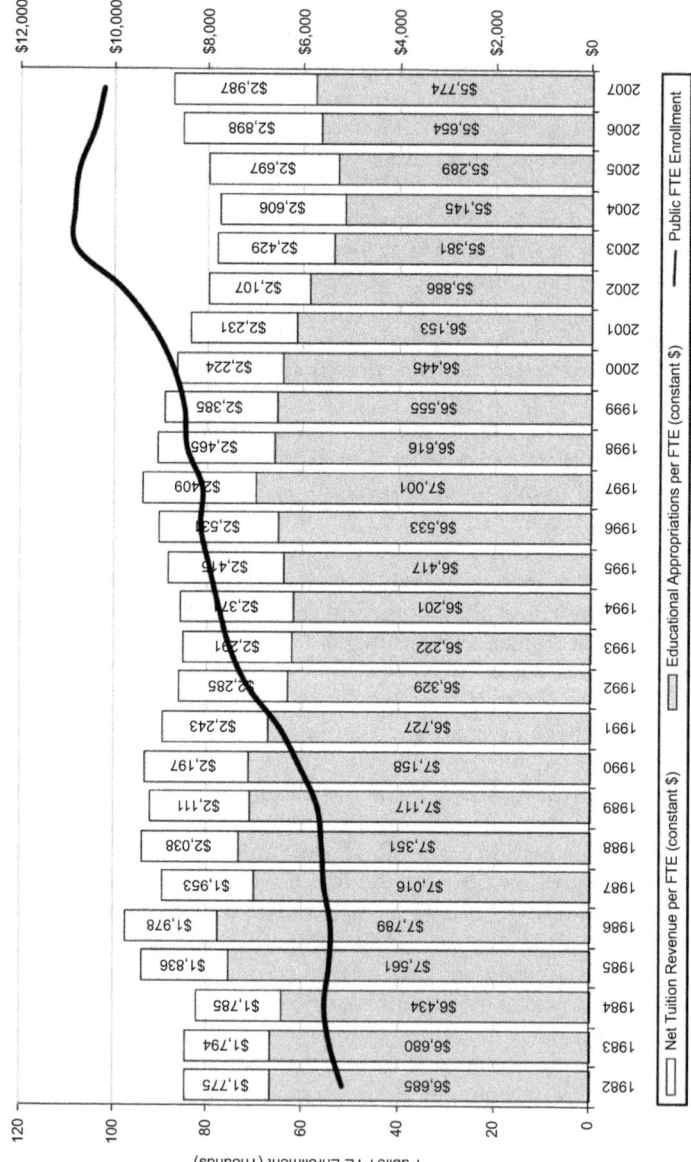

Figure 6.16 Public FTE enrollment, educational appropriations, and total educational revenue per FTE, Utah—fiscal 1982–2007.

Note: Constant 2007 dollars adjusted by SHEEO Higher Education Cost Adjustment (HECA), EMI, and CCLA.

Source: SHEEOSHEF.

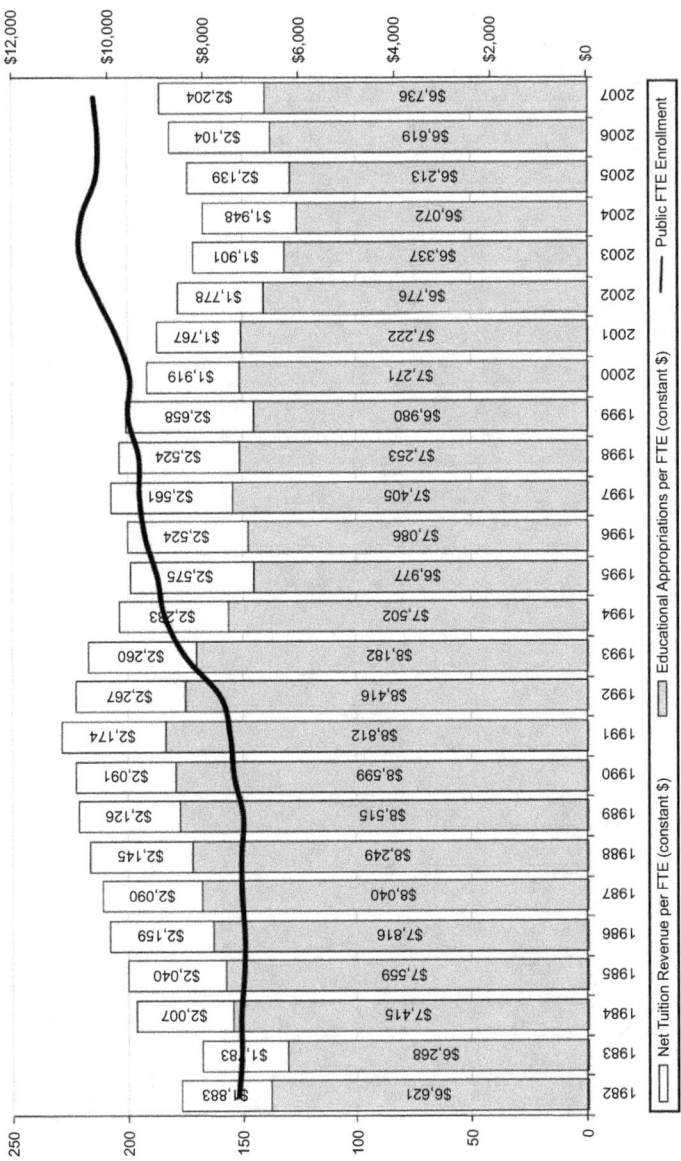

Figure 6.17 Public FTE enrollment, educational appropriations, and total educational revenue per FTE, Washington—fiscal 1982–2007.

Note: Constant 2007 dollars adjusted by SHEEO Higher Education Cost Adjustment (HECA), EMI, and CCLA.

Source: SHEEOSHEF.

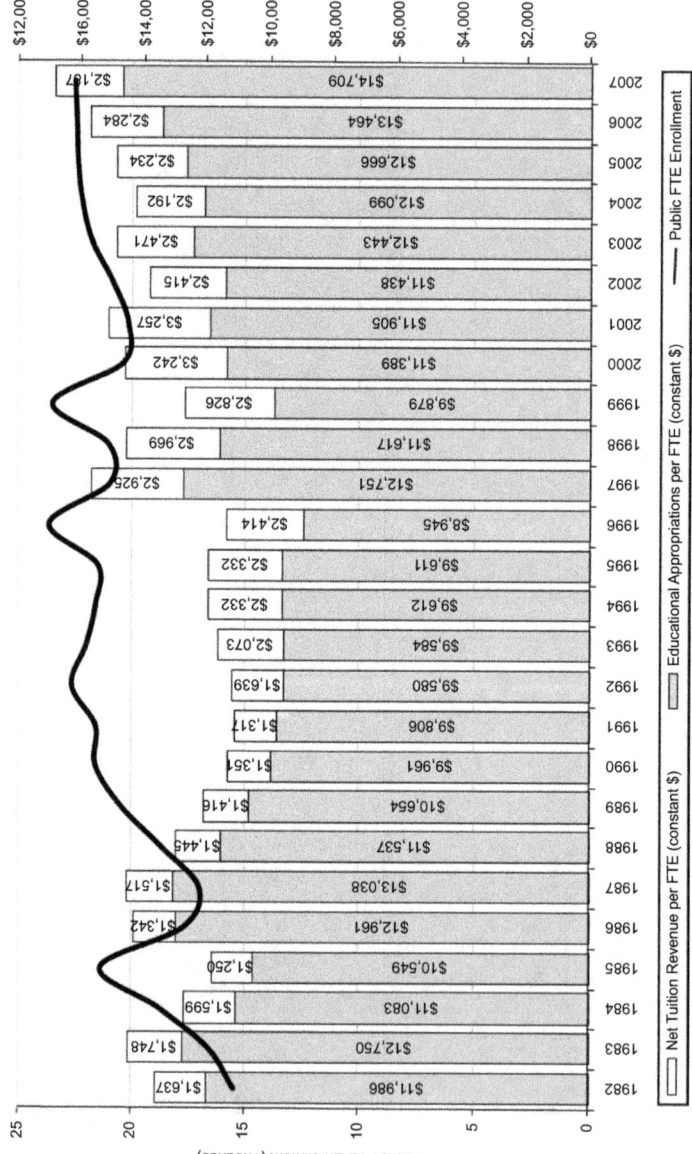

Figure 6.18 Public FTE enrollment, educational appropriations, and total educational revenue per FTE, Wyoming—fiscal 1982–2007.

Note: Constant 2007 dollars adjusted by SHEEO Higher Education Cost Adjustment (HECA), EMI, and CCLA.

Source: SHEEOSHEF.

- Wyoming, a geographically large state with a small and dispersed population, is served by one public four-year institution (University of Wyoming) and seven public two-year institutions with separate institutional governing boards. Wyoming's wave chart (figure 6.18) shows comparatively high Educational Appropriations per FTE student, among the highest in the region and in the nation, reaching over $14,000 per FTE student in 2009. In 2012, Wyoming had Net Tuition Revenue of $1,971 which is far below both the national average and the western states as a region. Wyoming has had consistently and comparatively low Net Tuition Revenues, in constant dollar values approximately the same per FTE student in 2012 as in 1980. A well-funded state financial aid program contributes to Wyoming having significantly less Net Tuition Revenue (and correspondingly more Educational Appropriations) than other Western states. With 20 percent growth in Wyoming's population between 1980 and 2010, FTE enrollments have increased 82 percent since 1980, with three distinct enrollment surges between 1988 and 2000, then a gradual increase since 2000 and another surge between 2009 and 2010. Educational attainment among adults is slightly lower than regional and national averages, with 35 percent of adults over age 25 with an associate's degree or higher; 9 percent of the adult population over 18 was enrolled in some postsecondary education in 2010.

OBSERVATIONS AND CONCLUSIONS

The conclusion of SHEEO's *State Higher Education Finance Report, FY2012* reads, in part, as follows:

> Since the beginning of the 21st century, higher education enrollment has grown faster than any decade since the 1960s. Simultaneously, state and local funding for higher education stagnated twice due to recessions...(With) federal economic stimulus funds...no longer available, enrollment stabilized in 2012, and constant dollar state and local support per student declined 8.9 percent from 2011...Institutions have stretched to accommodate enrollment demand, but in some states students have been turned away due to inadequate resources. Students and their families have paid higher tuition, but rising costs...have likely deterred or reduced some enrollment. Total revenue per student (in higher education) has fallen in nearly every state. (SHEO, 2012, p. 43)

This national outlook applies to western states, some much more evidently and consequentially than others. However, as all westerners know well, our region of the United States is an area of contrasts: flat plains broken by mountain ranges, cities separated by sparsely populated areas. Similar contrasts characterize higher education in the western states: research universities coexist with many smaller colleges, public and private institutions (nonprofit and for-profit) providing an array of educational choices. The data and graphs provided in this chapter also show significant variation in the ways western states finance their higher education systems. Although trends in higher education financing in the West are not dramatically different from national trends, important distinctions emerge when comparing western states to the rest of the nation and across states within the region.

Over the past 32 years, most states in the West have had high rates of enrollment growth and many have continued a "historical preference" for lower public institution tuition rates, compared to the nation as a whole. However, significant differences in enrollment growth are apparent across states: in 11 of the 15 Western states, higher education enrollments have increased more rapidly than population growth, and attainment rates are above the national average. The patterns are complicated, because of the many contributing factors which are difficult to decipher. If the western states are to remain economically competitive and attractive, they must grow their college education workforce. This suggests important and growing roles for WICHE in working with its 15 member states to help them expand opportunities for higher education in the West. Higher education has other important roles to play if the West is to remain a region of opportunity and innovation that can deal with the impending demographic and social changes.

For the nation as a whole, Total Educational Revenue per student (the combination of state and local support plus Net Tuition Revenue at public institutions) increased more than 15 percent between 1980 and 2012 in constant dollars, compared to the West, where it decreased slightly and now stands 14 percent below the national average. While tuition has increased rapidly in the West, it has not increased as rapidly as the nation as a whole. Educational Appropriations per FTE student have decreased 28 percent in the West, compared to 22 percent nationally in constant dollars since 1980. In spite of lower state and local support and the shifting of the cost burden to the student, the West has done reasonably well in maintaining educational opportunity and increasing educational attainment over the three decades. The situation may not be grim but surely needs close scrutiny and well-informed decisions. And given the significant differences across states in their needs, structures, and funding for higher education, it really must be addressed on a state-by-state basis.

Many western states, particularly California, with its large community college sector, have a history of comparatively low tuition charges. This is reflected in the relatively low proportion of public institution educational revenue derived from tuition charges and a correspondingly heavy dependence on Educational Appropriations from state and local funding to support educational services. However, this pattern is far from uniform across the western states and has become less characteristic of the region than in the past. While several states have maintained low tuition rates in public institutions, others have now moved above the national average. The proportion of tuition-derived revenue in Total Educational Revenue rose from less than 14 percent in the West in 1980 to nearly 38 percent in 2012, and five western states now derive more than 50 percent of Total Educational Revenue at their public institutions from tuition payments.

The trends and current conditions in the West's funding for higher education require, we believe, much closer examination than they currently get. Higher education leaders and state policymakers need to see how discrete, year-by-year decisions contribute to broader and more consequential patterns of change over time. And the public, including students and families, will need to understand this context and its consequences as they think about and prepare for the future.

Our intent in this chapter was to provide an overview and way of using higher education financial indicators that will prompt and support better understanding and decision making. However, examining the data can only be a starting point in addressing the tough questions and difficult budgetary choices that states face—questions and choices that include:

- How will changes to the sources, patterns, and levels of support from state and local governments impact higher education access and opportunity?
- How can higher education institutions maintain and improve their quality and competitiveness, given growing enrollment needs and budgetary constraints?
- What consequences will result from states and institutions continuing to shift the burden to pay from public investment to tuition charges, and what levels of student financial aid are essential to broaden access and improve completion rates as college prices go up?
- And most importantly, will current patterns in enrollment, financing, and education delivery meet the needs of the future; and if not, what steps will need to be taken?

These questions have no simple answers, but they need to be asked and discussed. We hope our analysis will help states and the public to ask the right questions and to respond appropriately.

Notes

*The coauthors are current or former SHEEO staff members who have contributed to annual State Higher Education Finance (SHEF) reports; currently, SHEF is primarily the responsibility of Andy Carlson (acarlson@sheeo.org).

1. Net Tuition Revenue is not a measure of "net price" (the cost for students to attend public institutions after deducting assistance from federal, state, and institutional grants). Several factors make the calculation of net price very complex and Net Tuition Revenue per FTE student should not be treated as a substitute. For example, SHEF does not deduct federal grant assistance (primarily from Pell Grants) from gross tuition revenue because nontuition costs (room and board, transportation, books, and incidentals) may also be covered by federal aid, while the tuition-supporting portions of federal aid are available for institutional use. Other factors, including the availability of federal tuition tax credits help reduce "net price" for middle and lower-middle-income students. These tax credits have no impact on the "Net Tuition Revenue" received by institutions, although they do reduce the "net price" paid by students.

References

Center for Study of Education Policy. *Grapevine Summary Tables FY12—FY13*. Illinois State University, 2012. Retrieved from http://grapevine.illinoisstate.edu/tables/index.htm, in June 7, 2013.

State Higher Education Executive Officers. *State Higher Education Finance FY2012*, 2012. Retrieved from www.sheeo.org/resources/publications/shef-%E2%80%94-state-higher-education-finance-fy12, in June 7, 2013.

US Census Bureau. *Census 2010*. Resident Population Data, Population Change, 2010. Retrieved from www.census.gov/2010census/data/apportionment-pop-text.php, in June 7, 2013.

———. *2010 American Community Survey 1-Year Estimates*. S1501: Educational Attainment [data], 2010. Retrieved from www.census.gov/acs/www/, in June 7, 2013.

———. *2010 American Community Survey 1-Year Estimates*. S1401: School Enrollment [data], 2010. Retrieved from www.census.gov/acs/www/, in June 7, 2013.

7

Technology and Distance Education

Challenges Facing the American West

Sally M. Johnstone* and J. Ritchie Boyd**

The western states have unique geographical challenges compared to the rest of the United States. Vast spaces and very small communities of people contributed to making colleges and universities in the West among the first to adopt technological solutions for reaching people. Since the mid-1980s, Alaska, California, Colorado, Hawaii, North Dakota, South Dakota, Washington, and Utah have played a leading role in developing technological and/or administrative systems to serve students who were not able to come to a campus.

Distance was only one of the driving factors for these developments. Another was the rapid growth of the high-tech industry that began in the 1980s and progressed through the 1990s. Companies needed highly skilled and up-to-date engineers who needed to continue to work while they studied. The only way to accomplish that was to use distance learning. In California and in Colorado, different solutions arose that foreshadowed developments to come.

The Genesis of Technology-Based Distance Learning

In California, a single campus approach was developed. The Chico campus of the California State University (CSU) system began working with one of the Silicon Valley high-tech companies in 1984. They had been serving students in a large area in northeastern California (33,000 square miles), using a microwave technology known as Instructional Television Fixed Service (ITFS) since the mid-1970s. CSU-Chico expanded to using a satellite-delivered master's degree program to serve the engineers and computer scientists at Hewlett-Packard. Initially, this program was only offered in California, but as the company grew, so did the program. Soon other companies were taking advantage of Chico's programs. Twenty years later, the Chico campus has several well-developed distance learning programs that offer courses and degrees to hundreds of students in several states and abroad through a web-based system with streaming video.[1]

In Colorado, Colorado State University in 1984 recognized the need for further education for engineers in high-tech companies. These engineers moved around the country for new assignments within their companies and also moved between companies. Since the faculties at the colleges of engineering had their hands full serving on-campus students, Colorado State dean Lionel Baldwin began weaving together a network of engineering schools to create the National Technological University (NTU). With the support of major technology companies, such as IBM, Motorola, Boeing, and Hewlett-Packard, NTU began delivering academic courses via satellite directly to corporations' training facilities. In 1984, NTU began offering degree programs using courses supplied by seven universities, helping realize Baldwin's vision of allowing students to take courses on site without having to spend hours getting to and from a university campus. NTU went on to develop into a network that included almost 50 partner universities and eventually merged with Walden University to become the NTU College of Engineering and Applied Science.

Within a few years many other universities and colleges began using Instructional Television Fixed Service (ITFS), cable television, and the Public Broadcasting Network to serve students away from campuses. By the early 1990s, several western states built their own networks to ensure that citizens in their rural areas could have access to college and university programs. In one example, the North Dakota University System's planners recognized the growing need to extend educational services to everyone who needed and wanted them statewide. In the early 1990s, the North Dakota Interactive Video Network (IVN) became operational. The initial programs linked the state's 11 public universities so that nursing and social work programs were available statewide. Today, IVN's services include statewide videoconferencing, audio conferencing, and web streaming for higher education, tribal colleges, government agencies, and secondary schools. Staff members also assist all education sectors in troubleshooting their technological problems.

Elsewhere, California's universities also developed video network links among campuses. In Utah, both higher education institutions and high schools were linked through Utah's EdNet. Oregon created Oregon Ednet. Hawaii created Distance Learning and Instructional Technology (DLIT) that utilizes all forms of media to link educational activities between the islands. In Arizona, community colleges were linked via video to a single university (University of Northern Arizona) that provided the remote courses and services. In addition to NTU, Colorado's university systems, community colleges, and multicampus institutions were finding ways to offer classes remotely. Most of the western states had developed some type of education-linking network by the mid-1990s.

The Impact of Regional Networks

While interactive video services were being expanded and upgraded in the 1980s, regional computing networks were being created with encouragement and funding from the National Science Foundation. The evolution of NorthWestNet serves as an example of how regional networks were initiated and coalesced to serve higher education.

In 1986, phase one of the National Science Foundation Network (NSFNET) established a three-tiered network architecture, with one of the goals being to connect multiple regional networks and peer networks to a major backbone—the core of NSFNET. In the northwest, the NorthWest Academic Computing Consortium (NWACC), which was composed of eight academic institutions in addition to the Western Interstate Commission for Higher Education (WICHE) plus Boeing as the corporate partner and host, was selected in 1987 to administer the initial grant to establish a network that eventually became NorthWestNet. This network's initial objective was to connect state universities in Alaska, Idaho, Montana, North Dakota, Oregon, and Washington, while spurring economic development of the region. The primary focus of this effort was to involve land-grant institutions and a handful of smaller universities and research centers.

During the late 1980s, networking protocols were just being developed (TelNet was used in the earliest days), and the very first routers built by Cisco were being manufactured. This initial network relied on 19.2K and 56K modems. For example, the entire state of Montana was served by a single 19.2K modem connection. By the close of the 1980s the NSF backbone had much faster T1 connections to a total of 13 sites (as a result of an award to Merit Network, Inc. and its partners).

In 1991, NWACC hired a full-time dedicated staff to manage NorthWestNet and upgrade it to T1 lines. Within three years NorthWestNet was up to about 25 staff, and membership grew rapidly during this period. By 1993 more than 120 institutions were connected, some with multiple T1 lines. During this period a number of text-based search and delivery tools, such as Archie and Gopher, were being developed and used.

In 1995 NWACC spun off NorthWestNet as a for-profit entity, and in 1997 sold it to Verio, which acquired a number of regional networks during this period. Verio was bought by NTT (Japan) several years later. At least two significant outcomes of this process are worth noting. First, a considerable amount of network infrastructure is a direct consequence of the efforts of NWACC from 1987 to 1997. And, second, the funds received from the sale of NorthWestNet allowed NWACC to establish a grant program to distribute funds to support institutions in their efforts to undertake collaborative projects between faculty and students and to build communities of practice for instructional and academic technologies among institutions.

The steady expansion of national and international high-speed networks continues to this day, as projects, such as Internet2 and the National Lambda

Rail, come online and expand to reach more institutions, in addition to accepting memberships from K-12 school districts.

THE CREATION OF THE WESTERN COOPERATIVE FOR EDUCATIONAL TELECOMMUNICATIONS

In 1989, WICHE founded a new organization to assist the states and their institutions in dealing with all the issues around the educational uses of information and communication technologies. The Western Cooperative for Educational Telecommunications (WCET) began with about 100 people coming together. These delegates were mostly from WICHE states with a few delegates from Oklahoma also attending. The Oklahomans petitioned the gathering to open up membership for institutions and organizations beyond the West. This enabled WCET staff to both import and export expertise to benefit the western states.

One the first issues targeted by WCET was the quality of the video-classroom experience for faculty and students. In part due to the technology being used, the form these classes took generally was referred to as exporting the classroom. A faculty member would stand in front of whiteboard (just a high-tech chalkboard) and conduct a class as usual. The students sitting in the same room as the instructor may have been impressed by the high-tech surroundings, but they soon began to complain about the attention the remote students were getting. The students sitting in remote classrooms had variable environments, but frequently they complained about not being able to see all the material written on the board and the awkwardness of trying to ask questions. The leaders of the National Technological University (NTU) were among the first to recognize the potential devastating effects this situation could have. They began an intensive program to help their campus members increase the quality of the video-classroom experience. Instructors beginning to teach in a video-classroom were required to go through some training on how to use it. Some campuses developed teams of student workers to assist the faculty members in creating better graphics to support their lectures. Time was spent with students at remote locations to help them understand how to get the most out of their distance learning experience. These developmental activities soon spread throughout the educational network community.

Once the networks were in place and students and faculty members were getting used to working together in new ways, some additional issues arose. In the early 1990s staff at the University of Arizona had begun offering electronically delivered classes to support students in New Mexico working on graduate degrees from the University of Arizona. At that time none of the universities in New Mexico offered Master's degrees in Library Science (MLS). There were several other western states that did not have MLS programs either. The University of Arizona turned to WCET to assist them in offering the program electronically to students in other states. WCET was funded by the US Department of Commerce to not only help the University of Arizona offer MLS programs regionally, but also to allow the University of North Dakota to offer its Masters in Space Science along with three other programs from different universities. By the spring of 1996, students from around the WICHE region were enrolling in five degree and certificate programs that were offered in a variety of distance learning formats.

In creating this interstate brokering activity, WCET staff quickly learned that each state had its own regulatory structure and none of them were designed to take into account academic programs developed electronically. Consequently, WCET developed a project to help states be more welcoming to these types of programs while still fulfilling their consumer protection function to assure the quality of the programs. This project was funded by the US Department of Education's Fund for the Improvement of Postsecondary Education (FIPSE), and resulted in a set of Principles of Good Practice for Electronically Offered Academic Degree and Certificate Programs. These principles became the basis for most of the western states' standards for programs offered electronically to its citizens, whether from higher education institutions inside or outside the state. Several states developed reciprocal agreements based on the principles.

The First Virtual Universities

The idea that states could affordably share higher education resources electronically attracted a great deal of interest at the summer 1995 meeting of the Western Governors' Association (WGA). Over the coming year, WCET staff worked closely with the WGA and the National Center for Higher Education Management Systems (NCHEMS) staff to create a framework for a Western Governors University (WGU). It was designed to allow the 18-member states to share higher education resources electronically and to be an institution that granted degrees based on student outcomes, not credit-hours earned. Utah governor Mike Leavitt and Colorado governor Roy Romer took the lead in shaping this institution under the leadership of its administrative officers, Jeffery Livingston (Utah) and Robert Albrecht (Colorado). WGU began enrolling its first students in 1999 under the leadership of President Robert Mendenhall. While it was originally co-located in both states, it is now headquartered in Utah but continues to serve students throughout the region, the nation, and the world. By the end 2013, WGU had five state affiliatiates with their own chancellors (Indiana, Washington, Texas, Missouri, and Tennessee), enrollments of more than 40,000 and about 25,000 graduates.

While many states across the country watched the development of WGU, several of them began developing their own statewide "virtual universities." Only one of the western states—California—decided not to participate in the WGU activities. At the time that WGU was being discussed, the CSU was actively engaged in developing its own intercampus distance learning system to serve its more than 20 campuses. Several of the University of California campuses were already linked and many of the 100-plus community colleges were quite active in using technology to serve students. The California

Virtual University (CVU) was launched as a marketing opportunity for all of California higher education, but, despite the backing of the state governor's office, there was little funding available for the institutions to keep them engaged and the project faded away in a few years.

WGU and CVU were not the only ones to arise in the United States in the late 1990s. By 2000, almost every state had created or was participating in something like a "virtual university" (Epper and Garn, 2003). As these distance learning activities escalated in both number and visibility, the regional accrediting associations were getting involved. In order to evaluate WGU, three of the regions had to work together. The Western Association's Senior and Junior Divisions, the Northwest Association, and the North Central Association all worked on assessing and eventually accrediting WGU.

Quality Assurance

After their experience assessing and accrediting WGU, the heads of the regional accrediting associations formed the Council for Regional Accrediting Commissions (C-RAC) to include all the associations. By 2000, C-RAC realized that it made no sense to have separate sets of standards or principles for distance learning, when an institution could be located anywhere in the United States and serving students anywhere else. They called on WCET to help in creating a common set of Principles of Good Practice (see table 7.1). Within the next two years, these principles had been adopted by all the regional accrediting associations.

One important aspect of these principles is that they place a great deal of importance on distance learning institutions fully supporting their students. This marked a shift from the usual emphasis on faculty support and training (included as well) and institutional resources. In general, the principles suggest that institutions serving distance students must:

- Provide honest information to the public about the program. This means that an institution should actually do what it says it will do.
- Students must have adequate skills to begin the program. The student should be told clearly what academic and technical skills he/she should have in order to successfully complete a program.
- Students must have access to needed support. If a student needs access to specialized library resources to be successful in a program of study, it is the institution's responsibility to ensure a means to that access.
- Students must have access to information from the institution and to be able to communicate with critical people within the institution, including faculty and other students.

All these services taken together reflect how an institution is expected to support its students who do not come to the campus. It also reflects services available on campuses for students either physically or virtually. In addition to being incorporated into campus evaluations by accreditors, these principles

Table 7.1 Summary of principles of good practice for electronically offered academic degree and certificate programs

CURRICULUM AND INSTRUCTION

Each program of study results in learning outcomes appropriate to the rigor and breadth of the degree or certificate awarded.

An electronically offered degree or certificate program is coherent and complete.

The program provides for appropriate real-time or delayed interaction between faculty and students and among students.

Qualified faculty provide appropriate oversight of the program electronically offered.

INSTITUTIONAL CONTEXT AND COMMITMENT

Role and Mission

The program is consistent with the institution's role and mission.

Review and approval processes ensure the appropriateness of the technology being used to meet the program's objectives.

Faculty Support

The program provides faculty support services specifically related to teaching via an electronic system.

The program provides training for faculty who teach via the use of technology.

Resources for Learning

The program ensures that appropriate learning resources are available to students.

Students and Student Services

The program provides students with clear, complete, and timely information on the curriculum, course and degree requirements, nature of faculty/student interaction, assumptions about technological competence and skills, technical equipment requirements, availability of academic support services and financial aid resources, and costs and payment policies.

Enrolled students have reasonable and adequate access to the range of student services appropriate to support their learning.

Accepted students have the background, knowledge, and technical skills needed to undertake the program.

Advertising, recruiting, and admissions materials clearly and accurately represent the program and the services available.

Commitment to Support

Policies for faculty evaluation include appropriate consideration of teaching and scholarly activities related to electronically offered programs.

The institution demonstrates a commitment to ongoing support, both financial and technical, and to continuation of the program for a period sufficient to enable students to complete a degree/certificate.

EVALUATION AND ASSESSMENT

The institution evaluates the program's educational effectiveness, including assessments of student learning outcomes, student retention, and student and faculty satisfaction. Students have access to such program evaluation data.

The institution provides for assessment and documentation of student achievement in each course and at completion of the program.

were used to guide newly developing distance learning projects at the state and campus level throughout the western states and the nation.

BEYOND WGU: TODAY'S VIRTUAL UNIVERSITIES

While WGU was a trendsetter in offering virtual educational opportunities, it is by no means alone as we enter the second decade of the twenty-first century. The more recent institutions offering online educational opportunities can be divided into three broad groups: (1) traditional university and college subsidiaries and consortia, (2) private not-for-profit institutions, and (3) for-profit colleges and universities. Intuitions in the first two categories seem to fit fairly well into the usual practices on which regulators and accreditors focus, but as noted below the third category has challenged many of the assumptions about what constitutes appropriate practices in higher education. All of these virtual institutions usually target adult students and consequently offer degree and certificate programs in areas related to workforce demands.

UNIVERSITY AND COMMUNITY COLLEGE SUBSIDIARIES

Among the university and college subsidiaries offering virtual higher education opportunities, two noteworthy examples are the Colorado Community Colleges Online and Rio Salado Community College, which is part of the Maricopa Community Colleges system in Arizona. Colorado Community Colleges Online (CCCOnline, www.ccconline.org) combines the resources of 13 community colleges in Colorado and single institutions in Montana and Missouri to offer career and technical programs to their students. In the CCCOnline model, the system produces the courses and the individual institutions feed students into the process. Thus, the transcript comes from the partner institution rather than the consortium. This mixture of students and instructors from around the system is intended to foster a rich experience for all involved. Since its inception in 1999, enrollment in CCCOnline courses increased in excess of 20 percent per year through 2005. In addition, CCCOnline has been an innovator in providing centralized support and services to students, such as an online writing lab that offers tutor resources that may not otherwise be available to all. In 2003, CCCOnline was recognized as one of the top three virtual consortiums in the United States by the Center for Academic Transformation at Rensselaer Polytechnic Institute, and the consortium's quality assurance practices garnered it a 2004 WCET WOW! award (WCET, 2004).

On the other hand, Rio Salado College Online (www.riosalado.edu), the distance learning arm of Arizona's Maricopa Community Colleges system, utilizes a different model for online education that emphasizes high-quality courses with rolling start dates such that students can begin a course each week based on when they are ready. Rio Salado now serves more than 60,000 students annually, with about one-half online, and is often described as one of the best online community college efforts in the United States. Rio Salado College may also offer an indication of where distance and online learning is headed. The college has been a leader in implementing a robust package of online student services well beyond what might be considered traditional. It has moved into the realm of personalized and social applications that at times mimic the social networking services that engage many students already. In particular, they have paired the RioLounge social portal with their RioLearn curricular environment with the goal of creating a seamless community for students in and outside of the formal learning process. The lounge portal allows students to do many of the things they may be familiar with already from other popular applications—connecting with other students, forming groups, and sharing profile information, while the learning environment provides access to courses, examinations, and online library resources. The lounge then goes beyond the common social tools to include direct links to academic and support services and information that would usually be parked on an institution's main web pages—thus, making the experience simpler and closer to the "one-stop shopping" that many who live in the online world have come to expect. These services are complemented by a live chat tool that provides access to academic and financial advising and technical support, in addition to both an online technology support help desk and an online instructional support help desk.

Beyond these examples, a number of states have established infrastructure models where the state supplies the hardware infrastructure and individual institutions have the opportunity to capitalize on this to serve students across their state. Examples of extensive statewide resources include the Utah Educational Network (UEN) and its counterparts in Hawaii, North Dakota, and South Dakota.

Private Not-for-Profit Institutions

The largest exemplars of private virtual universities in the West are National University in California (and Nevada), the Western Governors University, and the City University of Seattle (now international). The not-for-profit structure has allowed these institutions to keep prices to students reasonably low. WGU is one of the few virtual universities that have been able to take real advantage of the promise of technology to lower costs of higher education by using the competency-based approach. Both the National University and the City University are not completely virtual, but have large numbers of students in their online divisions. However, they still use a faculty-centric teaching model. WGU's faculty offer direct support to students, while the learner resources are acquired from existing providers.

For-Profit Institutions

There are now dozens of for-profit entities offering online degrees either exclusively or alongside location-based courses. Most online providers offer flexibility for mobile professionals. In this sense, these distance learning providers continue to honor the original impetus for coming into existence—to help professionals further their education without having to leave their places of employment or families. Some of the larger for-profit providers in the West include the University of Phoenix, Jones International, International University in Colorado, and Ashford University in California:

- The for-profit and publicly traded University of Phoenix Online (www.phoenix.edu) is the most successful in this category. Since its creation in 1989, it has grown to become the largest private accredited online university in the United States (indeed, the largest private university in North America), with more than 300,000 students in more than 200 physical locations, and more than 100 undergraduate-through-doctoral degree offerings.
- Jones International University (www.jiu.edu) is a successor to Glenn Jones' cable television-based Mind Extension University, which enabled as many as 30,000 students to take courses from more than 30 colleges and universities via television. Jones started JIU in 1993—the first university anywhere to exist completely online—and in 1999 gained the distinction of being the first entirely virtual institution in the United States to receive regional accreditation.
- Ashford University began as a small Franciscan college in Iowa. When it was acquired by Bridgepoint Education in 2005, enrollments in the online division quickly outpaced the campus-based enrollments. With the online division enrolling thousands more students and employing more people in California than in Iowa, the Higher Learning Commission of the North Central Association requested Ashford University apply for accreditation with the western association. This is an interesting example in the development of the use of technology in higher education. As corporations move into the field, the whole regulatory structure needs to accommodate to the changing practices.

The rapid growth of online degree programs has pushed both the states and the federal government to take a closer look at this segment of higher education. By 2011, the US Department of Education reminded institutions offering online degrees (both public and private) that they must comply with the state requirements in which the students are located (not just the location of the institution). While some institutions were complying with state requirements, not all were doing so. Since each state had unique requirements, WICHE's WCET with the State Higher Education Executive Officers organization (SHEEO) took the lead in collecting and tracking all states' requirements for the distance education community nationwide. Since this level of compliance can be very expensive (some institutions reporting spending hundreds of thousands of dollars annually to comply) and time consuming, several national projects evolved to simplify the process. In early 2013 all these projects came together under the leadership of WICHE. The plan is to use WICHE's sister organizations in the other regions of the country to assist in forming reciprocity agreements among their states to have each state take on the consumer protection role for the institutions located in the state thus allowing institutions to serve students in reciprocating states. As noted below, the US Congress has become involved in consumer protection issues as well.

As a result of the ubiquitous availability of information and communication technologies, new models of education are being offered to students to allow them to accelerate their time to degree and to take advantage of the growing number of high-quality learning resources becoming available. Since 2011 several new ventures have arisen out of Stanford University's faculty in California. New Silicon Valley–backed companies are making Massive Open Online Courses (MOOC) available to thousands of learners around the world. These courses are led by instructors from well-regarded universities and utilize social networking to support students who enroll in the courses. StraighterLine is offering learners low cost courses in a wide variety of subjects that are typically required in traditional collegiate general education programs. These offerings raise interesting policy issues. Can students who take advantage of cost savings by using these options have access to financial aid? Can they transfer these courses readily into the home institutions for credit? The jury is still out but the interest is high among state and federal policymakers looking for ways to decrease the costs of higher education while increasing the number of Americans with postsecondary degrees.

Why the West?

It is fair to ask what it is about the West that has given rise to the number and diversity of online educational opportunities that we see today. One of the earliest uses of excess bandwidth capacity on communication satellites was education. The first western telecommunications education project was established by Louis Bransford in Colorado, because from Colorado it was possible to "hit" the transponders of satellites that covered both the Atlantic and Pacific regions. These activities in Colorado attracted professionals that were involved in both education and the communications industry to the region. In addition, the rural distribution of the western states' relatively low populations and large land mass demanded a viable response from educators to provide access to learning opportunities to residents who wanted to stay in their own communities. The early development and availability of computing and telecommunications networks, as mentioned earlier, set up the conditions for institutions to reach the entire rural West.

Technology has given us the ability to flatten the world in many ways, to reduce or remove barriers to communicating and collaborating with people around the world. For westerners this provides the ability to bring rich learning opportunities from around the world to the West and to extend educational resources from the West to the world. Finally, the organizations in the western states (e.g., WICHE, NorthWestNet, and others) acted as catalysts to encourage states to work together and to learn from one another.

As the dot-com bust of the late 1990s and early 2000s manifested itself throughout the United States and the world, statewide educational technology projects began to focus more heavily on programs and projects for workforce development. They also were encouraged by policymakers to begin to share more resources. In South Dakota, the university regents created a policy by which there would not be any state funding for duplicative courses developed for electronic delivery. That is, if one campus produced an online calculus course that could be delivered statewide, the other campuses were expected to use it. This was an excellent strategy to gets things started but ran into difficulties when a different set of faculty at another campus developed a better version of a calculus course. The rate of change of the techniques and tools for using online technologies made public policy quite difficult.

The early 2000s were a cooling-off period for large-scale educational technology investments, but a few other things were happening to influence the use of technology in the western states. The biggest was the popularization of electronic commerce and the wide use of the Internet by the broader population. This meant that the older video networks that had been developed in the late 1980s and early 1990s could be "replaced" with webcasting that could reduce telecommunications charges, while reaching a wider audience. By 2005, most of the original players, like Cal State, Chico, and NTU, had switched to webstreaming distribution of their video classes.

Consumer Protection

As additional players moved into online delivery, the venture capital world became enchanted with the success of institutions like the University of Phoenix. Investments flowed into "virtual universities" in the early 2000s. By the end of that decade Kaplan University (a subsidiary of the Washington Post Company); Capella University; Career Education's InterContinental University, Bridgepoint's Ashford University, Le Cordon Bleu North America, and Sanford-Brown colleges; plus dozens of other for-profit organizations were serving hundreds of thousands of students. Since such a large proportion of these students were using federal financial aid to pay their fees to these companies, the US Congress became interested in how quality was being controlled and whether there were sufficient safeguards for the protection of federal dollars. The regional accrediting community found itself in the middle of Congressional inquiries. The rise of these for-profit institutions was so fast, the usual practices and expertise of the accreditation commissions' staffs were not equipped to fully understand them. States began again to assert their role in protecting their citizens from abuse and the federal government insisted that all online providers adhere to state rules regarding permission to operate. By 2010 the regional accrediting commissions began changing their standards and ways to examine different types of institutions in response to the shifting higher education landscape.

Table 7.2 Selection of issues in *The Distance Learner's Guide*

Technologies used in distance learning	Who offers distance learning
Synchronous versus asynchronous communication: a critical difference	Characteristics of successful distance learners
Is distance learning for you?	Beware of "diploma mills"
Choosing a distance learning provider	Overcoming the personal barriers to success in distance learning
Questions to ask any distance learning provider	Setting personal and academic goals
Why you need a computer	Health and wellness: relationship to college success
Power-user tips for using the web	Learning to learn
Are you ready for online courses?	Study guides and tips
Shopping for computing equipment and software	Time and stress management
Distance learner's library	Writing papers
What library services are available and how effective are they?	Tips for becoming a better student

Source: Western Cooperative for Educational Telecommunications, *The Distance Learner's Guide*, 2nd ed. Upper Saddle River, NJ: Prentice Hall, 2005.

WCET members realized early in this process that regulation and accrediting were not enough to help these consumers of online higher education. To get information into the hands of consumers, WCET staff worked with commercial publisher Prentice Hall to create and distribute *The Distance Learner's Guide* in 1999. The publication was successful enough that an updated and revised edition was released by Prentice Hall in 2005 to keep pace with the ever-changing online world. Samples of issues raised in the second edition of this book are listed in table 7.2.

As one looks at this list, it is easy to recognize many of the same issues any college student faces. Online students are rarely made aware of all the challenges they will face. Studying online is quite different from shopping online.

Now to the Future

By 2005, most colleges and universities in the West were using online technologies to serve students, either on- or off-campus. The emphasis shifted from how to reach new students to how technology can help offer better and more cost-effective services to students and faculty members. Higher education leaders, like their corporate counterparts, have ceased to be simply enamored by technology and are now trying to sort out the most appropriate uses of technology to help institutions achieve their missions.

Most institutions of higher education now have uniform course management software systems and faculty members are incorporating online resources into their classes (on- or off-campus). One foundation based in the West, the William and Flora Hewlett Foundation in California, saw an opportunity to take advantage of these online educational resources. Along with the Mellon Foundation, they funded the Massachusetts Institute of Technology (MIT) to put their courseware online. Almost all MIT course materials are now online and shared freely and openly worldwide. There are now dozens of other projects that fall into the Open Educational Resources (OER) movement. For instance, the Connexions project at Rice University in Texas allows faculty all over the world to contribute materials and use one another's materials. This is allowing multicampus courses to be developed. Adding to this collaboration is the work of Professor David Wiley of Utah who is leading efforts to build self-supporting social communities around these activities. This exciting movement allowed WCET to work directly with the United Nations Educational Scientific and Cultural Organization (UNESCO) for the worldwide development of open course materials. WCET staff has been part of the group that developed the concepts and understanding of OER for people at universities and colleges throughout the world.

Another project out of the western states has provided a tool that removes a tricky barrier to the sharing of intellectual "property" through OER. Creative Commons began at Stanford University in California and is now offering intellectual content licenses in multiple languages and national legal systems. The licenses available through Creative Commons for educational material, music, graphics, and so on, posted to the Internet allow the original creator of the material to let others know what they can do with the material. Some authors requite attribution, others require only noncommercial use of their materials, others permit their materials to be free for anyone to use and modify. Creative Commons is having a profound effect on opening access to human intellectual capital throughout the world.

Another area of rapidly emerging interest is the study of predictive analytics reporting (PAR). In 2011, WCET announced the federation of datasets from six institutions, comprising more than 640,000 anonymized student records and more than three million course-level records, focusing on 33 common variables. The goal of the PAR Framework is to identify variables that influence student retention and progression and to investigate the existence of unique demographic, pedagogical, or institutional factors affecting loss/retention and momentum/completion. One of the unique project goals is to explore patterns that emerge when the datasets from considerably different institutions are analyzed as a single, unified sample.

Forming an overlay on top of all of the recent activities and advances in higher education is the increasing impact of mobile devices and associated resources on the entire academic enterprise. It seems difficult to overstate the role that mobile devices, supplied both by institutions as well as individual students, will have on the way we teach, learn and do much of our daily business. Recent studies by Forrester Research, Inc., and others suggest that mobile devices, primarily tablet computers, will quickly become the preferred primary learning device for millions of knowledge workers and students.[2] This trend suggests we are on the cusp of substantial challenges (and opportunities) in creating and/or adapting content for such devices, whether it is for the delivery of educational content, professional development, or productivity-based activities. And for brick and mortar institutions, the rapid appearance of so many wireless devices has already strained infrastructures to the extent that many will continue to play catch-up as the number of devices per student (and employee) continue to grow.

While some of the earliest projects to successfully use technology to reach students began in the West, organizations in the region are now helping to lead the rest of the world in using technology for access to quality higher education resources.

Notes

*Sally Johnstone wishes to thank the early WCET staff members who facilitated the progression of quality distance learning practices and policies, Mollie McGill and Russ Poulin. More thanks go to Paul Albright for documenting western higher education progress.

**Ritchie Boyd would like to thank Bob Gillespie, Dan Jordt, and Marty Ringle for their lively discussions of the history of NorthWestNet and the future of academic computing. In addition, thanks go to Russ Poulin and Mike Offerman for their reflections on emerging educational consortia and companies in the West.

1. From a conversation with Debra Barger, dean of continuing education at California State University, Chico, and Ralph Mueter, previous dean of continuing education at California State University, Chico.
2. See Gillett, F. E. *Tablets Will Rule the Future Personal Computing Landscape* (Forrester Research, Inc., April 23, 2012), at www.forrester.com.

References

Atkins, D. E., J. S. Brown, and A. L. Hammond. *A Review of the Open Educational Resources (OER) Movement: Achievements, Challenges, and New Opportunities.* Retrieved from www.oerderves.org/wp-content/uploads/2007/03/a-review-of-the-open-educational-resources-oer-movement_ final.pdf, 2007, in January 2009.

Boyd, D. *Social Network Sites: Public, Private or What?* Retrieved from The Knowledge Tree http://kt.flexiblelearning.net.au/tkt2007/edition-13/social-network-sites-public-private-or-what/, 2007, in September 2008.

Dirr, P. *Putting Principles into Practice: Promoting Effective Support Services for Students in Distance Learning Programs: A Report on the Findings of a Survey.* Retrieved from www.wiche.edu/wcet/Resources/publications/index.htm, 1999.

Epper, R., and M. Garn. *Virtual College and University Consortia, A National Study.* Retrieved from www.wcet.info/resources/publications/vcu.pdf, 2003, in December 2004.

Johnstone, S. M. "Open Educational Resources." *Proceedings of the First Global Forum on Quality Assurance, Accreditation and Recognition of Qualification.* United Nations Educational Scientific and Cultural Organization, 2002.

——. "Signs of the Times: Change is Coming for E-Learning." *Educause Review,* Nov/Dec (2002): 15–24.

——. "Quality Issues in Electronic Delivery of Higher Education," *Journal for Public Service and Outreach,* 2 (3) (1997): 12–17.

Johnstone, S. M., and Connick, G. (eds.). *The Distance Learner's Guide*, 2nd ed. Upper Saddle River, NJ: Prentice Hall, 2005.

Johnstone, S. M., and D. Jones. "New Higher Education Trends Reflected in the Design of the Western Governors University," *On the Horizon* (1997).

Johnstone, S. M., and R. Poulin. "So, How Much Do Technologies Really Cost?" *Change*, 34 (2) (2002): 21–23.

Jones, D. P. *Technology Costing Methodology Handbook—Version 1.0*, Western Interstate Commission for Higher Education. Retrieved from www.wiche.edu /telecom/projects/tcm/TCM_Handbook_Final.pdf, 2001.

National Center for Educational Statistics. *Distance Education at Postsecondary Education Institutions*. US Department of Education, OERI Publication #2000–013, NCES, 1999.

Tapscott, D., and A. Williams. *Wikinomics: How Mass Collaboration Changes Everything*. New York, Portfolio, 2006.

Trombley, W. "Electronic Education," *CrossTalk* (California Higher Education Policy Center) 4 (3) (1969): 1, 12.

Western Cooperative for Educational Telecommunications. "WCET Announces Awards for Outstanding Work in Using Technology for Education" (press release). Retrieved from www.wcet.info/ documents/WOWAwardsPressRelease2004.asp, 2004, in January 2009.

———. *When Distance Education Crosses State Boundaries: Western States' Policies*. Boulder, CO: Western Interstate Commission for Higher Education, 1995.

8

THE GROWTH OF COMMUNITY COLLEGES IN THE WEST

CONDITIONS AND PUBLIC POLICY CHALLENGES

*Cheryl D. Lovell**

Community colleges have served as a way to deliver general education initially and then later training programs for many who were not able to attend traditional colleges. In this way they served as a point of access to postsecondary education since their inception. The history of community colleges has been documented extensively (Baker, 1994; Brint and Karabel, 1989; Cohen and Brawer, 1989; Goodchild and Wechsler, 1997). Expansion of these colleges in simple numbers has grown since the first community college was established in Joliet, Illinois, in 1901 (Deegan and Tillery, 1985) to more than 1,700 today (NCES, 2010). We know from these and other accounts that community colleges provided access for millions all over the United States (Cohen, 2001).

More than increased access has been gained with the evolution of community colleges. Greater reliance on these colleges became a significant strategy for the states to meet the educational needs of the growing diversity of student populations. Community colleges have been especially noteworthy in being a first point of entrance for diverse populations (Simmons, 1994). Many community colleges enrolled large minority populations in their programs, enabling them to graduate for careers or transfer to baccalaureate institutions.

The reader should notice that the "regional" chapters in the companion volume document the importance and growth of the community college "movement" in every subregion in the West, except for the mountain-plains states of North Dakota, South Dakota, and Montana. The evidence of the importance of community colleges throughout the rest of the West is noted throughout that volume. It seems appropriate, therefore, to designate one chapter to highlight their development across the West with particular attention to the policy issues related to their historical development.

In this chapter in the present book, I provide descriptive data to lay the foundation of the sweeping influence of the community colleges in today's postsecondary environment on the national scene. I chronicle the growth of community colleges in the 15 Western Interstate Commission for Higher Education (WICHE) states over the last six decades and explore the recent public policy issues involving the community colleges in these states. Growth is presented numerically in terms of the percent of students enrolled in community colleges and as a percentage of the state's community college enrollment, compared to the total postsecondary enrollment to illustrate this tremendous increase in participation. Specific attention is offered noting the range of community colleges that serve special populations, such as Tribal Colleges and Universities (TCU) and Hispanic-Serving Institutions (HSI).

Since this growth often required new resources to meet these demanding needs, an exploration of the state funding patterns shows how community colleges faired compared to the total funding for higher education. The state data revealed that community colleges received a larger share of the state's budget than their four-year counterparts in many of the western states. While simple descriptive data are presented in this chapter, it is important to note that these kinds of summary data of this magnitude are not available anywhere else in this format. Multiple sources of state data were used in addition to federal data. The key factor that made the compelling case for this chapter was an historic overview of their development and then the longitudinal nature of the data. Six decades of data on any issue or subject matter showed key data points in the 15 WICHE states over 60 years in their dramatic growth. In addition, this chapter includes a matrix that summarizes state policy issues affecting community colleges. These policy issues represent those for 2003 (the 50th year of WICHE) through the 2011 legislative calendars. These legislative policy issues are presented state-by-state for the 15 WICHE states. Finally, this chapter concludes with a few observations about the continued growth and reliance on community colleges in the West as well as a brief glance at the future for community colleges in the region.

COMMUNITY COLLEGES NATIONALLY

An overview of community colleges nationally portrays the growth and expansive nature of the community colleges across the United States. The US Department of Education recognizes a total of 1,721 two-year institutions, including 1,000 public colleges, 85 independent colleges, and 636 for-profit colleges (NCES, Fall 2010). In 2005, there were 31 classified as tribal colleges (Phillippe and Sullivan, 2005) and today that number has increased to 37 (American Indian Higher Education Consortium, 2011). In total, these 1,721 colleges enroll approximately 12 million students, with just over 7.4 million taking courses for credit (NCES, 2008).

Community colleges are truly serving as a first point of access to postsecondary education as demographic data reveals. About 43 percent of all freshmen at community colleges are first-time enrollees, as noted by the American Association of Community Colleges (Fast Facts, AACC, 2011). Whether attending a community college for a terminal vocational degree or as a point of transfer to complete the bachelor's degree, the community colleges play a critical role in the nation's postsecondary system. In total, the community colleges enroll 44 percent of all undergraduates. Of this student population, 58 percent are female and 42 percent are male, and most (60 percent) attend part-time (Fast Facts, AACC, 2011). Community colleges enroll 52 percent of all Hispanics attending undergraduate postsecondary education, as well as 44 percent of African Americans, 45 percent of Asian/Pacific Islanders, and 55 percent of Native Americans. The average age of all students attending community colleges in the United States is 28 (Fast Facts, AACC, 2011). Almost 47 percent of students attending a community college receive financial aid of some type. Of those with federal assistance, one-third receive Pell grants, about 6 percent utilize the subsidized Stafford loans, and about 5 percent receive the unsubsidized Stafford loans (AACC, 2011).

COMMUNITY COLLEGES IN THE WICHE STATES

As displayed in table 8.1, the 15 WICHE states have 597 two-year institutions within their borders, which is just over a third (35%) of the national number of two-year institutions (AACC, 2011). Also, 14 percent of the independent two-year colleges are located in WICHE states. Of the two-year colleges located in the WICHE states, almost 50 percent of them are for profit—a dramatic 60 percent increase from 2000. A clear majority of the TCUs are located in the WICHE states (74.2%) (AIHEC, 2011).

Table 8.1 Number and type of two-year institutions, by decade

States	# Publics	# Independent	# For profit	# Tribal	Total # CCs	# HSI
1950						
Alaska	0	0	0		0	
Arizona	3	0	1		4	
California	50	9	4		63	
Colorado	4	0	1		5	
Hawaii	3	1	0		4	
Idaho	1	0	0		1	
Montana	3	0	0		3	
Nevada	0	0	1		1	
New Mexico	4	0	0		4	
North Dakota	5	0	1		6	
Oregon	1	1	0		2	
South Dakota	0	2	0		2	
Utah	3	1	0		4	
Washington	12	2	1		15	
Wyoming	3	0	0		3	

Continued

Table 8.1 Continued

States	# Publics	# Independent	# For profit	# Tribal	Total # CCs	# HSI
1970						
Alaska	1	0	0		1	
Arizona	8	0	8		16	
California	93	12	15		120	
Colorado	12	0	4		16	
Hawaii	7	1	0		8	
Idaho	2	0	4		6	
Montana	6	0	0		6	
Nevada	2	0	4		6	
New Mexico	12	0	0		12	
North Dakota	5	0	2		7	
Oregon	12	1	13		26	
South Dakota	3	3	0		6	
Utah	6	1	4		11	
Washington	23	2	4		29	
Wyoming	7	0	0		7	
1990						
Alaska	2	0	0	0	2	0
Arizona	19	0	16	0	35	9
California	111	17	48	1	177	58
Colorado	16	1	12	0	28	5
Hawaii	7	1	2	0	10	0
Idaho	2	0	6	0	8	0
Montana	7	1	0	6	13	0
Nevada	4	0	5	0	9	0
New Mexico	16	0	1	3	19	17
North Dakota	5	0	5	4	14	0
Oregon	16	1	22	0	38	0
South Dakota	4	4	2	1	11	0
Utah	7	1	15	0	23	0
Washington	31	3	19	1	54	1
Wyoming	7	0	2	0	9	0
2000						
Alaska	3	0	1	0	4	0
Arizona	19	5	16	1	41	10
California	111	17	59	1	187	53
Colorado	16	1	16	0	32	4
Hawaii	7	1	2	0	10	0
Idaho	3	0	7	0	10	0
Montana	7	1	3	6	17	0
Nevada	4	0	5	0	9	0
New Mexico	16	0	1	3	20	15
North Dakota	5	0	5	4	14	0
Oregon	17	1	23	0	40	0
South Dakota	4	4	2	1	11	0
Utah	7	1	15	0	23	0
Washington	33	3	20	1	57	0
Wyoming	7	0	2	0	9	0

Continued

Table 8.1 Continued

States	# Publics	# Independent	# For profit	# Tribal	Total # CCs	# HSI
2010						
Alaska	2	1	1	1	5	0
Arizona	20	0	20	1	41	18
California	119	6	112	0	237	125
Colorado	15	1	34	0	50	12
Hawaii	6	0	1	0	7	0
Idaho	4	0	16	0	20	0
Montana	12	1	6	6	25	0
Nevada	1	1	16	0	18	1
New Mexico	20	0	5	2	27	18
North Dakota	6	1	7	3	17	0
Oregon	17	1	24	0	42	0
South Dakota	5	4	3	1	13	0
Utah	8	1	25	0	34	0
Washington	27	3	22	0	52	2
Wyoming	7	0	2	0	9	0

Sources: Numerous state reports, state websites, WICHE reports, and NCES data were utilized in constructing this table.

Access Gained through Growth of HSIs and TCUs

Historically, minority populations in the United States have been underrepresented in attendance and completion patterns in postsecondary education. Lack of experience with higher education can often make it difficult for individuals to attend (Warren, 1985). Participation can be further limited due to geographic and psychological barriers. Many states and institutions provide funds for minority or underrepresented populations to attend college in the hopes of maintaining a diverse student body. The western region tends to have high concentrations of Hispanic and Native American populations. Institutions dedicated to serving these populations provide a critical point of access and participation in postsecondary education (Guyden, 1999; Laden, 1999; Pavel, Inglebret, and VanDenHende, 1999; Simmons, 1994; Warren, 1985). Furthermore, Katsinas, D'Amico, and Friedel (2011) note, "community colleges are the portal of entry into higher education for millions of academically-talented minority, low income, first generation, and adult students" (p. 1). They further state that "access threats are acute in large states with fast-growing minority populations" (p. 2), which accurately describes some of the WICHE states, such as California, Colorado, Arizona, and New Mexico. Clearly California's increase in Hispanic population is above all the other WICHE states with a 28 percent growth in Hispanic population from 2000 to 2010 alone (Katsinas et al., p. 7)!

As of Fall 2010, there were 293 HSIs throughout the United States (including Puerto Rico) with 123 classified as for-profit institutions, according to NCES. HSIs are defined "as institutions whose enrollment of Hispanic students reaches 25 percent of full-time equivalent undergraduate enrollment and not less than 50 percent of Hispanic students enrolled are low-income individuals" (20 USC 1061). The second criterion, related to income, is not currently utilized, and institutions are identified as HSIs solely on enrollments. HSI has only been used as a descriptor of colleges and universities since the late 1980s and not officially noted as a classification category until 1992 (Laden, 1999). The contribution of these institutions is significant to the higher education community as "approximately half of all Hispanic students enrolled in all of postsecondary education are enrolled in HSIs" (Laden, 1999, p. 151). When considering two-year institutions only, WICHE states account for nearly 60 percent (59.7%) of the HSIs. It is interesting to note that this percentage corresponds to the share of the nation's Hispanic population that calls the West home. In 2010, just about 42 percent (41.6%) of these HSIs located in WICHE states are labeled as for-profits, as derived from the data displayed in table 8.1. With the high concentration of Hispanic populations in several WICHE states, these institutions are critical providers of educational opportunities (Pardon, 1994). As much as one-third of California's population is Hispanic and close to one-fourth in Arizona (Laden, 1999). The data on HSIs match these population concentrations with Arizona, California, and New Mexico having the bulk of the HSIs among WICHE states.

On the other hand, TCUs are also heavily represented in the WICHE region. TCUs are defined as "postsecondary institutions where funding is provided by the US Department of the Interior to those institutions where 50 percent or more of student enrollment is American Indian" (25 USC 1801 et seq.). With a significant portion of the nation's American Indian population living within the WICHE region, about three-quarters (74.2%) of all TCUs are located in these 15 states. Pressures are great for these institutions to serve the needs of both the individuals and communities (Pavel and Colby, 1992). Pavel, Inglebret, and VanDenHende (1999) also note that "promoting access to postsecondary education among American Indians is perhaps one of the most central missions of tribal colleges" (p. 136). Accordingly, these institutions are key providers of local access to postsecondary education.

Enrollments in Community Colleges in the WICHE States

Community college enrollments in the WICHE states have escalated throughout this 50-year period, outstripping enrollments in the four-year sector. Table 8.2 displays the percentage of enrollments in the community colleges compared to the total state enrollments in postsecondary education. Each state reported enrollment data differently so that consistency of data across and even within western states could not be found. Further trend data are not always consistent, given various methods for calculating enrollment that may differ from year to year as well as often vary from state to state. The author derived this summary data from numerous datasets on enrollment for each state for each of the decades noted in table 8.2.

Table 8.2 Percent of state enrollments in community colleges for the WICHE states

	1950	1970	1990	2000	2010
Alaska	3.6	4.29	3.28	2.81	2.5
Arizona	28.53	43.74	44.37	49.56	51.3
California	35.29	47.5	53.67	59.78	60.28
Colorado	17.33	23.1	26.42	27.33	30.97
Hawaii	17.1	31.51	41	46.85	40.12
Idaho	6.44	9	12.84	16.63	24.95
Montana	7.22	8.65	9.89	12.12	21.61
Nevada	16.78	32.88	40.25	42.55	53
New Mexico	25.19	34.74	39.71	42.62	54.68
North Dakota	9.52	15.2	20.39	20.85	14.23
Oregon	29.87	42.39	43.81	43.62	45.33
South Dakota	1.42	3.72	9.91	14.94	12.36
Utah	11.89	19.49	31.12	18.61	21.71
Washington	33.79	43.65	55.52	57.77	42.55
Wyoming	24.18	38.9	51.72	52.28	66

Sources: Numerous state reports, state websites, interviews, and regional (WICHE) and national databases (HEGIS, IPEDS) were utilized in constructing this table.

As might be expected, enrollment growth occurred in every state across the last 60 years. The key trend to note is the magnitude of this growth in several states that reflect the importance of community colleges in these states. For example, in California 60 percent of the state's enrollment in postsecondary education is at the community college level. Washington has a sizable population attending community colleges as do Arizona, New Mexico, and Oregon. The pressure for access to postsecondary education is especially apparent in Wyoming with 66 percent of its enrollments at the community college level in 2010. Wyoming only has one public four-year institution so the need for community college opportunities is great. While these percentages are revealing in terms of understanding where students attend; they do not account for cross enrollments or dual enrollments. Nor do the data reveal anything about the recently named phenomena of "swirling and double dipping" enrollments (McCormick, 2003). Students could be simultaneously enrolled in a community college and baccalaureate institution or could attend the four-year institution first and then transfer to a community college. Although there are several enrollment patterns that are not accounted for in this table, it is nonetheless helpful to see how important community colleges serve the states' population within postsecondary education. Community colleges are clearly a key higher educational provider in the WICHE states.

FUNDING COMMUNITY COLLEGES IN THE WICHE STATES

Community colleges can receive local, state, and federal funding, depending on the local property laws and state funding mechanisms. Table 8.3

Table 8.3 Share of state budget allocated to all of higher education and share of higher education budget allocated to community colleges

	1950	1970	1990	2000	2010
Alaska					
all HED	9.92	10.79	12.33	9.38	7.48
to CCs	2.79	19.18	17.8	18.49	See text
Arizona					
all HED	6.42	15.49	18.4	14.89	12.04
to CCs	4.59	18.35	12.05	15.34	14.93
California					
all HED	14.02	17.23	14.35	11.86	9.35
to CCs	14.76	15.79	25.9	21.43	41.35
Colorado					
all HED	11.56	14.06	8.49	5.73	8.83
to CCs	19.25	13.79	14.31	24.32	26
Hawaii					
all HED	14.9	13.49	14.49	10.89	4.15
to CCs	5.82	13.71	25.69	16.38	33.4
Idaho					
all HED	11.99	8.02	9.65	10.47	13.75
to CCs	4.13	28.85	20.96	13.59	21.65
Montana					
all HED	5.97	14.83	12.41	8.68	11.17
to CCs	5.29	12.1	16.96	27.47	4.54
Nevada					
all HED	6.4	10.96	10.22	6.89	18.01
to CCs	8.68	23.81	15.08	28.85	28
New Mexico					
all HED	7.29	9.97	8.35	6.87	17.31
to CCs	60.79	17.36	23.4	28.19	19.05
North Dakota					
all HED	5.42	10.41	14.9	8.23	9.56
to CCs	7.86	13.36	17.67	22.62	15.16
Oregon					
all HED	6.52	12.23	11.61	6.49	5.2
to CCs	6.28	24.48	27.11	22.34	33.62
South Dakota					
all HED	9.63	16.4	9.57	6.46	17.52
to CCs	5.02	13.6	18.13	17.61	15
Utah					
all HED	7.23	11.5	8.91	8.34	6.65
to CCs	5.17	15.17	19.76	23.69	20
Washington					
all HED	4.53	10.51	9.96	6.21	11.66
to CCs	6.51	16.57	21.62	22.64	41.84
Wyoming					
all HED	4.15	16.44	7.71	8.23	
to CCs	5.79	18.35	16.23	26.69	

Sources: Numerous state websites, state reports, publications, interviews and regional (WICHE) and federal databases (HEGIS, IPEDS), as well as SHEEO and *Grapevine* data, were consulted to construct the table.

displays the percentage of state funds allocated to all of higher education and then the percent of that amount that went to community colleges. Figure 8.1 provides a graphic display of the same data. Trend data are difficult at best, given the various methodologies utilized by the states and the multiple state agencies within states that report financial data. For example, in some states, branch campuses of main universities that have two-year mission functions are counted in some years with the main campus and in some years in calculations for the community colleges in that state. Careful effort was made to keep the sources consistent within states for this table—nonetheless the reader should use caution with the results. The inclusion of stimulus, American Recovery and Reinvestment Act (ARRA), also complicates trend comparisons within states. The key point to notice about funding for community colleges in the WICHE states is that over the 60 years for most states the community colleges have received an increasing share of the higher education budget. State budgets overall have declined in most of the WICHE states. For example, in the last budget cycle, three WICHE states (California, Nevada, and Oregon) have experienced over 20 percent reductions in their state budgets. Three states (Washington, Arizona, and South Dakota) have had budget shortfalls in the 10 percent to 20 percent range. Five states (Idaho, Utah, Colorado, New Mexico, and Hawaii) have had less than 10 percent budget cuts. Only four WICHE states have had no budget shortfall (Wyoming, North Dakota, Montana, and Alaska). Clearly a range of financial ability across the WICHE states exists to fund higher education (Center on Budget and Policy Priorities, 2011), where some states have experienced severe budget shortfalls that they must make up. For example, in Arizona the recent state budget shortfall was over a billion dollars and in California shortfalls have been the topic of conversation for several years with upwards of several billion dollars.

To further illustrate the percentages, figure 8.1 visually shows the trends over the 50 years. This graphic representation reveals the magnitude of funding to higher education and specifically to community colleges. There is substantial growth in allocations to community colleges as well as wide variations in funding patterns that are better viewed in this graphic presentation.

Over the years, community colleges have received a good percentage of the total higher education funding in most of the WICHE states. When looking at the most recent decade, the funding percentages were especially strong for community colleges in every state. For Alaska, the recent decade data are not reported for the share going to community colleges in light of the changes in funding that followed the changes in community college governance with community college budgets now part of the university rather than as individual campuses. A caution should be offered about these data. In no way do the data displayed in table 8.3 or figure 8.1 imply implicitly or explicitly that funding is adequate for either higher education in general or community colleges specifically. These data only reveal the percentages allocated and do not suggest appropriateness of funding.

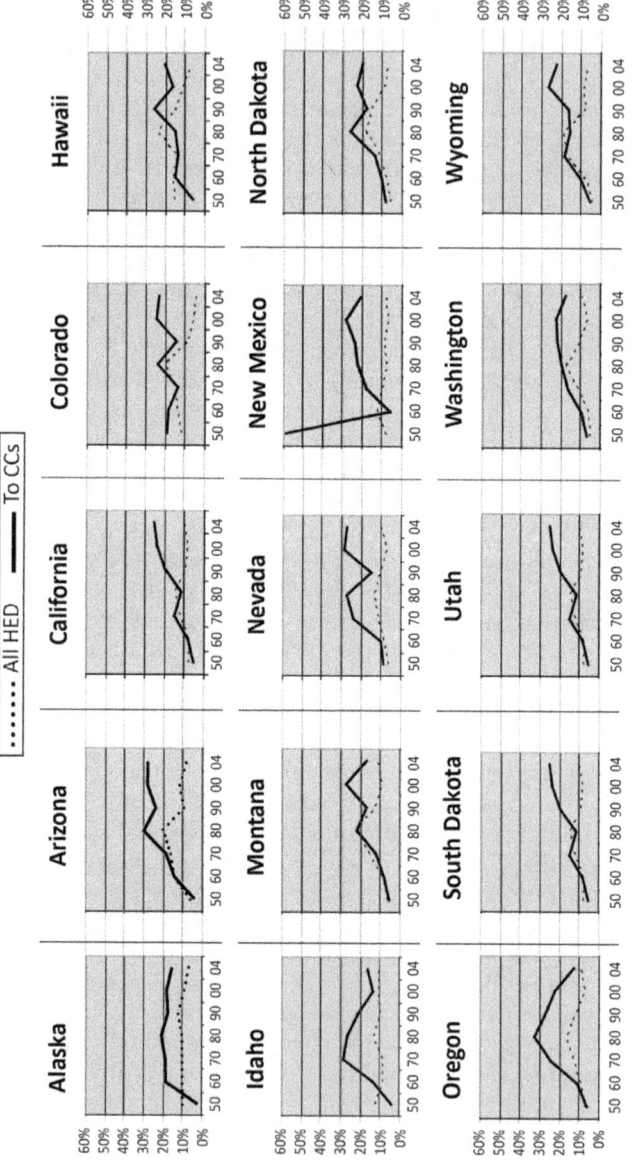

Figure 8.1 Share of state budget allocated to all of higher education and share of higher education budget allocated to community colleges—graphical representation.

Sources: Numerous Websites, state reports, WICHE data, and NCES data were consulted to construct these figures.

Public Policy Issues Confronting Community Colleges in the West

Nationally, postsecondary institutions are dealing (and have been for several decades) with a plethora of policy issues relating to: accountability, assessment, diversity, finance, governance, workforce development, homeland security, economic declines, increases in tuition, degree completions, and data-related issues. More recently, however, there are more state legislative enactments dealing with specific transfer, co-enrollments (with high schools), and early access issues, better ways to accomplish remediation, and institutional rewards for retention and completion. All of these support a clear interest in getting students into the postsecondary education pipeline as quickly as possible, keeping them moving forward as efficiently as possible, and making sure credits are accounted for that will allow students to complete the certificate or degree as promptly as possible. Each of these policy issues requires the time and energy of the institutional staff as well as system and statewide resources to propose workable remedies. The range and scope of public policy issues affect colleges and universities differently. Community colleges seem to be particularly influenced with the range of issues and potential implications. In a prior study, I observed that these local colleges tend to "feel" the impact of legislative enactments much quicker, and they seem to often have a much deeper effect on them than four-year institutions (Lovell, 2000). Cohen, however, takes a broader and more exhaustive view by noting that "government affects every enterprise" (Cohen, 2001, p. 3). At the federal level, I also noted that the typical range of public policy issues affect community colleges (Lovell, 2001), including funded mandates, unfunded mandates, federal tax policies, federal research funding, and federal student financial aid. These broad areas of federal policies vary in their influence on the community college. For example, when federal financial aid policies are changed by new legislation, it can have a high and immediate influence on the community college, while changes in federal research funding would have less influence on the community college than it might for a research university (Lovell, 2000). This is especially true, for example, when US Department of Labor initiatives provide targeted funding to institutions to make available certain curricular programs that support various business and economic opportunities. Community colleges are often the most appropriate institutions to receive these targeted funds, since they typically have the vocational-focused programs. Community colleges are also the institutions that most readily attract vocational-focused students who may also be eligible for special funding from the US Department of Labor. Thus, often new federal initiatives are felt first at the community college.

State legislation also influences the community colleges. Legislative issues in the WICHE states are similar to those of the rest of the country in terms of the campus being required to comply with new legislation and accommodate many new accountability mandates. For example, Townsend and Twombly (2001) explore policy matters in their book on future issues for community colleges. The issues they cite are similar to those passed by legislatures in the WICHE states.

As displayed in table 8.4, the examples of legislative enactments directly related to community colleges in the WICHE states are vast in scope and content. Represented here are policy issues from 2003, the year of WICHE's fiftieth anniversary, through the 2011 legislative year. This list is illustrative of policy issues facing community colleges to give the reader insight into the vast range of policy issues community colleges face on a regular basis. It is not intended to be exhaustive and does not include references to any of the typical annual enactments, such as: appropriations, authority to collect property taxes, tuition-setting bills, building projects, the issuance of bonds, revisions to statewide educational savings plans, or name changes of colleges. Most states have bills similar to these that on an annual basis deal with the mundane yet necessary and required actions of the state.

The table does display legislative enactments specifically relating to activities of the state and their community colleges. Many of the issues deal with a critical area of concern regarding economic development and workforce training. Alaska, California, Colorado, Hawaii, New Mexico, North Dakota, Washington, and Wyoming each had bills relating to some aspect of workforce training and economic development in 2003 and 2007–2008. In early years of this specific period as displayed in table 8.4, governance issues were of concern in California, Idaho, North Dakota, Oregon, Washington, and Wyoming. In Idaho, Nevada, and Oregon in 2003 and 2007, there were calls for studies to review aspects of the decision-making processes for institutions statewide. North Dakota and Washington had bills relating to statewide goals and strategic master plan expectations. The legislature in Nevada called for a statewide audit of the higher education system to review capital construction, athletic program costs, administrative costs, enrollment data, investment practices, and bidding policies. Special targeted funding were examples of key policy opportunities in North Dakota, South Dakota, and Oregon. Moreover, many other legislatures also have an interest in improving the efficiencies of their institutional systems. In the last legislative year, California, Colorado, Idaho, Montana, South Dakota, and Washington addressed governance issues. The focus for California was on integrating community college credits (via transcripts), which would help facilitate the transfer process and on requiring the development of a common college-readiness standard. Similarly, in Colorado, the legislature established an educational success taskforce to study the pipeline/transition benchmarks to ensure that support systems are in place to increase student successes. Washington's focus this last legislative year (2012) was to require common student identifiers to follow community and technical college students into the bachelor-level institutions to allow for tracking the success of a transfer.

Growth in enrollments can gain legislative notice, such as in Nevada, where the legislature passed a bill to allow better transfer of tuition credits from community colleges to the baccalaureate institutions. As previously noted, Nevada's growth in enrollment at the community college level has

Table 8.4 Examples of public policy issues involving community colleges in the WICHE region, 2003–2011

Policy Issue	Legislative Description	Bill #	Month/Year
ALASKA			
Finance/Enrollment	Allows for differential rates of tuition for CCs different from rates set by regional campus centers with approval	R05.10.030. Authority to Set Tuition Rates	May 2010
Workforce Development	Requires students who do not return to Alaska after earning postsecondary degrees in the medical field to repay financial aid provided by the state	HB 18	Jan. 2007
Economic Development	DOEED—AK Vocational Tech Center successes	HB 318	Feb. 2003
ARIZONA			
Adult Education	Describes funding guidelines for Adult Education	SB 1617	Mar. 2011
Admissions	Sets criteria for CC enrollment and credit-hour limits	SB 1152	Mar. 2011
Student Status Classification	Requires each CC to report in-state and out-of-state student classifications related to immigration status	15–1803/ Title 15	Feb. 2010
Transfer & Articulation	Initiates a statewide articulation and transfer system and common course numbering system	SB 1186	May 2010
Financial Aid	Establishes financial aid program for CC graduates transferring to private universities	SB 1012	Jan. 2008
Political Activities	Allows student orgs to meet on CC property	SB 1105	May. 2003
Governance	Eliminates CC board—Effective 7/20/03	SB 1360	Jan. 2003
CALIFORNIA			
Articulation	Establishes a process to ease transfer within the CA CC system	AB 1023	Sept. 2011
Articulation	Enacts the College Promise Partnership Act allowing for HS students to take college classes at CCs	SB 650	Oct. 2011
Governance-Board #	Allows CC governing board districts to change board election systems	AB 684	Oct. 2011
Governance/System Planning	Requires a procedure to facilitate the electronic receipt and transmission of student transcripts by districts	AB 1056	Oct. 2011

Continued

Table 8.4 Continued

Policy Issue	Legislative Description	Bill #	Month/Year
Governance/System Planning	Requires the development of a common college-readiness standard	AB 743	Oct. 2011
Workforce Training & Economic Development	Allocates funding to CCs to improve and expand career technical education and lower division public HE including the hiring of additional faculty	SB 1330	Sept. 2010
Governance & Articulation	Requires the CA State University and the Office of the Chancellor of the CA CCs to establish methods to inform students, college advisers, and the general public about specified transfer pathways	AB 2302	Sept. 2010
Governance/System Planning	Allows for "gifted students" identified by K-12 districts to attend college classes at CCs to ease college transition	AB 1713	Sept. 2010
Governance/System Planning	Requires the CC board to establish a taskforce to examine specified best practices and models for accomplishing student success	SB 1143	Sept. 2010
Governance/System Planning	Requires that a student who receives an associate degree be deemed eligible for transfer into a CSU institution, and conditions state funding for CCs on its development and granting of associate degrees for transfer	SB 1440	Sept. 2010
Workforce Training & Economic Development	Establishes the Pilot Program for Innovative Nursing and Allied Health Care Profession Education at CCs	AB 2385	Sept. 2010
Articulation	Requires the implementation of articulated nursing degree transfer pathways between CA CSU and CC system	AB 1295	Oct. 2009
Governance/System Planning	Refines HE reporting requirements to provide for more effective, manageable, and transparent reporting	AB 1182	Oct. 2009
Articulation	Requires that funds allocated for the Transfer Education and Articulation Program are available to support transfer and articulation projects and common course numbering projects	SBX 34	Feb. 2009

Continued

Table 8.4 Continued

Policy Issue	Legislative Description	Bill #	Month/Year
Workforce Training & Economic Development	Establishes new funding system for state CCs with criteria and standards developed by the board of governors	SB 361	Oct. 2006
Employment Fac.	Part-time faculty contracts	AB 654	Sept. 2003
Enrollment/ Cross-enrollment	Extends Donahoe Act permitting cross-campus enrollments— Allows fees to be charged	AB 1783	Sept. 2003
Governance-Board #	Revises membership of the Board of Governors	SB 644	Apr. 2003
COLORADO			
Governance/System Planning	Creates an educational success taskforce charged with collecting and reviewing P-20 data	SB 111	Apr. 2011
Financial Aid/ Workforce Training	Creates a scholarship program to assist persons employed in early childhood education to obtain an associate of arts degree	HB 1030	Jan. 2010
Articulation	Requires creation of statewide college degree transfer agreements between institutions of HE	HB 1208	Feb. 2010
Governance/System Planning	Authorizes CCs and JCs to offer two-year degree programs with academic designation	SB 088	Feb. 2010
Articulation	Requires creation of statewide college degree transfer agreements between institutions of HE	HB 1208	Feb. 2010
Governance/System Planning	Authorizes CCs and JCs to offer two-year degree programs with academic designation	SB 088	Feb. 2010
Workforce Training	Establishes postsecondary transitions program and fund to address retention and achievement issues among economically disadvantaged students	HB 07–1098	Apr. 2007
Financial Aid	Allows state-supported institutions (including CCs) to offer fixed-rate tuition contracts to incoming students	HB 07–1193	Feb. 2007
Workforce Training	Allows CCHE to approve education paraprofessional preparation programs in CCs or universities	HB 1159	Apr. 2003
HAWAII			
Workforce Training & Economic Development	Redesign of career and technical education from a "hobby style" curriculum to support of economic development	HCR 185	Jan. 2003

Continued

Table 8.4 Continued

Policy Issue	Legislative Description	Bill #	Month/Year
IDAHO			
Governance	Revises laws relating to election campaign contributions for CC trustees	SB 1107	Mar. 2011
Financial Aid	Forbids postsecondary benefits, including tuition assistance and scholarships, to undocumented students	SB 1303	Feb. 2010
Governance	Revises CC trustee election procedures and creates sub-districts	HB 663	Feb. 2010
Governance	Revises procedures and elections for formation of CC districts	HB 237	Apr. 2007
Governance/System Planning	Calls for a review of the higher education system (greater convergence of goals; transfer credits; maximum efficiencies; avoid duplication; reorganize governance system (cost savings)	HCR 31	Apr. 2003
MONTANA			
Governance/System Planning	Resolution urging the development of shared K-20 policy goals and accountability measures	SJ 8	Mar. 2009
Funding	Revises CC funding statutes with new cost calculations	SB 12	May 2007
NEVADA			
Accountability	Call for legislative audit of system (capital construction; athletic program costs; administrative costs; enrollment data; investment policies; bidding)	AB 148	June 2005
Articulation	Allows transfer of credits from CC to university	AB 507	May 2003
Academic Program Review	Creates Committee to Evaluate Higher Education Programs (needs analysis of academic programs; gaps in needs and offerings; feasibility of relocating existing resources to meet critical needs not currently being met; determine if funds are being distributed evenly to CCs and universities)	AB 203	June 2003
NEW MEXICO			
Articulation	Requires students to complete a final next-step plan during HS senior year/prior to graduation	SB 360	July 2010
Articulation	Establishes dual HS/College credit guidelines for Indian Education HS and Tribal Colleges	HB 90	July 2010

Continued

Table 8.4 Continued

Policy Issue	Legislative Description	Bill #	Month/Year
Funding	Creates a formula for allocating funds for adult education from a state endowed fund	SB 575	July 2010
Professional Development	Expands faculty endowment fund to include CCs	HB 983	Apr. 2007
Governance	Expands branch CC boards	SB 984	Apr. 2007
Workforce Training & Economic Development	Transfers the authority for adult basic education to the Commission on Higher Education (must provide statewide planning of adult education)	SB 691	Apr. 2003
NORTH DAKOTA			
Governance	Requires that the commissioner of HE improve the interplay between the university system and tribally controlled CCs	HB 1566	Jan. 2009
Funding	Provides targeted funding to tribally controlled community colleges	SB 2404	Mar. 2007
OREGON			
Transfer/Articulation	Requires Boards of Education to develop standards for ease of CC credit transfer for baccalaureate degrees and eases associate degree completion processes	HB 3521	Apr. 2011
Governance/System Planning	Specifies percentage of undergraduate courses to be taught by full-time tenured and tenure-track faculty at public institutions of HE	HB 2557	Feb. 2009
Governance/System Planning	Requires CCs offering new career pathways certificates to give notice to Department of CCs and Workforce Development	HB 3117	Apr. 2009
Workforce Training	Requires work toward the development of applied baccalaureate degree programs	HB 3093	May 2009
Governance/System Planning	Requires the development of a plan to increase collaboration among K-12, CCs, labor, business and industry in relation to career and technical education	HB 2732	June 2009
Workforce Training & Economic	Creates in the Department of CCs and Workforce Development the Oregon Career Readiness Certification Program	HB 2398	July 2009
Workforce Training	Awards grants to CCs for programs that help prepare students for college	HB 3144	Mar. 2007

reached almost 43 percent of the total enrollment in postsecondary education. With that level of community college enrollment, it is critical that policies and practices are in place to allow ease of transfer from the two-year to four-year level. California is equally concerned with allowing students to cross-enroll in both two- and four-year institutions. States with high-enrollment growths typically will find legislative enactments that support more access and greater efficiency across higher education systems in their states. Often legislative enactments are required to create policies from system to system. Several states, as noted on table 8.4, have addressed issues to increase transfer and articulation agreements. Focus on these statewide agreements can support student completion and can influence issues of efficiency and productivity.

Efficiency or performance-oriented legislative enactments were passed in some of the WICHE states in 2003, as were several bills to revise the way community colleges receive their state allocations. From previous legislative enactments, it is becoming clearer that efficiency-oriented legislation most likely will have an influence on all sectors of state government, and not just community colleges. Washington's bill will create performance-funding contracts between the state and the institution. New Mexico created a Higher Education Performance Fund to allow for incentive-funding schemes to alter state funding to colleges and universities. Reviews of the higher education systems are required as a result of legislative enactments in Idaho and Nevada. Colorado also created performance-funding requirements of the postsecondary systems and recently reinforced its prior commitment to performance contracts with additional legislation in the last legislative calendar year.

Across the WICHE region and throughout the United States, one policy problem that has been getting increasingly troublesome is the rapid rise of community college tuition over the past several decades, undermining their central role in access to higher education. Between 1994–1995 and 2007–2008, average tuitions in all community colleges in the WICHE region increased 106 percent; excluding California, where average tuition increased 116 percent. This compares with a rise in the Consumer Price Index (CPI) during the same time of about 40 percent (Brian Prescott, WICHE, personal communication, 2008).

CRITICAL WESTERN STATES AND RECENT COMMUNITY COLLEGE ACTIONS

Four western states have been chosen to profile new developments in community college action: Washington, Arizona, Oregon, and California. As Washington state funding for the community colleges has diminished over the past ten years, the college costs have doubled to about $4,200 annually during that time (SHEEO, 2013). Well above average for WICHE states, this level of tuition, while still significantly lower than for public four-year universities, influences access by placing more burden on financial aid. Critically federal financial aid is not currently available to part-time student, the majority of those attending community colleges. Thus costs adversely influence students' persistence, since they refrain from increasing their debt burdens for college. Tuition levels for ESL and ABE programs, historically lower, are also rising with the pressure of reduced state funding. The potential of new federal immigration laws that require English as a condition of the "path for citizenship" will only increase the pressures on these programs. To deal with these problems, state higher education leaders are increasing emphasis upon efficiency in the postsecondary system through new efforts to articulate better transfer policies from K-12 schooling to four-year institutions, to provide more funding for concurrent enrollment, and enable more flexible transfer of credit.

Arizona community colleges are the West's epicenter for seeking to overcome its postsecondary persistence and graduation crisis. In 2008, slightly more than half of its high school completers went on to higher education, making the state forty-fifth in the nation. A statewide initiative, Getting AHEAD, brought together all higher education leaders, the business community, and the legislature to fashion new approaches to improving degree completion. The Lumina Foundation also contributed a $1.5 million grant to assist the state's Maricopa 10 campus community college district in 2011. President Tom Anderes of the Arizona Board of Regents and Maricopa Chancellor Rufus Glasper joined to launch the initiative. Stakes are high since in Arizona 60 percent of all undergraduates attend community colleges and are two-thirds Hispanic, as Pat Callan notes in a recent Policy Alert, "Affordability and Transfer: Critical to Increasing Baccalaureate Degree Completion" from the National Center for Public Policy and Higher Education (June 2011). Importantly, while only 22 percent graduate and transfer to a four-year institution initially, in two more years another 25 percent transfer, resulting in an overall 47 percent of its students moving on to four-year institutions. However the report shows that from 1999 to 2009 Arizona's cost for community college education soared 120 percent in the state making it the highest rise of community college tuition in the nation, and a significant barrier for high school graduates attending college. Other state initiatives to improve Arizona's postsecondary workforce involve access to online and distance education with new online postsecondary advising, seek greater career specializations at regional universities, and increase more coordinated postsecondary planning to improve graduation through Arizona's University and Community College Joint Council of Presidents.

Like other western states, Oregon's community colleges have increased their tuition in response to the decline in state funding. Community college state funding dropped 25 percent from $6,083 to $4,547 per student. In response, the 2011–2012 tuition was increased to $4,400 annually, which represented an increase of 100 percent over the past decade. System efficiencies have also come under greater scrutiny: legislators have expressed concern about the amount of remedial work being required by the community colleges, which in turn has put pressure on them and the P-12 system.

Moreover, this holds greater difficulty for four-year institutions that are attempting to strengthen articulation between the systems. This "vertical articulation" has been accompanied by intensified "horizontal articulation" as the community college system has placed more emphasis on economic development. The name of the statewide board has been changed to reflect this new mission focus to now be the Department of Community Colleges and Workforce Development. This agency distributes funds from the federal Workforce Investment Act. Structural changes in statewide governance of the postsecondary system have also included greater devolving of decision-making to the individual community college campuses.

The effects of the Great Recession in California particularly affected its 112 community colleges and 2.4 million students. A recent study (Bohn, Reyes, and Johnson, 2013) of the country's largest community college system showed that it had lost $1.5 billion in state funding from 2007 to 2012, resulting from a drop in per student funding from $6,700 annually to $5,100 by 2011. Moreover, student fees doubled reaching $46 per unit or a 28 percent increase, even though this was still only one-quarter of the average community college cost in the rest of the nation. Both of these changes resulted in a 15-year low in course section offerings, as they declined from 420,000 in 2007 to only 334,000 in 2012 (p. 14). These funding changes and reduced course offerings thus affected student attendance that fell an estimated 21 percent or some 600,000 students over the six-year recession. Critically, first-time students and first-time transfer attendance dropped 25.6 percent and 28.7 percent, respectively (pp. 23, 25). Accordingly 77 top administrators noted that the "cuts in state funding had a strong impact in students' academic experience" (p. 2). While some recent good economic news in California by May 2013 points to a $1.1 billion surplus in the state budget for the coming fiscal year—the state's first surplus in a decade—it is not clear how this might affect positively community college funding and reduction of student costs. Hidden in these economic difficulties are some major academic questions that are being raised about the overall quality of these struggling two-year public institutions. Twenty out of the 27 colleges under accreditation review seem likely to have their degree granting authority suspended, because they are "in danger of losing accreditation" (California Competes, 2013). A shared governance challenge on the part of California Competes: Higher Education for a Strong Economy, a Community Initiatives Group (sponsored by Rockefeller Philanthropy Advisors) under the direction of Robert Shireman, claims in effect that 18 percent of the colleges are suffering from a lack of strong district involvement. Shireman is questioning the state's 1991 community college governance revision, and is seeking to have district involvement and decision-making restored. Community College Chancellor Brice Harris's response pointed to how this 22-year-old legislative change has succeeded this long without legislative intervention and should continue to stand. Yet the larger question under this governance controversy is the academic leadership and quality of the 20 community colleges under review. How has the Great Recession affected their overall institutional viability and service to community college students? As the state is seeking more educated workers and professionals to restore the state's economic might, one of its greatest economic engines is being severely hampered.

These four state community college powerhouses provide telling examples on how recent state economic and political troubles have been affecting postsecondary education. Moreover, they show how the critical public good that western community colleges contribute to the state's welfare by educating its citizens is being jeopardized in the economic downturn.

Observations on Growth and Looking Forward

Higher education plays an important role in expanding knowledge and creating opportunities for citizens to make productive contributions to the state economy. Community colleges and two-year institutions in general play a vital role in the economic successes of individuals as well as subsequently to the state and national economies. More financial support is necessary especially with the economic downturns we are currently experiencing. What to expect for the next decades is impossible to say with any certainty, but it is clear that the community colleges are a fixed component of the postsecondary landscape in the West and the entire nation. Community colleges provide an important contribution and have had tremendous success and impact. Their transfer function is a proven example of community colleges' significant influence in the postsecondary community, evidenced by the fact that as many as "82 percent of transfer students who had all of their credits accepted at four-year institutions completed a bachelor's degree in six years" (Callan, Ewell, Finney, and Jones, 2007, p. 12). Successes of this magnitude will entrench the role of the community colleges in our postsecondary future. The Integrated Basic Educational Skills Training (I-BEST) Program in Washington state is another excellent example of the expansive role the community colleges are providing in meeting the basic educational needs of adults (Callan et al., 2007). Interrelations among four elements—state funding, state tuition levels, financial aid, and student debt burdens—thus offer a sequence of cascading dominos that challenge the current successes of community college education for all persons.

Community colleges are vital providers of education and a key policy tool for state policymakers interested in expanding educational opportunities to its citizens. The future for community colleges is very bright and uplifting in general as a major positive influence in today's higher education environments, regardless of the state. Funding, however, is always critical to allow these key institutions to offer postsecondary education to the vast populations they have served so well over the past 50 years. Several authors in this book provided many details about the serious funding dilemmas existing in the WICHE states. More specifically, in chapter 5, Dennis Jones indicates that higher education should not count on state government having substantial additional resources to devote to higher education. This forces the question for community colleges, as the biggest provider of access to the higher education pipeline: How will the increased demand for admission be met in the midst of declining state resources? How far can community colleges go on increasing tuition, without jeopardizing their fundamental role as an access institution? These questions reveal critical policy issues that WICHE states must address to ensure the vitality of this critical sector of higher education. Further, with the new goal of curricular efficiency and intense focus on student degree completions and graduation, how will community colleges collaborate with four-year institutions to maintain a strong seamless transfer pipeline, not weakened by unnecessary leaks or cracks. Many states will need to continue their relatively rediscovered or newfound interests in transfer, remediation, and completion efficiencies to allow students continuous progress toward completion. Some state examples offer new ways of dealing with these issues: (1) North Dakota's great collaborative model where all the community colleges have a joint degree in nursing, (2) Arizona's limit on credit-hour accumulation, (3) Colorado's focus on statewide articulation agreements, and (4) California's focus on easing community college transfer. Each is worthy of close attention, as an example of expanding educational opportunities.

In addition to recent prior funding patterns, some community college leaders do not feel confident of their own state's financial outlook, as noted by Katsinas et al. (2011). In fact, according to their findings in a national study on community college funding, most state leaders were concerned that there were no long-term plans that would allow the community colleges to meet the expectations for increased enrollments. Most state leaders also believed that there was no funding and no incentive system to reward community colleges for increasing their transfer functions. Finally, they found that most state leaders believed that it would be difficult to increase graduation rates in light of state funding cuts. Community college leaders in WICHE states tended to express similar responses to the national leaders on questions of funding. Clearly, community colleges need new state financial strategies—as in some type of outcomes incentive system—for accomplishing their expanding educational functions in the states.

Any future of community colleges is predicated on a comprehensive view of statewide strategy for postsecondary planning that encompasses community colleges and four-year campuses. A focus to make sure community colleges and universities are planning together will support this statewide strategy. Also, tremendous collaborations and innovative educational endeavors can be possible where flexibility and incentives for such collaborations are rewarded. Rewarding institutions for outcomes, including transfers, will also be supportive of larger state goals with increased completions. Further, getting to a common definition of college readiness would also help citizens access and hopefully be ready to succeed in postsecondary education whether one starts at a community college or university. The current work in California, Colorado, Montana, New Mexico, North Dakota, Oregon, and Washington are great recent efforts that need to be studied to see their impact and effectiveness.

Economic development efforts are often linked to community colleges as they can play a key role in connecting local employers to a ready and well-trained workforce. Recent workforce studies note the need for some level of postsecondary education, and for some states as much as 60 percent of the new jobs and employment opportunities will require postsecondary course work. Continued focus on a vibrant workforce will be a long-standing issue that will influence community colleges to constantly assess their academic offerings to make sure they are focused on relevant needs of their students and local employers. A strong connection here can have lasting impact on the larger state economy, too.

Immigration laws and access to postsecondary education will be another continual issue for community colleges, since there is an open door for admission to these institutions. As the immigration debate for the country goes, so do the access points for students wishing to matriculate to the community colleges in the WICHE states, many of which have a high percentage of immigrants. The Hispanic Association of Colleges and Universities (HACU, 2005) indicates that "half of the nation's Hispanics reside in California... or Texas" with a sizable presence in Arizona, Colorado, and New Mexico (NCES, 2008). Careful consideration of new immigration policies and practices are required for all postsecondary leaders and especially for community college leaders in the WICHE states.

From the budget crisis to the increased expectations for completions, community colleges in the WICHE states have recently experienced an uphill struggle. How far can these historically open access institutions continue to serve the populations they have previously served? In light of all the current economic pressures and increased expectations, several states have seen a move to balance these increased pressures by limiting enrollments, long waiting lists for certain popular majors, capping class sizes, laying off support staff, and reducing the amount of financial aid available to students. Some reports over the last two years indicate thousands of students have been "closed out" of postsecondary opportunities in California, for example; other states, such as Colorado, are considering how much they will eliminate from the state financial aid program, since ARRA funding will not be available next year. A close monitoring of who is being served by these traditional open institutions is warranted.

In summary, the WICHE states historically have been supported by a growing and expanding community college sector. With close to 50 percent of a state's enrollment in community colleges, it is critical to explore this sector and to understand its contributions to a state's future. The colleges have been open-door institutions for decades and have provided excellent general education and training for transfer programs, for completion programs, and for various technical and skilled trades. The West's development has been closely linked to these colleges and its future economy will reflect their strong participation.

Note

*Author's Note: Appreciation is expressed to the reviewers who provided feedback and suggested edits. Also, gratitude is expressed to Ranee Tomlin, Ryan Barone, Jacquelynn Rich, and to all my former doctoral students in the Higher Education Program in the Morgridge College of Education at the University of Denver for assistance with data collection.

References

American Association of Community Colleges. *Fast Facts*. Retrieved from www.aacc.nche.edu.

American Indian Higher Education Consortium, (AIHEC). *Summary Data*. Retrieved from www.aihec.org/colleges, 2011.

Baker, G. (ed.). *A Handbook on the Community College in America: Its History, Mission, and Management*. Westport, CT: Greenwood Press, 1994.

Bogue, J. P. *The Community College*. New York: McGraw-Hill Book Company, Inc., 1950.

Bohn, S., B. Reyes, and H. Johnson. *The Impact of Budget Cuts on California's Community Colleges*. San Francisco: Public Policy Institute of California. Retrieved from www.ppic.org/content/pubs/report/R_313SBR.pdf, in March 2013.

Brint, S., and J. Karabel. *The Diverted Dream: Community Colleges and the Promise of Educational Opportunity in America, 1900–1985*. New York: Oxford University Press, 1989.

California Competes. "We Respond to Chancellor Harris' Refusal to Address Broken Decision-Making in California Community Colleges." Retrieved from http://californiacompetes.org/news_and_events/we-respond-to-chancellor-harris-refusal-to-address-broken-decision-making-at-california-community-colleges/, in February 2013.

Callan, P., P. Ewell, J. Finney, and D. Jones. *Good Policy, Good Practice Improving Outcomes and Productivity in Higher Education: A Guide for Policymakers*. Boulder, CO: National Center for Higher Education Management Systems, 2007.

Cass, J., and M. Birnbaum. *Comparative Guide to Junior and Two-year Community Colleges*. New York: Harper and Row, 1972.

Center on Budget and Policy Priorities. *The State Budget Crisis and the Economy*. 2011.

Cohen, A. "Government Policies Affecting Community Colleges: a Historical Perspective." In B. Townsend and S. Twombly (eds.), *Community Colleges: Policy in the Future Context*. Westport, CT: Ablex Publishing, 2001, pp. 3–22.

Cohen, A., and F. Brawer. *The American Community College*. San Francisco, CA: Jossey-Bass, 1989.

Deegan, W. L., D. Tillery, and Associates. *Renewing the American Community College: Priorities and Strategies for Effective Leadership*. San Francisco, CA: Jossey-Bass, 1985.

Goodchild, L. F., and H. S. Wechsler. *The History of Higher Education*. Needham Heights, MA: Simon and Schuster, 1997.

Guyden, J. (1999). "Two-year historically black colleges." In B. Townsend (ed.), *Two-year Colleges for Women and Minorities*. New York: Falmer Press, 1999, pp. 85–112.

Hansford, B. W. (ed.). *Community Junior Colleges*. Denver: Colorado Department of Education, 1967.

Hispanic Association of Colleges and Universities (HACU). *Facts.* HACU, Washington, DC, 2005.

Katsinas, S., M. D'Amico, and J. Friedel. *Challenging Success: Can College Degree Completion Be Increased as States Cut Budgets?* Education Policy Center, Tuscaloosa: The University of Alabama, 2011.

Laden, B. "Two-Year Hispanic-Serving Colleges." In B. Townsend (ed.), *Two-Year Colleges for Women and Minorities.* New York: Falmer Press, 1999, pp. 151–194.

Lovell, C. D. "Federal Policies and Community Colleges: a Mix of Federal and Local Influences." In B. Townsend and S. Twombly (eds.), *Community Colleges: Policy in the Future Context.* Westport, CT: Ablex Publishing, 2001, pp. 23–37.

———. "Understanding the Relationship of Federal Policies and Community Colleges: a Proposed Analytical Policy Framework," *Journal of Applied Research in the Community College,* 7 (2) (2000): 77–86.

McCormick, A. "Swirling and Double-Dipping: New Patterns of Student Attendance and Their Implications for Higher Education." In J. E. King, E. L. Anderson, and M. E. Corrigan (eds.), *Changing Student Attendance Patterns: Challenges for Policy and Practice,* New Directions for Higher Education, no. 121 (2003), p. 1324.

Morsch, W. *State Community College Systems: Their Role and Operation in Seven States.* New York: Praeger Publishers, 1971.

National Center for Education Statistics (NCES). *The Condition of Education 2001, 2004, 2008, 2010,* and *2011.* Washington, DC: US Department of Education, 2001 et seq.

National Center for Public Policy and Higher Education. *Affordability and Transfer: Critical to Increasing Baccalaureate Degree Completion.* Retrieved from www.highereducation.org/reports/pa_at/, 2011.

Pardon, E. J. "Hispanics and Community Colleges." In G. A. Baker, III (ed.), *A Handbook on the Community Colleges in America: Its History, Mission, and Management.* Westport, CT: Greenwood Press, 1994, pp. 82–93.

Pavel, D., and A. Colby. *American Indians in Higher Education: The Community College Experience.* ERIC Clearinghouse for Junior Colleges: University of California at Los Angeles, 1992.

Pavel, D., E. Inglebret, and M. VanDenHende. "Tribal Colleges." In B. Townsend (ed.), *Two-Year Colleges for Women and Minorities.* New York: Falmer Press, 1999, pp. 113–150.

Phillippe, K. A., and L. G. Sullivan. *National Profile of Community Colleges: Trends and Statistics,* (4). Washington, DC: American Association of Community Colleges, 2005.

Quigley, M. S., and T. Bailey. *Community College Movement in Perspective: Teachers College Responds to the Truman Commission.* Lanham, MD: Scarecrow Press, 2003.

Simmons, H. "Diversity Among Community College Student Populations." In G. Baker (ed.), *A Handbook on the Community College in America: Its History, Mission, and Management.* Westport, CT: Greenwood Press, 1994, pp. 454–461.

Townsend, B. (ed.). *Two-year Colleges for Women and Minorities: Enabling Access to the Baccalaureate.* New York: Falmer Press, 1999.

Townsend, B., and Twombly, S. (eds.). *Community Colleges: Policy in the Future Context.* Westport, CT: Ablex Publishing, 2001.

Warren, J. "The Changing Characteristics of Community College Students." In W. Deegan, D. Tillery, and Associates (eds.), *Renewing the American Community College,* pp. 53–79 San Francisco, CA: Jossey-Bass, 1985.

Part III

A Concluding Commentary

Afterword

Where Do We Go from Here

The Policy Nexus between the West and the Federal Government

David A. Longanecker

Geography and history—both fascinating—coalesce to form the soil in which western colleges and universities have been planted over the past century and a half. What has been built—by missionaries, state and local governments, boosters, and entrepreneurial leaders as well as more recently by Native American and Hispanic groups—is nothing short of magnificent. Across this landscape, we see powerful and in some instances world-renowned research universities, pioneering community colleges that continually reinvent themselves, urban colleges and universities that serve the unique needs of their communities, rural colleges and universities that provide broad geographic access to learners in the remote corners of the region, diverse independent institutions large and small, highly specialized institutions, a growing sector of proprietary institutions, and emerging cyber institutions. This vast array is supported by students and their parents, federal, state and local taxpayers, philanthropic individuals and foundations, Native American nations, and consumers. In the companion volume relating to the history of western higher education there is rich evidence of this impressive "postsecondary system," though none dare call it that for fear of abridging the independent spirit of the West.

Thus, we westerners can look back with pride, as the saying goes, of what has been accomplished. But, as this volume on policy and its companion volume on history make clear, the great challenges for these states and institutions at the beginning of the twenty-first century is to meet the needs of a changing population of students—to provide them with the ever-evolving career and life skills necessary to participate effectively in the global community with its insatiable demand for intellectual resources of higher-order skills.

A "Perfect Storm" to Challenge

Compounding this challenge at the time of this writing (winter 2013), the West, the nation, indeed the world, are beginning to recover from the worst recession since the Great Depression of the 1930s. The multiple consequences of these difficult economic times will require exceptional change and sacrifice from individuals, institutions, and governments in order to maintain and expand access to high-quality higher education in the West.

This challenge can fairly be described as a perfect storm:

- An economic recession that has constrained the pocketbooks of states as well as students, families, and donors;
- A growing college-age population with sharply increased numbers of students with historically poor educational achievement; and
- An educational enterprise that seems in many ways unprepared for these challenges.

The challenge seems daunting, to say the least. The details are described by noting the authors in this book. First, Cheryl Blanco describes the demographic challenge, particularly the growing diversity of the college-age population in the West, and the increasing numbers of less traditional students who historically have not been served well by higher education in the West. Second, Mikyung Ryu, using data from *Measuring Up, 2006,* paints a picture of western higher education's lagging grades on some measures of performance, especially the declining affordability of western institutions over the past decade and college-going rates of high school graduates, with mixed assessment in the category of college completion. Third, Dennis Jones lays out some of the consequent and critical financial challenges facing state and institutional policymakers on these issues. Fourth, Aims McGuiness demonstrates the weaknesses in state decision-making structures that are needed to solve the policy puzzles. He describes the difficult governance picture in the WICHE West where tight state budgets and tax resistant state leaders, cultures, and populace have made funding postsecondary education increasingly problematic now and in the future. Fifth, a collaboration by staff of the State Higher Education Executive Officers association, led by Charlie Lenth, demonstrates the exceptional financial challenges that public institutions have faced as states confront expanding claims on their limited tax dollars, a challenge that has led a number of western states to decrease funding of public institutions, coupled with the predictable and continued rise in tuition. In the companion volume on the history of higher education in the West, Patrick Callan (2014) describes the master planning process that California used to address the mid-twentieth century challenges of growth and explosive demand for higher education, a model that was lauded and replicated throughout the country. Callan (2014) and McGuinness make clear, however, that the process appears ill-suited for the needs of greater integration and coordination in the twenty-first century. Sixth, Sally Johnstone and

Ritchie Boyd document the explosive growth in technology-based higher education, both with respect to Internet-delivered learning and technology-mediated curricula on campus. However, they make no prediction about the likelihood of these technologies solving some of the basic problems of access, affordability, and completion. Lastly, community colleges in the West may be the most challenged sector of the higher education ecology. As Cheryl Lovell points out, increasing and increasingly diverse populations in many of the states and the dynamic requirements of the skill requirements for tomorrow's jobs have intensified the strain caused by the level or shrinking budgets in many of our states.

Confronting the Challenges

In an "all else being equal" scenario, these challenges could spell a dismal future for western higher education. However, "all else being equal" need not be the vision or reality of the West's future. Surely, the increasing diversity of the western states' college-age population represents as much an opportunity as a challenge as our population increasingly reflects the population of the globe. The West's immigrants from all of the Asian countries, from Mexico, as well as from Central and South America, who are bringing their postsecondary educational experiences and degrees, will help our states develop robust economic ties with those regions.

So, too, the western states' historic links with the federal government can be leveraged into stronger educational partnerships. Western community colleges, some of which lead the country and perhaps the world in linkages with the workplace and transfer routes to universities, can provide new models of skill training, open access, and community links that will be powerful engines driving both educational opportunity and economic development. Our major public and private universities, well-represented among the research powerhouses of the country and the world, will continue to provide research to fuel the leading-edge economies of many western states, as well as the highly trained professionals and "incubator" resources to translate that research into economic benefits.

Finally, the western states' heavy—although by no means exclusive—reliance on public higher education can offer new political and organizational models to more quickly and effectively muster the political creativity and political will to make all this work. Yet, this will not occur without significant change in the ways in which we effectively expand access, provide cost-effective, high-quality education, and produce competitive research. We must improve in almost every facet of the higher education enterprise if we are to succeed. And, we must accomplish this change agenda in the midst of the most economically distressed environment in modern history. Certainly this offers an opportunity; the current environment can supply the motivation, and perhaps the political will, to rethink the funding, organization, and operation of the education enterprise, and to make the next decades a time of renewal, energy, and new success for the West's colleges and universities.

Western higher education has no choice, really, but to accept the current circumstances as opportunities rather than as ordeals. As western historian Patty Limerick (2014) in the companion volume reminds us that the spirit of innovation has characterized the West and will seemingly continue to do so. We must collaborate with and encourage further learning among those populations that sadly we have historically disenfranchised. Not to do so would lead to a less economically viable and equitable society, neither of which is acceptable. We must increase the productivity and effectiveness of our higher education enterprise, especially for all groups. Not to do so would make it impossible to provide the broad access to high-quality postsecondary education that will be necessary to sustain vibrant economies and a high quality of life in the West.

The West is up to the task, given innovation has been our hallmark. As the companion volume on the history of higher education in the West has demonstrated (Goodchild, Jonsen, Limerick, and Longanecker, 2014), the West is capable of rapid expansion, creativity in responding to demands, and in developing the capacity to provide high-quality service with modest resources. All we need to do is to follow the lead that our predecessors have provided.

REFERENCES

Callan, P. M. "Higher Education in California: Rise and Fall." In L. F. Goodchild, R. W. Jonsen, P. Limerick, and D. A. Longanecker (eds.), *Higher Education in the American West: Regional History and State Contexts*. Higher Education and Society series. New York, NY: Palgrave Macmillan, 2014.

Goodchild, L. F., R. W. Jonsen, P. Limerick, and D. A. Longanecker, eds. *Higher Education in the American West: Regional History and State Contexts*. Higher Education and Society series. New York, NY: Palgrave Macmillan, 2014.

Limerick, P. "Forty-Five Years in the Academic Saddle: The American West, Higher Education, and the Invitation to Innovation." In L. F. Goodchild, R. W. Jonsen, P. Limerick, and D. A. Longanecker (eds.), *Higher Education in the American West: Regional History and State Contexts*. Higher Education and Society series. New York, NY: Palgrave Macmillan, 2014.

Contributors

Allison C. Bell
Former Policy Analyst, State Higher Education Executive Officers (SHEEO), Boulder, Colorado
Allison Bell was with the State Higher Education Officers from 2008 to 2011 when she coauthored her chapter. She now works for the US Department of Education's National Center for Education Statistics. While with SHEEO, Bell had the lead responsibility for data collection and analysis for the annual State Higher Education Finance (SHEF) report. She also worked on the State Policy Resource Connections initiative, which involves major types and sources of demographic and economic data as well as SHEF financing data. Through these projects, she played major roles in developing SHEEO's data collection and management procedures. Bell completed her doctorate in higher education at the University of Michigan with a dissertation on the role of costs and financing in college aspiration formation. She earned her undergraduate degree in sociology at Stanford University and her MA in higher education at University of Michigan. Among other employment experiences, Bell has worked in institutional research at the University of California-San Diego and Washtenaw Community College in Michigan. She is also a qualified sailing instructor. Bell is a westerner by birth (southern California) and by choice (Colorado) before her move to Washington, DC.

Cheryl D. Blanco
Vice President for Special Projects, Southern Regional Education Board (SREB), Atlanta, Georgia
Cheryl Blanco is vice president for special projects at SREB. She oversees special initiatives on college readiness and college completions and develops new projects. Her work focuses on policy and research related to postsecondary education issues and the nexus between higher education and K-12. Publications include *Promoting a Culture of Student Success: How Colleges and Universities Are Improving Degree Completion* and *No Time to Waste: Policy Recommendations for Increasing College Completion*. She has coauthored chapters in such reports as *Integrating Financial Aid and Financing Policies: Case Studies from the Changing Direction Technical Assistance States*. Previously, Blanco was vice president for National College Access Programs and executive director of the Pathways to College Network at TERI, vice president for policy and research at the Council for Adult and Experiential Learning, senior program director for policy analysis and research at the

Western Interstate Commission for Higher Education, and educational policy director at the Florida Postsecondary Education Planning Commission. She held positions at Arecibo Technological University College, University of Puerto Rico, including assistant to the vice president for academic affairs, director of the division of continuing education, coordinator for professional development, and tenured associate professor in the Department of English. She received her PhD in higher education leadership from Florida State University.

J. Ritchie Boyd
Academic Technology Specialist, Montana State University, Bozeman, Montana
J. Ritchie Boyd is an academic technology specialist and a web scientist at Montana State University (MSU). He has spent the majority of his career developing and supporting instructional technology and e-learning opportunities for university faculty and students, in addition to creating professional development opportunities and resources for K-12 teachers and administrators. Boyd led the implementation, training, and support efforts for MSU's first learning management system and has been an advocate for appropriate and innovative uses of a broad range of technologies across the curriculum. Specifically, he has been involved in numerous projects related to instructional design and support for online courses, whose goal was to increase the science content knowledge of in-service teachers. He has presented at a number of national conferences on such topics as emerging web-based technologies (i.e., social networking and collaboration tools) and their application in providing innovative student services and engaging instructional opportunities. Prior to joining MSU, Boyd was involved in faculty development and support for instructional technologies at the University of Wyoming and at the University of Wisconsin-Madison. He has a BA and MA in geology and geophysics from the University of California at Santa Barbara.

Andrew M. Carlson
Senior Policy Analyst, State Higher Education Executive Officers (SHEEO), Boulder, Colorado
Andrew M. Carlson is a higher education senior policy analyst at the State Higher Education Executive Officers, where he began in September 2011. He manages and compiles the annual State Higher Education Finance Report (SHEF) and works on various other policy studies, typically related to higher education finance, tuition policy, and financial aid. Previously, Carlson worked at the Colorado Department of Higher Education as the director of budget and financial aid. In this role, he managed and developed governing board and state-level budget appropriation requests. In addition he was responsible for the collection, analysis, and presentation of institution-level financial data, including tuition and fee, student FTE, and detailed revenue and expenditure reporting. Prior to being there, he had worked at the Colorado Office of the State Auditor and the Bighorn Center for Public Policy. He holds an MPA degree from the University of Colorado-Denver and a BA degree in history from Indiana University.

Lester F. Goodchild
Distinguished Professor of International and Comparative Education and Advisor to the Provost, University of Massachusetts Boston, Boston, Massachusetts and Professor of Education, Emeritus, Santa Clara University, Santa Clara, California

Lester F. Goodchild is distinguished professor of international and comparative education and advisor to the provost at the University of Massachusetts Boston since September 2012, and professor of education, emeritus at Santa Clara University. He had served as dean of Santa Clara's School of Education and Counseling Psychology and director of its Higher Education Program. Previously, Goodchild was dean of the School of Education and Human Development at the University of Massachusetts Boston, as well as earlier interim dean of education, director of the Higher Education Program, and associate professor of education at the University of Denver. His specialty is the study of higher education, with emphases on its history, public policy, administration, and professional ethics. He has coedited five books: *Advancing Higher Education as a Field of Study: In Quest of Doctoral Degree Guidelines—Commemorating 120 Years of Excellence* (2014); *The History of Higher Education* (1989, 1997, 2007); *Public Policy and Higher Education* (1997); *Rethinking the Dissertation Process: Tackling Personal and Institutional Obstacles* (1997); and *Administration as a Profession* (1991). He wrote 61 refereed articles, book chapters, and other publications. Goodchild received his PhD in higher education from the University of Chicago, M.Div. from St. Meinrad School of Theology (Indiana), MA in religious studies from Indiana University, and BA in sociology from the University of St. Thomas (Minnesota).

Sally M. Johnstone
Vice President for Academic Advancement, Western Governors University, Salt Lake City, Utah

Sally M. Johnstone is vice president for academic advancement at the Western Governors University. From 2006 to mid-2011 she was the provost and vice president for academic affairs at Winona State University in Minnesota. Prior to 2006 she was the executive director of Western Cooperative for Educational Telecommunications (WCET) at the Western Interstate Commission for Higher Education for almost two decades. Johnstone continues to work on policy issues for higher education institutions and system organizations, inter-institutional collaborations, quality assurance issues, project development and evaluation, and international projects. She serves on the US National Commission for the United Nations' Educational, Scientific and Cultural Organization (UNECSO) as well as the editorial boards for *Change* magazine and the *Journal of Open Learning* (UK). She has written dozens of articles, books, and reports on issues of integrating information and communication technology into academics. Johnstone earned her PhD in experimental psychology from the University of North Carolina at Chapel Hill.

Dennis P. Jones
President, National Center for Higher Education Management Systems (NCHEMS), Boulder, Colorado
Dennis Jones is president of NCHEMS, a nonprofit research and development center founded to improve strategic decision-making in institutions and agencies of higher education. A member of the staff since 1969, Jones is widely recognized for his work in such areas as: (1) developing "public agendas" to guide state higher education policymaking; (2) financing, budgeting, and resource allocation methodologies for use at both state and institutional levels; (3) linking higher education with states' workforce and economic development needs; and (4) developing and using information to inform policymaking. Jones has written many monographs and articles on these topics, has presented his work at many regional, national, and international conferences, and has consulted with hundreds of institutions and state higher education agencies on management issues of all kinds. Prior to joining NCHEMS, Jones served as an administrator (in business and in institutional planning) at Rensselaer Polytechnic Institute. He received his graduate and undergraduate degrees from that institution in the field of management engineering.

Richard W. Jonsen
Former Executive Director, Western Interstate Commission for Higher Education (WICHE), Boulder, Colorado
Richard W. Jonsen retired in 1999 as executive director of WICHE. He held that position since 1990. Recently, he taught ESL at Front Range Community College in Westminster, Colorado. He had been at WICHE since 1977, first as project director and then as deputy director. He held previous positions at the Education Commission of the States, Syracuse University (NY), and University of Santa Clara (CA). He has held faculty positions in higher education at Syracuse, University of Denver (visiting) and the Autonomous University of Tamaulipas, Mexico (visiting). Jonsen holds degrees in English from Santa Clara University and San Jose State University, and a PhD in higher education from Stanford University.

Charles S. Lenth
Vice President for Policy Analysis and Academic Affairs, State Higher Education Executive Officers (SHEEO), Boulder, Colorado
Charles S. Lenth is vice president for policy analysis and academic affairs for the State Higher Education Executive Officers (SHEEO) association in Boulder, Colorado. Previously Lenth held positions with the Minnesota Private College Council, the Education Commission of the States, the Western Interstate Commission for Higher Education, and the Illinois Board of Higher Education. He holds a PhD in political science from the University of Chicago and an A.B. in government from Dartmouth College. His professional experience includes state, regional, and national studies on higher education financing and tuition policies, and directing projects related to higher education access, affordability, and success. At SHEEO his areas of

responsibility include state-level academic planning and policy, relationships with K-12 education, regulation and quality assurance, and other areas of policy concern. Since late 2010, Lenth has been one of two higher education members of the Smarter Balanced Assessment Consortium Executive Committee, working with 26 states and territories to develop new Common Core-based college readiness assessments. From 2010 through 2012, he was a member of the Group of National Experts and project manager for US participation in the OECD Assessment of Higher Education Learning Outcomes Feasibility Study.

Patricia ("Patty") Nelson Limerick
Professor of History and Director of the Center of the American West, University of Colorado, Boulder, Colorado
Patty Limerick is the faculty director and chair of the board for the Center of the American West at the University of Colorado, where she is also a professor of history. She received her PhD from Yale University in 1980, and has dedicated her career to demonstrating the benefits of applying historical perspective to contemporary dilemmas and bridging the gap between academics and the general public. She is the author of many books, most notably *The Legacy of Conquest* (1987), as well as a prolific essayist and sought-after speaker. Her scholarship and her commitment to teaching have been recognized with a number of honors, including the MacArthur Fellowship (1995–2000), and she has served as president of several professional organizations, advised documentary film projects, done two tours as a Pulitzer Prize nonfiction jurist, and been a guest columnist for the *New York Times*. In 1986, Limerick was one of the principal founders of the Center of the American West, and since 1995 it has been her primary affiliation. Under her leadership, the center serves as a forum committed to the civil, respectful, problem-solving exploration of important, often contentious, public issues.

David A. Longanecker
President, Western Interstate Commission for Higher Education (WICHE), Boulder, Colorado
David A. Longanecker has served as the president of WICHE since 1999. This regional compact was created between the 15 western states to assure access and excellence in higher education through collaboration and resource sharing among the higher education systems of the West. Previously, Longanecker served for six years as the assistant secretary for postsecondary education at the US Department of Education. He has been the state higher education executive officer in Colorado and Minnesota. He was also the principal analyst for higher education for the Congressional Budget Office. Longanecker serves on numerous national boards and commissions. He writes extensively on higher education issues. His primary higher education interests are: expanding access to successful completion for students within all sectors of higher education, promoting student and institutional performance, assuring efficient and effective finance and financial aid strategies, and fostering educational technologies. These activities seek to sustain

America's educational strength in the world and increase the quality of life for all Americans, particularly those who have traditionally been left out in the past. He holds an Ed.D. from Stanford University, an MA in student personnel work from George Washington University, and a BA in sociology from Washington State University.

Cheryl D. Lovell
President, Rocky Vista University, Parker, Colorado
Cheryl Lovell is president of Rocky Vista University in Parker, Colorado. Its College of Osteopathic Medicine is a leader in global, rural/wilderness, and military medicine. Previously, Lovell was professor of higher education and associate academic dean with the University of Denver's Morgridge College of Education. She also served as chief academic officer for the State of Colorado in its Department of Higher Education. She was responsible for its academic and student affairs, research/information/data policy analyses, and student access division. Lovell has edited the ASHE Reader on *Public Policy and Higher Education* (2010), and published book chapters on "Federal Public Policy Issues and Community Colleges" in *Community Colleges for the Future* and "Community Colleges in a Global Society: Is There One Best Model?" in *Globalization: Education Research, Change, and Reform*. Lovell was also vice president of the National Association of Student Personnel Administrators' IV-West region. She helped create NASPA's Public Policy Division. As its chair, she served on NASPA's Board of Directors for four years. Prior to the University of Denver, Lovell staffed with the State Higher Education Executive Officers, the National Center for Higher Education Management Systems, and the Florida Board of Regents. Her PhD is from Florida State University.

Aims C. McGuiness Jr.
Senior Associate, National Center for Higher Education Management Systems (NCHEMS), Boulder, Colorado
Aims McGuinness is a senior associate with the National Center for Higher Education Management Systems (NCHEMS), a nonprofit policy center in Boulder, Colorado. He specializes in state governance and coordination of higher education, strategic planning and restructuring higher education systems, roles and responsibilities of public institutional and multicampus system governing boards, and international comparison of education reform. Prior to joining NCHEMS in 1993, he was director of higher education policy at the Education Commission of the States. Before joining ECS in 1975, he was executive assistant to the chancellor of the University of Maine System. For 31 years, McGuinness has advised states on their higher education systems and reforms. Recent governance and other system projects involved Arkansas, California, Colorado, Kentucky, Louisiana, Massachusetts, Mississippi, New York, Oregon, Texas, Washington, and Wisconsin. International policy projects through the OECD and the World Bank included the Baltic States, Dominican Republic, Egypt, Greece, India, Israel, Ireland, Kazakhstan, Korea, Japan, Malaysia, Russia, and Turkey. He chaired the international taskforce for the 2011 OECD report, *Strong*

Performers and Successful Reforms: Education Policy Advice to Greece. McGuinness earned his BA from the University of Pennsylvania, an MBA from George Washington University, and a PhD in social science from the Maxwell School, Syracuse University.

Mikyung Ryu
Interim Director, Center for Policy Analysis, American Council on Education (ACE), Washington, DC
Mikyung Ryu as the interim director currently leads the policy research center at the nation's premier higher education association that represents 1,800 institutions and organizations. She oversees ACE's expansive research portfolio, focusing on postsecondary attainment, accountability, college pathways for adults, financial aid, diversity, institutional leadership, and internationalization on campus. Her publications include: *Credit for Prior Learning* (ACE, forthcoming), *With Degree in Hand: Analysis of Minority College Graduates and Their Lives after College* (ACE, 2013), *The Education Gap: Understanding African-American and Hispanic Attainment Gaps in Higher Education* (ACE, 2012), and *Mapping Internationalization on U.S. Campuses* (ACE, 2012). Previously, Ryu served as the lead analyst for the unprecedented 50 state report cards for higher education, titled *Measuring Up*, for the National Center for Public Policy and Higher Education. In recognition for its profound impacts on the public policy for higher education, Ryu was named one of the ten higher education's new generation of thinkers by *The Chronicle of Higher Education*. Prior to leading higher education advocacy work, Ryu was on the faculty at Wagner College. She holds a PhD from the State University of New York at Buffalo.

Kathleen J. Zaback
Policy Analyst, State Higher Education Executive Officers (SHEEO), Boulder, Colorado
Kathleen J. Zaback joined SHEEO as a higher education policy analyst in 2010. She supports SHEEO's efforts to help improve access for state policymakers to quality information to inform education policy decisions. Zaback has helped support SHEEO's partnership with Complete College America to create a streamlined data collection process to meet state needs, and she has been involved with its efforts to inform development and encourage adoption and implementation of the Common Education Data Standards. Zaback also performs policy analysis as part of the State Policy Resource Connection (SPRC) project and to support the State Higher Education Finance report (SHEF). Her prior experience in higher education includes being research associate and institutional researcher at Regis University and project associate with the National Survey of Student Engagement. Zaback earned a master's degree in public affairs with a concentration in policy analysis from the School of Public and Environmental Affairs at Indiana University at Bloomington, and she holds a BA in economics and political science from Hastings College and a master's certificate in database design from Regis University.

Index

academic preparation
 See preparation
accessibility, xv–xvi, 31–2, 39–40
 completion and, 48, 49, 51
 enrollment growth and, 176
 for historically underserved
  populations, 48
 at HSIs, 9
 low income and, 43, 48–9
 open access institutions, 181, 189
 racial/ethnic gaps and, 39
 shift away from, 73
 at TCUs, 19
accountability, 66, 82
 accountability mandates, 169
 for institutional performance, 72, 83
 linked with financing policy, 75
 in Oregon, 81
 public policy issues in, 174
 reforms in, 73, 74, 76–8, 79
Accountability for Better Results: A National Imperative for Higher Education (National Commission on Accountability in Higher Education), 76
accreditation for online universities, 152, 155
admissions, 171, 181
adult education, 150, 171
 vs. traditionally aged students, 5, 43, 47, 49, 55, 56
adult literacy, 33, 96
Advanced Placement test program, 33, 50, 53, 54, 55, 56
affordability, 188
 in Alaska, 50
 in Arizona, 50
 in California, 51
 in Colorado, 51

 vs. enrollment, 108
 federal government and, 62–3
 in Hawaii, 52
 in Idaho, 52
 as *Measuring Up* report card category, 32–4, 40, 42, 43, 47, 72
 in Montana, 53
 in Nevada, 53
 in North Dakota, 54
 in Oregon, 54–5
 in South Dakota, 55
 technology and, 151
 tuition and, 101
 in Utah, 56
 in Washington, 56
 in Wyoming, 57
"Affordability and Transfer: Critical to Increasing Baccalaureate Degree Completion" (Policy Alert), 177
African-Americans
 See Blacks (African-Americans)
age demographics, 5–7, 15–16
AIHEC (American Indian Higher Education Consortium), 19
Alabama
 funding in, 46, 100, 102
 high school graduation rates in, 44
 immediate college-going rates in, 45, 93
 Measuring Up scores for, 41–2
 public *vs.* private institutions in, 92
 state coordinating board in, 86
 tuition in, 94, 103–4
Alaska, xii
 affordability in, 50
 community colleges in, 161–3, 165, 166, 168, 170, 171
 degree completion in, 47, 50, 135
 Educational Appropriations in, 119, 135

200 INDEX

Alaska—*Continued*
　educational attainment in, 37, 113, 132, 135
　enrollment rates in, 50, 113, 119, 135, 165
　finance policy in, 171
　financial aid in, 50, 135
　FTE enrollment in, 119, 135
　funding in, 50, 100, 102, 119, 132, 135, 166, 168
　governance in, 86
　high school graduation rates in, 44
　immediate college-going rates in, 45, 93
　Measuring Up scores for, 34–5, 41–2, 47, 50
　natural resource extraction in, 132, 135
　Net Tuition Revenue in, 119, 135
　population of, 132, 135
　preparation in, 50
　public *vs.* private institutions in, 92
　race/ethnicity in, 37
　SHEF wave chart of, 119
　system configurations in, 135
　taxes in, 95
　Total Educational Revenue in, 119, 135
　tuition in, 94, 103–4
　University of Alaska system, 135
　university research in, 132, 135
Alaska Commission on Postsecondary Education, 88n3, 135
Albrecht, Robert, 147
algebra, 54
American Association of Community Colleges, 161
American Association of Universities, 62
American Indian College Fund (AICF), 20
American Indian Higher Education Consortium, 19
American Indians/Alaska Natives
　colonial colleges and, 20
　at community colleges, 161
　demographic information on, 8, 10–11, 15–16, 26n2
　educational attainment of, 37–8
　population growth of, 10–11
　TCUs and, 9, 18–20, 161, 163–4
American Recovery and Reinvestment Act (ARRA) (2009), 61, 62, 167, 181

American Taxpayer Relief Act (2012), 62
American West
　See Alaska; Arizona; California; Colorado; Hawaii; Idaho; Montana; Nevada; New Mexico; North Dakota; Oregon; South Dakota; Utah; Washington; Wyoming
Anderes, Tom, 177
anti-intellectualism, 61
anti-tax sentiment, 95
Archie and Gopher, 145
Arizona, xii
　affordability in, 50
　American Indian population in, 11
　budget shortfalls in, 167
　community colleges in, 161–3, 165, 166, 168, 171, 177
　degree completion in, 50, 118, 177
　distance learning in, 144, 146–7, 150–1, 177
　Educational Appropriations in, 118, 120
　educational attainment in, 37, 113, 118
　enrollment rates in, 50, 113, 118, 120, 165
　financial aid in, 50
　FTE enrollment in, 120
　funding in, 46, 50, 100, 102, 120, 166, 168, 177
　Getting AHEAD, 177
　governance in, 79, 86, 87n(m)
　high school graduation rates in, 44, 68
　Hispanic population in, 8, 15, 164, 177
　immediate college-going rates in, 45, 93, 177
　Maricopa Community Colleges, 118, 150, 177
　Measuring Up state grades for, 34–5, 41–2, 47, 50
　Navajo Community College, 19
　Net Tuition Revenue in, 120
　Pima Community College, 118
　population growth in, 4, 118
　public *vs.* private institutions in, 92
　race/ethnicity in, 37, 38
　Rio Salado Community College, 150–1
　SHEF wave chart of, 120
　system configurations in, 118
　Total Educational Revenue in, 120

tuition in, 94, 103–4, 177
University and Community College Joint Council of Presidents, 177
University of Arizona, 146
University of Phoenix Online, 152, 154
workforce in, 177
working-age population in, 50
Arizona State Board of Directors of Community Colleges, 87n(m)
Arkansas
funding in, 46, 100, 102
high school graduation rates in, 44
immediate college-going rates in, 45, 93
Measuring Up scores for, 41–2
public *vs.* private institutions in, 92
state coordinating board in, 86
tuition in, 94, 103–4
articulation
between 2-year and 4-year institutions, 171, 172, 173, 174, 176, 179, 180
between education levels, 72, 177
of TCUS and four-year institutions, 20
vertical and horizontal, 178
Ashford University, 152
Asians/Pacific Islanders
at community colleges, 161
demographic information on, 7, 8, 11–12, 15, 16
educational attainment of, 37
population growth of, 7, 11–12
attainment level/rates
See educational attainment

Baldwin, Lionel, 144
Bell, Allison, xx, 107, 191
benefits, as *Measuring Up* report card category, 33, 35, 39, 72
Bill and Melinda Gates Foundation, 76
Blacks (African-Americans)
at community colleges, 161
demographic information, 7–8, 12–13, 15, 16, 36
educational attainment of, 37
enrollment rates for, 22–3
population growth of, 12–13
Blanco, Cheryl, xiv, xix, 3, 188, 191
Board of Regents of the Montana University System, 80
Boeing, 145

Boyd, Ritchie, xx, 143, 188–9, 192
Bransford, Louis, 153
Bridgepoint Education, 152
Bureau of Census
See US Bureau of the Census
Bush administration, 66
Bush, George W., 63

California, xii
affordability in, 51
budget shortfalls in, 167
community colleges in, 51, 117, 161–3, 165, 166, 168, 170–3, 176, 178–80
cross-enrollment in, 176
degree completion in, 51, 128
distance learning in, 143–4, 144, 147–8, 151, 152, 153, 156
educational attainment in, 37, 80, 113, 128
enrollment rates in, 50, 113, 122, 125, 128, 165
FTE enrollment in, 122, 125
funding in, 43, 46, 100, 102, 122, 125, 140, 166, 168, 178, 178–9
governance in, 79, 80, 86, 87n(o), 178–9, 188
Great Recession and, 178
high school graduation rates in, 44
Hispanic population in, 8–9, 15, 163, 181
immediate college-going rates in, 45, 93
Measuring Up state grades for, 34–5, 41–2, 47, 51
National University, 151
Net Tuition Revenue in, 122, 125
population growth in, 125
public *vs.* private institutions in, 92
race/ethnicity in, 7, 37, 38
reducing levels of service in, 97
SHEF wave chart of, 122
Stanford University, 153, 156
system configurations in, 125, 128
Total Educational Revenue in, 122, 125
tuition in, 94, 97, 103–4, 117, 140, 178
University of California system, 125
California Competes
Higher Education for a Strong Economy, a Community Initiatives Group, 178

California Master Plan (1960), 60
California Postsecondary Education Commission (CPEC), 79, 80, 85, 87n(o)
California State University (CSU)
  Chico campus, 143–4, 157n1
  distance learning at, 147
California State University system, 125
California Virtual University (CVU), 147–8
Callan, Patrick, 188
capacity building *vs.* capacity utilization, 75, 82
Carlson, Andrew, xx, 107, 192
Caucasians
  See Whites
Census Bureau
  See US Bureau of the Census
Center for Academic Transformation at Rensselaer Polytechnic Institute, 150
Center for the Study of Education Policy, 110
Chambers, M. M, 110
Cisco, 145
City University of Seattle, 151
Closing the Gaps initiative (TX), 75
Cohen, Arthur, xiv, 159, 169, 182
collaboration
  across state sectors, 73, 74–5, 83
  between community colleges and universities, 180
  between faculty and students, 145
  through online educational resources, 156
College Board, the, 65
College Opportunity Fund, 51
College Participation
  See participation
college subsidiaries, 150–1
colonial colleges, 20
Colorado, xii, 176
  affordability in, 51
  articulation agreements in, 180
  community colleges in, 161–3, 165, 166, 168, 170, 173
  degree completion in, 118
  Degree Dividend, The: Building Our Economy and Preserving Our Quality of Live, 80–1
  distance learning in, 144, 147, 150, 153
  educational attainment in, 37, 81, 112, 113, 118
  enrollment rates in, 113, 118, 119, 123, 165
  financial aid in, 51, 181
  FTE enrollment in, 118, 123
  funding in, 46, 100, 102, 118, 119, 123, 166, 168, 181
  governance in, 80–1, 80–1, 86
  high school graduation rates in, 44
  immediate college-going rates in, 45, 51, 93
  in-migration to, 51
  Jones International University, 152
  low-income students in, 51
  Measuring Up state grades in, 34–5, 41–2, 51
  Net Tuition Revenue in, 118, 119, 123
  population growth in, 118
  public *vs.* private institutions in, 92
  racial/ethnic gaps in, 38, 51
  SHEF wave chart of, 123
  system configurations in, 118
  Total Educational Revenue in, 118, 123
  tuition in, 94, 103–4
  Whites in, 51
Colorado Commission on Higher Education, 80–1, 118
Colorado Community Colleges Online (CCCOnline), 150
Colorado Department of Higher Education, 118
Colorado Higher Education Strategic Planning Committee, 80
Colorado State University, 144
Commission on the Future of Higher Education, 66
community colleges, xiv, 159–81, 189
  in Alaska, 161–3, 165, 166, 168, 170, 171
  in Arizona, 161–3, 165, 166, 168, 171, 177
  in California, 51, 117, 161–3, 165, 166, 168, 170–3, 176, 178–80
  in Colorado, 161–3, 165, 166, 168, 170, 173
  degree completion in, 49, 66, 181
  demographic information on, 160–1
  distance learning at, 150–1
  dropout rates at, 55

economic developments and, 178, 181
emergence of, 23–4
enrollment in, 8–9, 48, 160, 164–5, 170, 176, 177, 181
financial aid at, 161, 176–7, 181
vs. four-year institutions, 48, 180
funding for, 160, 165–8, 176–7, 177, 179–80, 181
future of, 179–82
governance in, 178–9
growth of, 60, 160
in Hawaii, 161–3, 165, 166, 168, 170, 173
Hispanics and, 8–9
in Idaho, 161–3, 165, 166, 168, 170, 174
immigration laws and, 177, 181
increases in tuition in, 176, 180
low-income students and, 48–9
minority populations and, 159
in Montana, 161–3, 165, 166, 168, 170, 174
in Nevada, 161–3, 165, 166, 168, 170, 176
in New Mexico, 161–3, 165, 166, 168, 170, 174–5
in North Dakota, 161–3, 165, 166, 168, 170, 175, 180
Obama initiatives and, 66
in Oregon, 55, 161–3, 165, 166, 168, 170, 175, 177–8
public policy issues and, 160, 169–6
in South Dakota, 170
state economy and, 179, 181
transfer function of, 179, 180, 181
in Washington, 56, 161–3, 165, 170, 176–7
workforce and, 181
See also articulation
competition for state resources, 100
Complete College America, 73, 76
completion rates
See degree completion
Congress, 61, 66, 152, 154
Connecticut
funding in, 46, 100, 102
high school graduation rates in, 44
immediate college-going rates in, 45, 93
Measuring Up scores for, 41–2

public *vs.* private institutions in, 92
state coordinating board in, 86
tuition in, 94, 103–4
Connexions project, 156
Consumer Price Index (CPI), 176
Cost of Living Adjustment (COLA), 111
Council for Regional Accrediting Commissions (C-RAC), 148
Creative Commons, 156
cross-enrollment, 165, 176

defaulting on loan payment, 65, 66
degree completion, 24–5, 112–13
accessibility and, 48, 49, 51, 73
in Alaska, 47, 50, 135
in Arizona, 50, 118, 177
in California, 51, 128
in Colorado, 118
at community colleges, 49, 66, 176, 181
at for-profit institutions, 49
funding and, 141–2, 180
in Hawaii, 135
for Hispanic students, 8
in Idaho, 52, 128
increases in, 23–4
as *Measuring Up* report card category, 33, 35, 39, 40, 42, 47, 48–57, 72
in Montana, 53, 121
in Nevada, 47, 53, 128
in New Mexico, 53, 128, 132
in North Dakota, 54
in Oregon, 54, 55, 121
in South Dakota, 55, 125
in US, 23–4, 25, 67
in US *vs.* OECD, 31, 47, 68
in Utah, 55–6, 132
in Washington, 47, 56
in Wyoming, 47, 57, 139
See also educational attainment
Degree Dividend, The: Building Our Economy and Preserving Our Quality of Live (Colorado Higher Education Strategic Planning Committee) (2010), 80–1
Delaware
funding in, 46, 100, 102
high school graduation rates in, 44
immediate college-going rates in, 45, 93
Measuring Up scores for, 41–2

Delaware—*Continued*
    public *vs.* private institutions in, 92
    state service agency in, 86
    tuition in, 94, 103–4
demographic information, xix, xvi, 3–25
    on age, 5–7, 15–16
    for American Indian/Alaska Native population, 8, 10–11, 15–16, 26n2
    for Asians/Pacific Islanders, 7, 8, 11–12, 15, 16
    on Blacks in the United States, 7–8, 12–13, 15, 16, 36
    on community colleges, 160–1
    on enrollment and degree completion, 22–4, 24
    on Hispanics, 7, 8–10, 13–15, 16, 26n3, 36, 52, 68
    on institutions of higher education, 18, 21, 22
    for Midwest region, 4, 5, 39
    on race/ethnicity, 7–8, 15–16
    on secondary schools, 17–18
    for US, 3–4
    for West, 4, 95–6
    on Whites, 4, 7–8, 13–14, 15, 16, 36, 39, 52, 68
    for young population, 36, 39
Department of Community Colleges and Workforce Development (OR), 178
Department of Education, 17, 66, 152, 160
Diné College (AZ), 19
direct democracy, 95, 97
Distance Learner's Guide, The (WCET), 155
distance learning, xiv, 143–57
    in Arizona, 144, 146–7, 150–1, 177
    in California, 143–4, 147–8, 151, 152, 153, 156
    collaboration through, 156
    in Colorado, 144, 147, 150, 153
    consumer protection for, 154–5
    financial aid for, 153, 154
    at for-profit institutions, 151–3
    future of, 155–7
    genesis of, 143–4
    in Hawaii, 144
    in Iowa, 152
    in Missouri, 150
    in Montana, 150
    in New Mexico, 146
    in North Dakota, 146–7
    in Oregon, 144
    regional networks and, 145–6
    in South Dakota, 154
    at university subsidiaries, 150–1
    in Utah, 144, 147, 151, 156
    virtual universities and, 147–50
    WCET and, 146–7
    in West, 153–4
    workforce and, 177
    See also virtual universities
Distance Learning and Instructional Technology (DLIT), 144
District of Columbia, governance in, 86
dropout rate, 55, 57

economic development
    community colleges and, 178, 181
    educational attainment and, 73, 82, 105
    public policy issues in, 171, 172, 173, 175
    regional networks and, 145
EdNet, 144
"Education and General" (E&G) expenditures, 108, 111
education "fees," 109
    See also tuition
Educational Appropriations (SHEF category), 122, 125
    in Alaska, 119, 135
    in Arizona, 118, 120
    in Colorado, 118, 123
    definition of, 110
    in Hawaii, 124, 132, 135
    in Idaho, 126, 128
    in Montana, 121, 127
    in Nevada, 128, 129
    in New Mexico, 128, 130
    in North Dakota, 131, 132
    in Oregon, 121, 133
    in relation to other SHEF categories, 111
    in South Dakota, 121, 134
    in US, 114, 115, 140
    in Utah, 132, 136
    in Washington, 125, 137
    in WICHE states, 116, 117, 125, 132, 135, 140
    in Wyoming, 132, 138, 139

educational attainment
  in Alaska, 37, 113, 132, 135
  in Arizona, 37, 113, 118
  in California, 80, 128
  in Colorado, 81, 112
  disparities in, 49
  economic development and, 73, 82, 105
  generation gap and, 47
  global competitiveness in, 72
  goals in, 76, 81, 83
  in Hawaii, 37, 80, 113, 132, 135
  of Hispanics, 49, 68
  in Idaho, 37, 113, 128
  in Kentucky, 75
  Measuring Up state report cards and, 40
  in Montana, 37, 80, 113, 121
  in Nevada, 37, 112, 128
  in New Mexico, 37, 113, 128, 132
  in North Dakota, 37, 113, 132
  in Oregon, 37, 113, 121
  race/ethnicity and, 37–8, 39, 68
  in South Dakota, 37, 113, 125
  state policy leadership and, 76
  state strategies for, 72
  in US, 48, 113
  in Utah, 37, 72, 113, 132
  in Washington, 80, 125
  of Whites, 68
  in WICHE states, 112–13, 140
  workforce and, 31, 66, 72, 76, 181
  of working-age population, 39
  in Wyoming, 37, 113, 132, 135, 139
  of young population *vs.* older adults, 47, 49
  See also degree completion
efficiency/effectiveness of higher education, 66–7, 75, 169, 170, 176, 177, 190
electronic commerce, 154
enrollment, 22–5, 47, 96, 111–12
  vs. affordability, 108
  in AIHEC colleges, 19–20
  in community colleges, 8–9, 48, 160, 164–5, 165, 170, 176, 177, 181
  in four-year institutions *vs.* community colleges, 48
  funding and, 114
  at HSIs, 9
  increases in, 22–3, 25, 59
  of low-income students, 48
  policy issues in, 171, 173
  population mobility and, 16
  in secondary schools, 17–18
  State and Local Support and, 112, 114
  of traditional college-age students, 43, 47, 48, 93. (*See also* immediate college-going rates)
  in US *vs.* OECD, 31, 47
  See also Full-Time-Equivalent Enrollment (FTE) (SHEF category)
enrollment growth, 112–17, 139
  access and, 176
  vs. growth of US population, 112, 140
enrollment "load," 111
Enrollment Mix Index (EMI), 111
enrollment rates
  in Alaska, 50, 113, 119, 135, 165
  in Arizona, 50, 113, 118, 120, 165
  of Blacks, 22–3
  in California, 50, 113, 122, 125, 128, 165
  in Colorado, 113, 118, 119, 123, 165
  in Hawaii, 113, 124, 135, 165
  of Hispanics, 8, 23, 52
  in Idaho, 52, 113, 126, 128, 165
  in Montana, 53, 113, 121, 127, 165
  in Nevada, 53, 112–13, 128, 129, 165, 170, 176
  in New Mexico, 113, 128, 130, 165
  in North Dakota, 113, 131, 132, 165
  in Oregon, 113, 121, 133, 165, 177
  vs. population growth, 22, 140
  in South Dakota, 113, 121, 134, 165
  of traditional college-age youth, 47, 48, 50, 53, 55, 56
  in US, 45, 113, 115
  in Utah, 112, 113, 132, 136, 165
  in Washington, 56, 125, 137, 165
  of Whites, 22–3, 52
  in WICHE states, 113–14
  of working-age population, 43, 50, 53, 54
  See also immediate college-going rates
equity gaps
  generational, 5, 43, 47, 49, 55, 56
  racial/ethnic, 38, 39, 51, 66

"essentialist" model of higher education, 67
Experimental Program to Stimulate Competitive Research (EPSCoR), 61

faculty-centric teaching model, 151
federal assistance
    See financial aid; funding, federal; grants
federal budget, 61–2
"federal connection" in the West, 60, 61, 189
federal domestic funding programs
    See funding, federal
federal economic stimulus funds, 139
federal education policy, 66
federal funding
    See funding, federal
federal immigration laws, 177
federal need-based aid
    See Federal Pell Grant Program
Federal Pell Grant Program, 46, 48, 52, 161
    vs. federal tax credit, 62–3
    vs. state financial aid programs, 64
federal programs
    fiscal integrity of, 66
    See also funding, federal
federal student aid program
    See financial aid; funding, federal
federal student loan program, 65
federal tax credit
    See also tax policy
federal tax credit for higher education expenses, 62–3, 142n1
Federal Termination Policy, 19
fertility rates, 14, 15, 16
finance policy, 91–106
    accountability and, 75
    affordability and, 72
    in Alaska, 171
    current state of, 91, 95–6
    linked with public agenda, 73, 75, 82
    options for changes in, 96–9, 101, 105
    in Oregon, 81
    for public purposes, 74
    reforms in, 77–8, 79
    See also funding, federal; funding, institutional; funding, state; tax policy; tuition policy

financial aid, 106, 109
    in Alaska, 50, 135
    in Arizona, 50
    in Colorado, 51, 181
    at community colleges, 161, 176–7, 181
    as component of affordability, 72
    decreases in, 181
    degree completion rates and, 141–2
    for distance learning, 153, 154
    federal, 62–6, 98, 110–11, 142n1, 169, 177
    in Hawaii, 52
    for Hispanic students, 9
    in Idaho, 52
    in Indiana, 64
    vs. institutional funding, 98, 101, 105
    for low-income students, 48, 50, 52, 53, 54, 55, 56, 57
    in Montana, 53
    in Nevada, 53
    in North Dakota, 54
    in Oklahoma, 64
    in Oregon, 55, 64, 81
    Pell Grant Program, 46, 48, 52, 62–3, 64, 161
    public policy issues in, 171, 173, 174
    Rethinking Financial Aid (The College Board), 65
    scholarship aid, 64
    "shared responsibility" program, 64
    in South Dakota, 55
    state, 43, 46, 48
    student financing policy, 72
    in Utah, 56
    in Washington, 43, 56, 64
    in West, 43
    in Wyoming, 139
    See also funding, federal; funding, state; low-income students
flagship universities, 60, 61
Florida
    funding in, 46, 100, 102
    high school graduation rates in, 44
    immediate college-going rates in, 45, 93
    Measuring Up scores for, 41–2
    public vs. private institutions in, 92
    state governing board in, 86, 87n(a), 87n(l)
    tuition in, 94, 103–4

Florida State Board of Education, 87n(1)
for-profit institutions, 151–3, 154
   degree completion rates in, 49
   low-income students and, 48–9
   workforce and, 150
   See also under *individual institutions*
"40-40-20" plan, 72
four-year institutions *vs.* community colleges, 48
frontier state universities, 61
FTE enrollment
   See Full-Time-Equivalent Enrollment (FTE) (SHEF category)
Full-Time-Equivalent Enrollment (FTE) (SHEF category)
   in Alaska, 119, 135
   in Arizona, 120
   in California, 122, 125
   in Colorado, 118, 123
   definition of, 111
   in Hawaii, 112, 124, 135
   in Idaho, 126, 128
   in Montana, 121, 127
   in Nevada, 112, 128, 129
   in New Mexico, 128, 130
   in North Dakota, 131, 132
   in Oregon, 121, 133
   population growth and, 112
   in South Dakota, 121, 134
   in US, 112, 114, 115
   in Utah, 132, 136
   in Washington, 125, 137
   in WICHE states, 113, 114, 116
   in Wyoming, 138, 139
   See also Educational Appropriations (SHEF category); Total Educational Revenue (SHEF category)
Fund for the Improvement of Postsecondary Education (FIPSE), 147
funding
   equitable distribution of, 106
   family share of, 94
   public policy issues in, 174, 175
   See also finance policy; financial aid
funding, federal, 68–9
   for community colleges, 177
   for distance learning, 154
   earmarked, 60, 62
   for E&G expenditures, 108

federal tax credit, 62
financial aid, 62–6, 98, 110–11, 142n1, 169, 177
   Great Society programs, 59–60
   for middle- *vs.* low-income students, 62–3
   Servicemen's Readjustment Act (1944), 59
   as share of national gross domestic product, 60
   vs. state funding, 43
   for TCUs, 20
   for university research, 60–2, 111, 169
   Workforce Investment Act, 178
   See also Federal Pell Grant Program
funding, institutional, 99, 101, 107–41
   for community colleges, 160, 165–8, 176–7, 177, 179–80, 181
   vs. student aid funding, 98, 101, 105
   for TCUs, 20
   See also tuition
funding, state, 91–106, 107–41
   for community colleges, 160, 165–8, 179–80
   current revenue *vs.* service demands, 107
   degree completion and, 180
   enrollment and, 114
   vs. federal funding, 43
   increased demand for, 63
   for low-income students, 48
   policy options for, 96–101, 105–6
   SHEF analysis of, 108–12, 114–41
   for TCUs, 20
   in Wyoming, 132
   See also finance policy; *individual states*
funding, student
   See financial aid

G. I. Bill
   See Servicemen's Readjustment Act (1944)
Geiger, Roger, xiv
generation gap, 5, 43, 47, 49, 55, 56
Georgia
   funding in, 46, 100, 102
   high school graduation rates in, 44
   immediate college-going rates in, 45, 93

Georgia—*Continued*
  Measuring Up scores for, 41–2
  public *vs.* private institutions in, 92
  state governing board in, 86
  tuition in, 94, 103–4
Getting AHEAD, 177
Glasper, Rufus, 177
global community, 187
global competitiveness, 31, 49, 66, 72, 76, 108
  for research and development, 60–1
global economy, 66, 67, 68, 91
Goodchild, Lester F., xii–xiii, xix, 190, 193
governance, 71, 84–7
  in California, 79, 80, 178–9, 188
  of community colleges, 178–9
  institutional, 73, 81, 83, 101
  public policy issues in, 171–5
  reforms in, 77–8, 79
  See institutional governing boards; state coordinating boards; state governing boards
Governor's Excellence Commission (Utah) (2010), 72
grants, 61, 68, 98, 102, 145
  See also Federal Pell Grant Program; funding, federal
Grapevine survey, 110
Great Depression, the, 4
Great Recession, The (2008), 61, 76, 95, 98–9, 115, 117, 188
  community colleges and, 178, 179
  decline of White high school graduates and, 14
Great Society programs, 59–60
growth states, 4, 47, 96, 97, 98

Halstead, Kent, 110
Harris, Brice, 178
Harvard, establishment of, 3
Hatch Act (1887), 59
Hawaii, xii
  affordability in, 52
  community colleges in, 161–3, 165, 166, 168, 170, 173
  degree completion in, 135
  distance learning in, 144
  Educational Appropriations in, 124, 132, 135
  educational attainment in, 37, 80, 113, 132, 135
  enrollment rates in, 113, 124, 135, 165
  entry into statehood of, 11
  FTE enrollment in, 112, 124, 135
  funding in, 46, 52, 100, 102, 133, 135, 166, 168
  high school graduation rates in, 44, 52
  immediate college-going rates in, 45, 52, 93
  inclusion in census, 26n1
  low-income students in, 52
  Measuring Up state grades for, 34–5, 41–2, 51–2
  minority populations in, 7, 11, 12, 37
  Net Tuition Revenue in, 124, 135
  Performance Measures, 2011, 80
  population growth in, 135
  public *vs.* private institutions in, 92
  residents sent to out-of-state colleges from, 17
  SHEF wave chart of, 124
  state governing board in, 86
  student achievement gaps in, 51
  system configurations in, 135
  Total Educational Revenue in, 124
  tuition in, 52, 94, 97, 103–4
  University of Hawaii Board of Regent, 135
  university research in, 135
Hewlett-Packard, 143
high school graduates
  college-going rate of, 22, 43, 45, 48, 50, 93, 188
  demographic information on, 17, 39
  racial/ethnic backgrounds of, 17, 68
high school graduation rates, 43, 48, 71, 95–6
  in Arizona, 68
  Great Recession and, 14
  in Hawaii, 52
  in Idaho, 52
  in Montana, 53
  in Nevada, 68
  in New Mexico, 54
  in North Dakota, 54, 96
  in Oregon, 54
  in Washington, 56
  in Wyoming, 44, 57
  See also immediate college-going rates

Higher Education Accountability Act (2008), 66
Higher Education Act (1965), 9, 62, 66
Higher Education and Public Policy (Goodchild, Lovell, Hines, and Gill), xvi
Higher Education Coordinating Commission (HECC) (OR), 79, 81
Higher Education Cost Adjustment (HECA), 111, 114
Higher Education in the American West: Regional History and State Contexts (Goodchild, Jonsen, Limerick, and Longanecker), xi–xii, xiv, 159, 187, 188, 190
higher education service agencies *See* state governing boards
Higher Learning Commission, 152
high-income students, 52
high-speed networks, 145–6
Hines, Edward, 110
Hispanic Association of Colleges and Universities (HACU), 9, 181
Hispanics
  in Arizona, 8, 15, 164, 177
  in California, 8–9, 163, 164, 181
  in Colorado, 51
  at community colleges, 8–9, 161
  degree completion rates of, 8
  demographic information on, 7, 8–10, 13–15, 16, 26n3, 36, 52, 68
  educational attainment of, 37–8, 49, 68
  enrollment rates for, 8, 23, 52
  financial aid allocated to, 9
  generational gap for, 49
  in Idaho, 52
  immigration of, 14
  in New Mexico, 8, 9, 15, 164
  population of, 7, 8, 14–15
  in Texas, 8, 9, 15, 181
  in US, 7
  in West, 163
Hispanic-Serving Institutions (HSIs), xiv, 8–10, 163–4
historically underserved populations, 31, 48, 66, 190
human capital, 51, 105, 108, 156

Idaho, xii
  affordability and, 52
  American Indian population in, 11
  community colleges in, 161–3, 165, 166, 168, 170, 174
  degree completion in, 52, 128
  Educational Appropriations in, 126, 128
  educational attainment in, 37, 113, 128
  enrollment rates in, 52, 113, 126, 128, 165
  FTE enrollment in, 126, 128
  funding in, 46, 52, 100, 102, 166, 168
  high school graduation rates in, 44, 52
  Hispanics in, 52
  immediate college-going rates in, 45, 52, 93
  low-income students in, 52
  Measuring Up state grades for, 34–5, 41–2, 52
  Net Tuition Revenue in, 126, 128
  out-of-state students in, 17
  participation in, 52
  preparation in, 52
  public *vs.* private institutions in, 92
  race/ethnicity in, 37
  residents sent to out-of-state colleges from, 17
  SHEF wave chart of, 126
  state governing board in, 85, 86
  system configurations in, 128
  Total Educational Revenue in, 126
  tuition in, 52, 94, 103–4
  Whites in, 52
  working-age population in, 52
Idaho State Board of Education, 128
Illinois
  funding in, 46, 100, 102
  high school graduation rates in, 44
  immediate college-going rates in, 45, 93
  Measuring Up scores for, 41–2
  policy reforms in, 77
  public *vs.* private institutions in, 92
  state coordinating board in, 86
  tuition in, 94, 103–4
Illinois State University, 110
immediate college-going rates, 43, 45, 48, 50, 71–2, 93, 188
  in Colorado, 51

immediate college-going rates—*Continued*
  in Hawaii, 52
  in Idaho, 52
  in Nevada, 53
  in New Mexico, 54
  in Oregon, 54
  in South Dakota, 55
  in WICHE states, 67, 91
  in Wyoming, 57
  See also enrollment rates
immigration, 177, 181
  of Asians/Pacific Islanders, 11
  of Hispanics, 14
income tax, 95, 97
indebtedness, 49
Indiana
  financial aid in, 64
  funding in, 46, 100, 102
  high school graduation rates in, 44
  immediate college-going rates in, 45, 93
  Measuring Up scores for, 41–2
  policy reforms in, 78
  public *vs.* private institutions in, 92
  Reaching Higher, Achieving More, 76
  state coordinating board in, 86
  tuition in, 94, 103–4
  "Twenty-first Century Scholars" program, 64
inflation rates, 109
information and communication technologies, 146, 153
in-migration, 16, 118
  to Colorado, 51
  to Washington, 56
institutional closure/consolidation, 96
institutional governing boards, 73, 101
  in Oregon, 81
institutional mission, 73
  expansion of, 59
  State of the Union address (2013) and, 66–7
  for TCUs, 19, 164
  technology and, 155
  at virtual universities, 149
Instructional Television Fixed Service (ITFS), 43
Integrated Basic Educational Skills Training (I-BEST) Program, 179
Internet, 2, 145–6

Iowa
  Ashford University, 152
  distance learning in, 152
  funding in, 46, 100, 102
  high school graduation rates in, 44
  immediate college-going rates in, 45, 93
  Measuring Up scores for, 41–2
  public *vs.* private institutions in, 92
  state governing board in, 86
  tuition in, 94, 103–4

Johnstone, Sally, xx, 143, 188–9, 193
Jones, Dennis, xix–xx, 91, 95, 106, 158, 179, 182, 188, 194
Jones International University (JIU) (CO), 152
Jonsen, Richard, xii–xiii, xix, 190, 194

K-12 education, 32, 33, 47, 71, 99, 105, 177
  in California, 51
  high-speed networks and, 146
  in Montana, 53
  in Utah, 55
Kansas
  funding in, 46, 100, 102
  high school graduation rates in, 44
  immediate college-going rates in, 45, 93
  Measuring Up scores for, 41–2
  public *vs.* private institutions in, 92
  state governing board in, 86, 87n(d)
  tuition in, 94, 103–4
Kansas Board of Regents, 87n(d)
Kentucky
  educational attainment in, 75
  enrollment rates in, 45
  funding in, 46, 100, 102
  high school graduation rates in, 44
  immediate college-going rates in, 45, 93
  Measuring Up scores for, 41–2
  policy reforms in, 78
  public *vs.* private institutions in, 92
  state coordinating board in, 86
  tuition in, 94, 103–4
Kentucky Postsecondary Education Reform Act (1996), 75
Kerr, Clark, xiv–xv

land-grant institutions, 19, 59, 145
Latinos
   See Hispanics
learning
   See student learning, as *Measuring Up* report card category
Leavitt, Mike, 147
Lenth, Charles, xx, 107, 188, 194
Limerick, Patricia Nelson, xii, xvi, xix, 69, 190, 195
Livingston, Jeffery, 147
Longanecker, David A., xii, xvi, xix, xx, 59, 187, 195
Louisiana
   funding in, 46, 100, 102
   high school graduation rates in, 44
   immediate college-going rates in, 45, 93
   Measuring Up scores for, 41–2
   policy reforms in, 77
   public *vs.* private institutions in, 92
   state coordinating board in, 86
   tuition in, 94, 103–4
Lovell, Cheryl, xx, 159, 189, 196
low-income students, 96, 99
   in Arizona, 50
   college access for, 43, 48–9
   in Colorado, 51
   community colleges and, 48–9
   enrollment and, 48
   federal funding and, 62–3
   financial aid for, 43, 48, 50, 53, 54, 55, 56, 57
   for-profit institutions and, 48–9
   in Hawaii, 52
   vs. high-income students, 52
   at HSIs, 163–4
   in Idaho, 52
   in Montana, 53
   in North Dakota, 54
   in Oregon, 55
   Pell Grant Program and, 46, 48, 52, 62–3, 64, 161
   in secondary school, 18
   in South Dakota, 55
   student achievement gaps and, 51
   in Utah, 56
   See also financial aid
"low tuition, low aid" approach, 43
Lumina Foundation, 72, 76, 177

Magnuson, Warren, 60
Maine
   funding in, 46, 100, 102
   high school graduation rates in, 44
   immediate college-going rates in, 45, 93
   Measuring Up scores for, 41–2
   policy reforms in, 77
   public *vs.* private institutions in, 92
   state governing board in, 86
   tuition in, 94, 103–4
Maine Maritime Academy, 87n(e)
major minority regions, 7, 17
   See also minority populations
Malone, Michael, xii
Maricopa Community Colleges (AZ), 118, 150, 177
Maryland
   funding in, 46, 100, 102
   high school graduation rates in, 44
   immediate college-going rates in, 45, 93
   Measuring Up scores for, 41–2
   public *vs.* private institutions in, 92
   state coordinating board in, 86
   tuition in, 94, 103–4
Massachusetts
   funding in, 46, 100, 102
   high school graduation rates in, 44
   immediate college-going rates in, 45, 93
   Measuring Up scores for, 41–2
   public *vs.* private institutions in, 92
   state governing board in, 86, 87n(j)
   tuition in, 94, 103–4
Massachusetts Institute of Technology, 156
Massive Open Online Courses (MOOC), 153
McGuiness, Aims, xix, 188, 196
Measuring Up 2006: The State Report Cards for Higher Education (National Center for Public Policy and Higher Education), 32, 188
   See also under *specific report card categories; specific states*
Measuring Up state report cards, 32–5, 39–47, 50–7, 71–2, 81
Medicaid, 99
Mellon Foundation, 156

Index

Mendenhall, Robert, 147
metropolitan areas, 59
"metropolitanization," 4
Michigan
   funding in, 46, 100, 102
   high school graduation rates in, 44
   immediate college-going rates in, 45, 93
   Measuring Up scores for, 41–2
   public *vs.* private institutions in, 92
   state governing board in, 86, 87n(g)
   tuition in, 94, 103–4
Michigan State Board of Education, 85, 87n(g)
middle-income families, 62–3
Midwest, demographic information on, 4, 5, 8, 39
migration trends, 4, 8, 15–16
Mind Extension University, 152
Minnesota
   funding in, 46, 100, 102
   governance in, 86
   high school graduation rates in, 44
   immediate college-going rates in, 45, 93
   Measuring Up scores for, 41–2
   public *vs.* private institutions in, 92
   TCUs in, 20
   tuition in, 94, 103–4
minority populations, xvi, 7, 17
   community colleges and, 159
   educational attainment and, 37–8, 39
   growth of, 8
   participation and, 52, 163
mission
   See institutional mission
Mississippi
   funding in, 46, 100, 102
   high school graduation rates in, 44
   higher education reform in, 77
   immediate college-going rates in, 45, 93
   Measuring Up scores for, 41–2
   public *vs.* private institutions in, 92
   state governing board in, 86
   tuition in, 94, 103–4
Missouri
   distance learning in, 150
   funding in, 46, 100, 102
   high school graduation rates in, 44
   immediate college-going rates in, 45, 93
   Measuring Up scores for, 41–2
   public *vs.* private institutions in, 92
   state coordinating board in, 86
   tuition in, 94, 103–4
mobile devices, 156–7
Montana, xii
   affordability in, 53
   American Indian population in, 11
   Board of Regents of the Montana University System, 80
   community colleges in, 161–3, 165, 166, 168, 170, 174
   degree completion rates in, 53, 121
   distance learning in, 150
   Educational Appropriations in, 121, 127
   educational attainment in, 37, 80, 113, 121
   enrollment rates in, 53, 113, 121, 127, 165
   FTE enrollment in, 121, 127
   funding in, 46, 53, 100, 102, 166, 168
   governance in, 80, 86
   high school graduation rates in, 44, 53
   immediate college-going rates in, 45, 93
   low-income students in, 53
   Measuring Up state grades for, 34–5, 41–2, 53
   modem connection in, 145
   Net Tuition Revenue in, 121, 127
   out-of-state students in, 17
   policy reforms in, 77
   population growth in, 121
   preparation in, 53
   public *vs.* private institutions in, 92
   race/ethnicity in, 37
   Salish Kootenai College, 20
   SHEF wave chart of, 127
   system configurations in, 121
   TCUs in, 20
   Total Educational Revenue in, 121, 127
   traditional college-age youth in, 53
   tuition in, 94, 104
   working-age adults in, 53
Montana University System, 80, 121
Morrill Act (1862), 59

National Assessment of Educational Progress, 54
National Center for Higher Education Management Systems (NCHEMS), 95, 99, 147
National Center for Public Policy and Higher Education, 76, 177
National Collaborative for Higher Education Policy (2003–2006), 75
National Commission on Accountability in Higher Education, 76
National Conference of State Legislatures, 76
National Governors' Association, 73, 76
National Institutes of Health, 61
National Lambda Rail, 145–6
National Research Initiative, 61
National Science Foundation, 61, 145
National Science Foundation Network (NSFNET), 145
National Student Clearinghouse Research Center, 17
National Technological University (NTU), 144, 146
National University (CA), 151
Native American Higher Education Initiative, 20
Native Americans
  See under American Indians
natural resource extraction revenue, 60, 132, 135
Navajo Community College (AZ), 19
Nebraska
  funding in, 46, 100, 102
  high school graduation rates in, 44
  immediate college-going rates in, 45, 93
  Measuring Up scores for, 41–2
  public *vs.* private institutions in, 92
  state coordinating board in, 86
  tuition in, 94, 103–4
need-based aid
  See Federal Pell Grant Program, state need-based aid; financial aid
"Need for State Policy Leadership, The" (National Center for Public Policy and Higher Education), 76
Net Tuition Revenue (SHEF category)
  in Alaska, 119, 135

  in all WICHE states, 116, 117, 125
  in Arizona, 120
  in California, 122, 125
  in Colorado, 118, 119, 123
  definition of, 110–11
  in Hawaii, 124, 135
  in Idaho, 126, 128
  in Montana, 121, 127
  in Nevada, 128, 129
  in New Mexico, 128, 130
  in North Dakota, 131, 132
  in Oregon, 121, 133
  in relation to other SHEF categories, 111, 112, 114
  in South Dakota, 121, 134
  in United States, 114, 115, 140
  in Utah, 132, 136
  in Washington, 125, 137
  in Wyoming, 138, 139
Nevada, xii
  affordability in, 53
  American Indian population in, 11
  audit of higher educational system in, 170
  community colleges in, 161–3, 165, 166, 168, 170, 176
  degree completion in, 47, 53, 128
  Educational Appropriations in, 128, 129
  educational attainment in, 37, 112, 128
  enrollment rates in, 53, 112–13, 113, 128, 129, 165, 170, 176
  FTE enrollment in, 112, 128, 129
  funding in, 46, 53, 100, 102, 128, 166, 168
  governance in, 80, 86
  high school graduation rates in, 44, 68
  immediate college-going rates in, 45, 53, 93
  Measuring Up state grades for, 34–5, 41–2, 47, 53
  Net Tuition Revenue in, 128, 129
  participation in, 53, 112–13
  policy reforms in, 77
  population growth in, 4, 128
  preparation in, 53
  public *vs.* private institutions in, 92
  race/ethnicity in, 37
  SHEF wave chart of, 129
  state taxes in, 97

Nevada—*Continued*
  system configurations in, 128
  System of Higher Education, 80
  Total Educational Revenue in, 129
  tuition in, 94, 103–4
  working-age adults in, 53
Nevada System of Higher Education, 80, 128
New Hampshire
  funding in, 46, 100, 102
  governance in, 86
  high school graduation rates in, 44
  immediate college-going rates in, 45, 93
  Measuring Up scores for, 41–2
  public *vs.* private institutions in, 92
  tuition in, 94, 103–4
New Jersey
  funding in, 46, 100, 102
  high school graduation rates in, 44
  immediate college-going rates in, 45, 93
  Measuring Up scores for, 41–2
  public *vs.* private institutions in, 92
  state coordinating board in, 86
  tuition in, 94, 103–4
New Mexico, xii
  community colleges in, 161–3, 165, 166, 168, 170, 174–5
  degree completion in, 53, 128, 132
  distance learning in, 146
  Educational Appropriations in, 128, 130
  educational attainment in, 37, 113, 128, 132
  enrollment rates in, 113, 128, 130, 165
  FTE enrollment in, 128, 130
  funding in, 46, 100, 102, 166, 168, 176
  governance in, 80, 86, 87n(h)
  high school graduation rates in, 44, 54
  Higher Education Performance Fund in, 176
  Hispanic population in, 8, 9, 15, 164
  immediate college-going rates in, 45, 54
  Measuring Up state grades for, 34–5, 41–2, 47, 53–4
  minority populations in, 7, 11
  Net Tuition Revenue in, 128, 130
  participation in, 53, 53–4

  population growth in, 128
  preparation in, 53
  public *vs.* private institutions in, 92
  race/ethnicity in, 7, 37, 38
  SHEF wave chart of, 130
  system configurations in, 128, 132
  taxes in, 95
  Total Educational Revenue in, 130
  tuition in, 94, 103–4
New Mexico Department of Higher Education, 85, 128
New Mexico Secretary of Higher Education, 80, 87n(h)
New York
  funding in, 46, 100, 102
  high school graduation rates in, 44
  immediate college-going rates in, 45, 93
  Measuring Up scores for, 41–2
  public *vs.* private institutions in, 92
  state coordinating board in, 85, 86, 87n(a)
  tuition in, 94, 104
New York Board of Regents, 85
Nippon Telegraph and Telephone Corporation (NTT), 145
North Carolina
  funding in, 46, 100, 102
  high school graduation rates in, 44
  immediate college-going rates in, 45, 93
  Measuring Up scores for, 41–2
  public *vs.* private institutions in, 92
  state governing board in, 86
  tuition in, 94, 103–4
North Central Association, 148, 152
North Dakota, xii, 3, 17, 180
  affordability in, 54
  American Indian population in, 11
  community colleges in, 161–3, 165, 166, 168, 170, 175, 180
  degree completion rates in, 54
  distance learning in, 146–7
  Educational Appropriations in, 131, 132
  educational attainment in, 37, 113, 132
  enrollment rates in, 113, 131, 132, 165
  FTE enrollment in, 131, 132
  funding in, 46, 54, 100, 102, 166, 168
  high school graduation rates in, 44, 54, 96

immediate college-going rates in, 45, 93
low-income students in, 54
Measuring Up state grades for, 34–5, 41–2, 54
Net Tuition Revenue in, 131, 132
participation in, 54
population growth in, 132
public *vs.* private institutions in, 92
race/ethnicity in, 37
SHEF wave chart of, 131
state governing board in, 86
state revenue in, 95
system configurations in, 132
taxes in, 95
TCUs in, 20
Total Educational Revenue in, 131, 132
traditional college-age youth in, 54
tuition in, 94, 103–4
University of North Dakota, 146–7
working-age adults in, 54
North Dakota Educational Roundtable, 75
North Dakota Interactive Video Network (IVN), 144
North Dakota University System, 132, 144
Northeast, demographic information on, 4, 5, 39
NorthWest Academic Computing Consortium (NWACC), 145
Northwest Association, 148
NorthWestNet, 145
NTU College of Engineering and Applied Sciences, 144

Obama, Barack, 31, 63, 66–7, 72, 76
OECD countries
  See Organization for Economic Cooperation and Development (OECD)
Ohio
  funding in, 46, 100, 102
  high school graduation rates in, 44
  immediate college-going rates in, 45, 93
  Measuring Up scores for, 41–2
  public *vs.* private institutions in, 92
  state coordinating board in, 86

Strategic Plan for Higher Education 2008–2017, 76
  tuition in, 94, 103–4
  University System of Ohio, 88n2
Oklahoma
  financial aid in, 64
  funding in, 46, 100, 102
  high school graduation rates in, 44
  immediate college-going rates in, 45, 93
  Measuring Up scores for, 41–2
  public *vs.* private institutions in, 92
  state coordinating board in, 86
  tuition in, 94, 103–4
  WCET and, 146
"Oklahoma Promise Scholarship," 64
online student services, 151
online writing lab, 150
open access institutions, 181, 189
open course materials, 156
Open Educational Resources (OER) movement, 156
Oregon, xii
  accountability in, 81
  affordability in, 54–5
  community colleges in, 55, 161–3, 165, 166, 168, 170, 175, 177–8
  degree completion in, 54, 55, 121
  distance learning in, 144
  Educational Appropriations in, 121, 133
  educational attainment in, 37, 113, 121
  enrollment rates in, 113, 121, 133, 165, 177
  finance policy in, 81
  financial aid in, 55, 64, 81
  "40–40–20" plan, 72, 81
  FTE enrollment in, 121, 133
  funding in, 46, 100, 102, 166, 168, 177, 177–8
  governance in, 79, 81
  high school graduation rates in, 44, 54
  Higher Education Coordinating Commission (HECC), 79, 81
  immediate college-going rates in, 45, 54, 93
  low-income students in, 55
  Measuring Up state grades for, 34–5, 41–2, 54–5
  Net Tuition Revenue in, 121, 133

Oregon—*Continued*
 out-of-state students in, 17
 policy reform in, 78
 public *vs.* private institutions in, 92
 race/ethnicity in, 37
 "shared responsibility" program, 64
 SHEF wave chart of, 133
 state coordinating board in, 81
 state governing board in, 86
 system configurations in, 121
 Total Educational Revenue in, 121, 133
 tuition in, 94, 103–4, 177
Oregon Department of Community Colleges and Workforce Development, 121
Oregon Education Investment Board (OEIB), 79, 81
Oregon University System, 121
Organization for Economic Cooperation and Development (OECD), 31
 countries in, 33, 40, 47, 68, 88n1
out-of-state students, 17

P-20 policy, 73, 79, 81, 82, 87n(l)
Palmer, James, 110
participation
 among working-age population, 53, 54
 in community colleges, 160
 in Idaho, 52
 income level and, 52
 as *Measuring Up* report card category, 32–4, 40, 41, 43, 52–6, 71–2
 in Nevada, 53, 112–13
 in New Mexico, 53–4
 in North Dakota, 54
 preparation and, 64
 race/ethnicity and, 52, 163
 in South Dakota, 55
 in Utah, 55–6
 in WICHE states, 91, 112–14
Pell Grant
 See Federal Pell Grant Program
Pennsylvania
 funding in, 46, 100, 102
 high school graduation rates in, 44
 immediate college-going rates in, 45, 93
 Measuring Up scores for, 41–2
 public *vs.* private institutions in, 92

 state coordinating board in, 85, 87n(a), 87n(i)
 state service agency in, 86
 tuition in, 94, 103–4
Pennsylvania Secretary of Education, 85
Pennsylvania State Board of Education, 85, 87n(i)
Performance Measures, 2011 (University of Hawaii System), 80
Pima Community College (AZ), 118
policy change, roadmap for, 32, 47–9, 96–106
policy leadership
 See state policy leadership
population
 See demographic information
population dispersion, 14–15, 132, 139, 153
population distribution by age groups, 5–7
population growth, 3–5, 112, 114
 of American Indians/Native Alaskans, 10–11
 in Arizona, 4, 118
 of Asians/Pacific Islanders, 7, 11–12
 of Blacks, 12–13
 in California, 125
 of children (0–14), 18
 in Colorado, 118
 distressed educational performance and, 68
 vs. enrollment rates, 22, 140
 FTE enrollment and, 112
 in Hawaii, 135
 for Hispanics, 7, 8, 14–15
 in Montana, 121
 in Nevada, 4, 128
 in New Mexico, 128
 in North Dakota, 132
 race/ethnicity and, 7
 of traditional college-age youth, 36, 47
 in Utah, 132
 in Wyoming, 139
 See also growth states; *individual states*
population mobility, 16–17
 federal immigration laws, 177
 immigration, 11, 14, 177, 181
 migration trends, 4, 8, 15–16
predictive analytics reporting (PAR), 156

preparation
 in Alaska, 50
 in Idaho, 52
 as *Measuring Up* report card category, 33–4, 39, 40, 41, 71
 in Montana, 53
 in Nevada, 53
 in New Mexico, 53
 participation and, 64
 by specific states in WICHE, 50–6
 "Twenty-first Century Scholars" and, 64
Principles of Good Practice for Electronically Offered Academic Degree and Certificate Program, 147, 148–50
private for-profit institutions, 151–3, 154
 low-income students and, 48–9
private institutions *vs.* public institutions, 21–2, 82, 91, 92
private not-for-profit institutions, 151
private servicing companies, 65
professional development, public policy issues in, 175
public 2-year colleges, tuition at, 104
public 4-year colleges, tuition at, 103
public agenda, 71–83
 short-term *vs.* long-term, 73–5
 state policies and, 73–5
Public Broadcasting Network, 144
public financing
 See funding, federal; funding, state
public institutions
 as enterprises, 105
 vs. private institutions, 21–2, 82, 91, 92
 tuition at, 103, 104
public interest
 See public agenda
public policy
 pertaining to community colleges, 160, 169–76
 population mobility and, 16
Public Policy Challenges Facing Higher Education in the American West (Goodchild, Jonsen, Limerick, and Longanecker), xi–xii, xiv, xvi
public services, 107
Puerto Rico, governance in, 86

quality of life linked with higher education, 71, 72, 73, 75, 80, 81, 82, 83, 190

race/ethnicity, 7–8
 age demographics and, 15–16
 educational attainment and, 37–8, 39, 68
 high school completion and, 17, 68
 participation and, 52, 163
 population growth and, 7
 young population and, 31, 36
racial/ethnic gaps, 38, 39, 66
 in Colorado, 51
Reaching Higher, Achieving More (Indiana Commission for Higher Education), 76
recession, 61, 109, 112, 115, 139
 See also Great Recession, The (2008)
reciprocity agreement, 152–3
reforms
 in accountability, 73, 74, 76–8, 79
 in higher education, 77–8
 in regulatory policy, 73, 74, 75, 82, 84–5
regional networks, 145–6
regulatory policy, 73, 74, 75, 77–8, 79, 82, 84–5
remote learning
 See distance learning
research funding, 60–2, 111, 169
research universities, 139
 in Alaska, 132, 135
 funding for, 60–2, 111, 169
 in Hawaii, 135
Rethinking Financial Aid (The College Board) (2008), 65
Rhode Island
 funding in, 46, 100, 102
 high school graduation rates in, 44
 immediate college-going rates in, 45, 93
 Measuring Up scores for, 41–2
 public *vs.* private institutions in, 92
 state governing board in, 86
 tuition in, 94, 103–4
Rice University (TX), 156
Rio Salado Community College
 RioLearn, 151
 RioLounge, 151

218　INDEX

Rio Salado Community College (AZ), 150–1
Rockefeller Institute of Government, 95, 99
Romer, Roy, 147
Ryu, Mikyung, xix, 31, 49, 57, 188, 197

sales tax, 95, 97
Salish Kootenai College (MT), 20
scholarship aid, 64
secondary schools, demographic information on, 17–18
Servicemen's Readjustment Act (1944), 59
Setting a Public Agenda for Higher Education in the States: Lessons Learned from the National Collaborative for Higher Education (National Collaborative for Higher Education Policy), 75
"shared responsibility" program (2007), 64
SHEF report
　See *State Higher Education Finance* (SHEF report)
SHEF wave charts by state
　all United States, 115
　all WICHE states, 116
　Alaska, 119
　Arizona, 120
　California, 122
　Colorado, 123
　Hawaii, 124
　Idaho, 126
　Montana, 127
　Nevada, 129
　New Mexico, 130
　North Dakota, 131
　Oregon, 133
　South Dakota, 134
　Utah, 136
　Washington, 137
　Wyoming, 138
Shireman, Robert, 178
social networking services, 151, 153
South Carolina
　funding in, 46, 100, 102
　high school graduation rates in, 44
　immediate college-going rates in, 45, 93
　Measuring Up scores for, 41–2

public *vs.* private institutions in, 92
state coordinating board in, 86
tuition in, 94, 103–4
South Dakota, xii, 3
　affordability in, 55
　college participation in, 55
　community colleges in, 161–3, 165, 166, 168, 170
　degree completion in, 55, 125
　distance learning in, 154
　Educational Appropriations in, 121, 134
　educational attainment in, 37, 113, 125
　enrollment rates in, 113, 121, 134, 165
　financial aid in, 55
　FTE enrollment in, 121, 134
　funding in, 43, 46, 100, 102, 166, 168
　high school graduation rates in, 44
　immediate college-going rates in, 45, 55, 93
　low-income students in, 55
　Measuring Up state grades for, 34–5, 41–2, 55
　Net Tuition Revenue in, 121, 134
　out-of-state students in, 17
　population growth in, 121
　public *vs.* private institutions in, 92
　race/ethnicity in, 37
　SHEF wave chart of, 134
　state governing board in, 86
　system configurations in, 121, 125
　Total Educational Revenue in, 121, 125, 134
　tuition in, 94, 103–4
South Dakota Board of Regents, 121
South, demographic information on, 4, 5, 8, 15, 39
Southwest, the, 8
Spellings, Margaret, 66
Stafford loans, 161
Stanford University, 153, 156
State and Local Support (SHEF category)
　decline in, 139, 140
　definition of, 110
　enrollment and, 112, 114
state budgets, 62, 74, 95, 98, 107
　state budget crises, 73, 74, 79
　state budget shortfalls, 167
state coordinating boards, 74, 84
　in California, 80
　in Colorado, 80–1, 86

in New Mexico, 80
in New York, 85, 86, 87n(a)
in Oregon, 81
in Pennsylvania, 85, 87n(a), 87n(i)
vs. state governing boards, 79
in Washington, 80
state economy, 73, 74, 75, 76, 80, 96, 98
   community colleges and, 179, 181
state funding
   See funding, state
state governing boards, 73–4, 79–81, 84–7
   See also under *specific governing boards*
State Higher Education Executive Officers (SHEEO), 108–12, 114, 139, 152, 188
State Higher Education Finance (SHEF report), 108–39
   analysis of individual WICHE states, 114–39
   conclusions drawn from, 139–41
   Full-Time-Equivalent Enrollment (FTE) (SHEF category)
   measuring enrollment growth through, 112–14
   Net Tuition Revenue (SHEF category)
   origins and development of, 108–12. (*See also* Educational Appropriations (SHEF category))
   SHEF wave charts by state
   State and Local Support (SHEF category)
   Total Educational Revenue (SHEF category)
state need-based aid, 43, 46, 52, 53
   See also financial aid; funding, state
State of the Union address (2013), 66–7
state policy leadership, 71–83
   challenges in, 73–5
   changing expectations in, 71–3, 74
   educational attainment and, 76
   governing boards and, 73–4, 79–81
   prerequisites for, 81–3
   reforms in, 75–81
   workforce and, 76
state report cards
   See *Measuring Up* state report cards
state service agencies, 84–7
state tax, 97, 110, 114
StraighterLine, 153

Strategic Plan for Higher Education 2008–2017 (University System of Ohio), 76
student achievement gaps, 51
student aid programs
   See financial aid
student financing policy, 72
   See also finance policy
student learning, as *Measuring Up* report card category, 32, 33, 39
"student load," 109
student status/classification, public policy issues in, 171
subsidies, 65, 108, 112
   See also funding, federal; funding, institutional; funding, state
system configurations
   in Alaska, 135
   in Arizona, 118
   in California, 125, 128
   in Colorado, 118
   in Hawaii, 135
   in Idaho, 128
   in Montana, 121
   in Nevada, 128
   in New Mexico, 128, 132
   in North Dakota, 132
   in Oregon, 121
   in South Dakota, 121, 125
   in Utah, 132
system planning, public policy issues in, 171–2, 173, 174, 175

T1 lines, 125
tax, income, 95, 97
tax policy, xvi, 91, 95, 97, 98, 102
   federal tax credits, 62–3, 142n1
tax revenue, 110, 114
   vs. service demands, 107
tax, sales, 95, 97
tax, state, 97, 110, 114
TCUs
   See Tribal Colleges and Universities (TCUs)
technology
   affordability and, 151
   institutional mission and, 155
   See also distance learning; *specific technologies*
TelNet, 145

Tennessee
  funding in, 46, 100, 102
  high school graduation rates in, 44
  higher education reform in, 78
  immediate college-going rates in, 45, 93
  Measuring Up scores for, 41–2
  public *vs.* private institutions in, 92
  state coordinating board in, 86
  tuition in, 94, 103–4
Tennessee Complete College Act (2010), 76
Test of Leadership, Charting the Future of U.S. Higher Education (Commission on the Future of Higher Education) (2006), 66
Texas
  Closing the Gaps initiative, 75
  funding in, 46, 100, 102
  high school graduation rates in, 44
  higher education reform in, 77
  Hispanic population in, 8, 9, 15, 181
  immediate college-going rates in, 45, 93
  Measuring Up scores for, 41–2
  public *vs.* private institutions in, 92
  Rice University, 156
  state coordinating board in, 86, 87n(f)
  tuition in, 94, 103–4
Texas Coordinating Board for Higher Education, 75, 87n(f)
Texas Higher Education Coordination Board, 75
Total Educational Revenue (SHEF category)
  in Alaska, 119, 135
  in all WICHE states, 116, 140
  in Arizona, 120
  in California, 122, 125
  in Colorado, 118, 123
  definition of, 111
  in Hawaii, 124
  in Idaho, 126
  in Montana, 121, 127
  in Nevada, 129
  in New Mexico, 130
  in North Dakota, 131, 132
  in Oregon, 121, 133
  in relation to other SHEF categories, 112, 114, 117
  in South Dakota, 121, 125, 134
  in United States, 115, 140
  in Utah, 132, 136
  in Washington, 118, 137
  in Wyoming, 138
traditional college-age youth
  vs. adult learners, 5, 43, 47, 49, 55, 56
  degree completion rates for, 55
  diversity of, 188, 189
  enrollment rates for, 43, 47, 48, 50, 53, 55, 56
  high school completion rates for, 54
  in Montana, 53
  in North Dakota, 54
  population growth in, 36, 47
  in Utah, 55–6
  in Washington, 56
traditionally disadvantaged students
  See historically underserved populations
transfer function of community colleges, 179, 180, 181
transfer/articulation, public policy issues in, 171, 175
Transforming Higher Education: National Imperative—State Responsibility (National Conference of State Legislatures) (2006), 76
Tribal Colleges and Universities (TCUs), xiv, 9, 18–20, 161, 163–4
tuition
  affordability and, 101
  in Arizona, 177
  in California, 97, 117, 140, 178
  in ESL and ABE programs, 177
  vs. family income, 50, 51, 52, 72
  in Hawaii, 52, 97
  in Idaho, 52
  increases in, 43, 64, 97, 99, 141, 176, 177, 180
  in Oregon, 177
  at public 2-year colleges, 104
  at public 4-year colleges, 103
  in Wyoming, 91, 138, 139
  See also Net Tuition Revenue (SHEF category)
tuition policy, 72, 101, 105, 106
  low tuition policies in WICHE states, 43, 51, 91, 95, 97, 99, 109
tuition tax credit, 62

tuition revenue, 101–6, 108–9, 112, 118
  See also Net Tuition Revenue
    (SHEF category)
"Twenty-first Century Scholars"
  program, 64
2008 recession
  See Great Recession, The (2008)

unemployment, 63, 107, 108, 114, 115
United Nations Educational Scientific
  and Cultural Organization
  (UNESCO), 156
United States
  degree completion in, 23–4, 25, 67
  economy of, 61, 66
  Educational Appropriations in, 114,
    115, 140
  educational attainment in, 48, 113
  enrollment rates in, 45, 113, 115
  FTE enrollment in, 112, 114, 115
  funding in, 46, 100
  high school graduation rates in, 44
  immediate college-going rates in,
    45, 93
  Measuring Up scores for, 41–2
  vs. OECD countries, 31, 33, 68
  public *vs.* private institutions in, 92
  racial/ethnic demographics of, 7
  SHEF wave chart of, 115
  Total Educational Revenue in, 115, 140
  tuition in, 94, 103–4, 114, 115, 140
University and Community College Joint
  Council of Presidents (AZ), 177
University of Alaska system, 135
University of Arizona, 146
University of California system, 125
University of Hawaii Board of Regents,
  135
University of North Dakota, 146–7
University of Phoenix Online, 152, 154
university subsidiaries, 150–1
University System of Ohio, 88n2
US budget deficit, 61
US Bureau of the Census, demographic
  information from, 3–4, 7–8, 10,
  14–15, 16, 26n1, 36
US Department of Commerce, 146
US Department of Education, 17, 66,
  152, 160
US Department of Labor, 169

US Department of the Interior, 164
Uses of the University, The (Kerr), xiv–xv
Utah, xii
  affordability in, 56
  college enrollment in, 55
  college participation in, 55–6
  community colleges in, 161–3, 165,
    166, 168
  degree completion in, 55–6, 132
  distance learning in, 144, 147, 151, 156
  Educational Appropriations in, 132, 136
  educational attainment in, 37, 72,
    113, 132
  enrollment rates in, 112, 113, 132,
    136, 165
  FTE enrollment in, 132, 136
  funding in, 46, 56, 100, 102, 166, 168
  governance in, 80, 86
  Governor's Excellence Commission
    (2010), 72
  high school graduation rates in, 44
  immediate college-going rates in,
    45, 93
  low-income students in, 56
  Measuring Up state grades for, 34–5,
    41–2, 55–6
  Net Tuition Revenue in, 136
  out-of-state students in, 17
  population growth in, 132
  preparation in, 55–6
  public *vs.* private institutions in, 92
  race/ethnicity in, 37
  SHEF wave chart of, 136
  system configurations in, 132
  Total Educational Revenue in, 132, 136
  traditional college-age youth in, 55–6
  tuition in, 94, 103–4, 132
Utah Board of Regents, 80
Utah Educational Network, 151
Utah System of Higher Education, 132

Verio, 145
Vermont
  funding in, 46, 100, 102
  high school graduation rates in, 44
  immediate college-going rates in, 45, 93
  Measuring Up scores for, 41–2
  public *vs.* private institutions in, 92
  state governing board in, 86, 87n(k)
  tuition in, 94, 103–4

Vermont Higher Education Council, 85, 87n(k)
video-classroom experience, 146
Virginia
 funding in, 46, 100, 102
 high school graduation rates in, 44
 higher education reforms in, 77
 immediate college-going rates in, 45, 93
 Measuring Up scores for, 41–2
 public *vs.* private institutions in, 92
 state coordinating board in, 86
 tuition in, 94, 103–4
virtual consortiums, 150
virtual universities, 147–55
 consumer protection for, 154–5
 first virtual universities, 147–8
 for-profit institutions, 151–3
 future of, 155–7
 institutional missions of, 149
 prevalence in the West of, 153–4
 private not-for-profit institutions, 151
 quality assurance for, 148–50
 university and community college subsidiaries, 150–1
 See also distance learning
voucher system, 51

Walden University, 144
Washington Higher Education Coordinating Board (HECB), 80
Washington state, xii
 affordability in, 56
 City University of Seattle, 151
 community colleges in, 56, 161–3, 165, 166, 168, 170, 176–7
 degree completion in, 47
 Educational Appropriations in, 125, 137
 educational attainment in, 37, 80, 113, 125
 enrollment rates in, 56, 113, 125, 137, 165
 financial aid in, 43, 46, 56, 64
 FTE enrollment in, 125, 137
 funding in, 100, 102, 166, 168, 176–7
 governance in, 80, 86
 high school graduation rates in, 44, 56
 I-BEST Program, 179
 immediate college-going rates in, 45, 93
 in-migration to, 56

 Measuring Up state grades, 34–5, 41–2, 47, 56
 public *vs.* private institutions in, 92
 race/ethnicity in, 37
 sales tax in, 95
 SHEF wave chart of, 137
 system configurations in, 125
 Total Educational Revenue in, 118, 137
 tuition in, 64, 94, 103–4, 118, 125, 137
Washington State Achievement Council, 80
Washington Steering Committee, 80
wave charts
 See SHEF wave charts by state
WCET
 See Western Cooperative for Educational Telecommunications (WCET)
webstreaming, 154
West, the
 See Alaska; Arizona; California; Colorado; Hawaii; Idaho; Montana; Nevada; New Mexico; North Dakota; Oregon; South Dakota; Utah; Washington; Wyoming
West Virginia
 funding in, 46, 100, 102
 high school graduation rates in, 44
 immediate college-going rates in, 45, 93
 Measuring Up scores for, 41–2
 public *vs.* private institutions in, 92
 state coordinating board in, 86
 tuition in, 94, 103–4
Western Association, 148
Western Cooperative for Educational Telecommunications (WCET), 146–7, 148, 152, 155, 156; WOW! award, 150
Western Governors' Association (WGA), 147
Western Governors University (WGU), 147–8, 151
Western Interstate Commission for Higher Education (WICHE), xii, 3, 8, 14, 17
Whites
 in Colorado, 51

demographic information on, 4, 7–8, 13–14, 15, 16, 36, 39, 52, 68
educational attainment of, 37–8, 68
enrollment rates of, 22–3, 52
in Idaho, 52
WICHE
See Western Interstate Commission for Higher Education
WICHE states, xii
SHEF wave chart of, 116
See also Alaska; Arizona; California; Colorado; Hawaii; Idaho; Montana; Nevada; New Mexico; North Dakota; Oregon; South Dakota; Utah; Washington; Wyoming
Wiley, David, 156
William and Flora Hewlett Foundation, 155–6
wireless devices, 156–7
Wisconsin
funding in, 46, 100, 102
high school graduation rates in, 44
immediate college-going rates in, 45, 93
Measuring Up scores for, 41–2
public *vs.* private institutions in, 92
state governing board in, 86
tuition in, 94, 103–4
W. K. Kellogg Foundation, 20
workforce
in Arizona, 177
community colleges and, 181
distance learning and, 177
educational attainment and, 31, 66, 72, 76, 181
for-profit institutions and, 150
Hispanics as future, 10
importance of West for, 49
job creation, 66
K-12 standards and, 71
state policy leadership and, 76
technology projects and, 154
workforce development, policy issues in, 171, 172, 173, 175
Workforce Investment Act, 178
working-age population
in Arizona, 50
college participation among, 53, 54
educational attainment of, 39
enrollment rates for, 43, 50, 53, 54
in Idaho, 52
in Montana, 53
in Nevada, 53
in North Dakota, 54
in Washington, 56
World War II, demographic information on, 4, 11, 17
Wyoming, xii
affordability in, 57
American Indian population in, 11
community colleges in, 161–3, 165, 166, 168, 170
degree completion in, 47, 57, 139
Educational Appropriations in, 132, 138, 139
educational attainment in, 37, 113, 132, 135, 139
enrollment rates in, 113, 138, 165
FTE enrollment in, 138, 139
funding in, 46, 57, 100, 102, 139, 166, 168
governance in, 79, 139
high school graduation rates in, 44, 57
immediate college-going rates in, 45, 57, 93
low-income students in, 57
Measuring Up state grades for, 34–5, 41–2, 47, 56–7
natural resource extraction in, 132
out-of-state students in, 17
population of, 132, 139
public *vs.* private institutions in, 92
SHEF wave chart of, 138
state funding in, 132
state governing board in, 86
taxes in, 91, 95
Total Educational Revenue in, 138
tuition in, 91, 94, 103–4, 138, 139

young population, 6, 7, 38
decline in, 15–16
demographic information for, 36, 39
educational attainment of, 47, 49
growth of, 47
vs. older adults, 47, 49, 52, 53, 54, 67
racial/ethnic makeup of, 31, 36

Zaback, Kathleen, xx, 107, 197
Zakaria, Fareed, xiii

Public Policy Challenges Facing Higher Education in the American West is the first regional public policy study of American higher education. Presidents of the Western Interstate Commission for Higher Education and the National Center for Higher Education Management Systems, alongside nationally recognized policy analysts and current western campus presidents, provosts, and administrators, tackle seven key public policy issues facing postsecondary education in the American West: student access, federal research funding, state governance, state financing, state appropriations and their relationship to institutional tuition, distance education and technology, and the role of community colleges. These analysts, researchers, and administrators offer a clear and complete analysis of the facts of each policy situation, the public policy options, and their connections to state and university relationships. Fifteen western states, including Alaska, California, and Hawaii, comprise the expansive region under discussion. With its companion volume, *Higher Education in the American West: Regional History and State Contexts*, this book is essential reading for higher education policymakers, scholars, and anyone who wants to know what the relationship between states and universities in the West has been and where it is going.

LESTER F. GOODCHILD is Distinguished Professor of International and Comparative Education at the University of Massachusetts Boston, USA.

RICHARD W. JONSEN is former Executive Director of the Western Interstate Commission for Higher Education, USA.

PATTY LIMERICK is Faculty Director and Chair of the Board of the Center of the American West at the University of Colorado Boulder, USA, where she is also Professor of History.

DAVID A. LONGANECKER is President of the Western Interstate Commission for Higher Education, USA.

GPSR Compliance

The European Union's (EU) General Product Safety Regulation (GPSR) is a set of rules that requires consumer products to be safe and our obligations to ensure this.

If you have any concerns about our products, you can contact us on

ProductSafety@springernature.com

In case Publisher is established outside the EU, the EU authorized representative is:

Springer Nature Customer Service Center GmbH
Europaplatz 3
69115 Heidelberg, Germany

www.ingramcontent.com/pod-product-compliance
Lightning Source LLC
LaVergne TN
LVHW051915060526
838200LV00004B/162